The Golden Builders

What are those golden builders doing? Where was the burying place
Of soft Ethinthus? Near Tyburns fatal tree? Is that
Mild Zions hills most ancient promontory: near mournful
Ever weeping Paddington? Is that Calvary and Golgotha?
Becoming a building of pity and compassion? Lo!
The stones are pity, and the bricks, well wrought affections:
Enameld with love and kindness, & the tiles engraven gold
Labour of merciful hands: the beams and rafters are forgivenness:
The mortar and cement of the work, tears of honesty: the nails,
And the screws & iron braces, are well wrought blandishments,
And well contrived words, firm fixing, never forgotten,
Always comforting the remembrance: the floors, humility,
The ceilings, devotion: the hearths, thanksgiving:
Prepare the furniture O Lambeth in thy pitying looms!
The curtains, woven tears & sighs, wrought into lovely forms
For comfort, there the secret furniture of Jerusalems chamber
Is wrought: Lambeth! The Bride the Lambs Wife loveth thee:
Thou art one with her & knowest not of self in thy supreme joy
Go on, builders in hope: tho Jerusalem wander far away,
Without the gate of Los: among the dark Satanic wheels.

Jerusalem XII.25-40. William Blake, 1804

The Golden Builders

Alchemists,
Rosicrucians, and
the First Freemasons

Tobias Churton

WEISER BOOKS
Boston, MA/York Beach, ME

This edition first published in 2005 by
Red Wheel/Weiser, LLC
York Beach, ME
With offices at:
368 Congress Street
Boston, MA 02210
www.redwheelweiser.com

Cataloging-in-Publication Data available upon request from the Library of Congress.

ISBN 1-57863-329-X

Printed in Canada
TCP

12 11 10 09 08 07 06 05
 8 7 6 5 4 3 2 1

CONTENTS

PART TWO THE TRUE STORY OF THE
ROSICRUCIANS

PART THREE   ELIAS ASHMOLE (1617-1692)

Preface

"Why are you so interested in alchemy, Rosicrucianism and things like that?" my mother asked me recently.

"There's something beautiful in magic." I replied, without thinking. When I suggested making this exchange the Preface to my new book she recommended I add the letter 'k' to 'magic': the old spelling, to distinguish it from stage conjuring.

Magick has always had to be qualified. Pico della Mirandola's Oration on the Dignity of Man (1486) sharply differentiated "magia", the science of the magi, from "goetia", a thing involving demons and a terrible thing – what we would now call black magic. The cradle of Christ in the New Testament welcomes the *magi* from the east, while the Acts of the Apostles pits Paul and Peter in regular conflict with 'magicians'. Mathematics in the middle ages and Renaissance was frequently classed, innocently, as 'natural magic' while sorcery was condemned. The word is used just as innocently today on the cover of a child's 'magic painting book' though its practitioner might be a little devil.

Magic in this sense denotes a startling effect that can be described with the adjective 'magical', but which is plainly a simple operation of natural laws that strikes us as special (the reaction of crystals in water). Not surprising then, that magic is often linked to the word illusion – the magic lantern deceives the eye. Cinema, which has done little else for a century, has naturally become the vehicle of global mythology.

That adjective, 'magical' though – does it not suggest something more than the operation of a natural law? Something we describe as *magical* somehow touches our most receptive part, that which we call the soul, in a way that can change our lives, or make our lives. With this kind of power, it is little wonder that magic has been used and abused by the wicked (from the evil eye to the Nuremberg Rallies), and puritans have come to suspect beauty as carrying a fatal attraction. But is ugliness preferable? Well, I suppose the generous puritan might opt for just plain *plain*. But that is to side step the issue. To the eyes that behold it, the universe contains beauty and ugliness in measureless measure, but not much that could be fully described as *plain*.

So what attracts me to these subjects? There is, I believe, a *hiddenness* to the universe, an inherent quality that does not meet the eye, at least not at first. I am not referring to microbes or DNA – though one might find this magic there as well. It was, according to one of the subjects of this book, Elias Ashmole, the "admirall wisdom of the Magi", to seek this quality, and work with it for the good. Another subject, Paracelsus, referred to the "divine signatures" inherent in the world, traces of a more than natural (though not unnatural) presence, something of the Maker's mark and transcendent mind, discernible in creation – a ladder, a clue, to something higher. One needs to see the world from a different perspective to that which has become familiar, or over-familiar. One needs to ascend the ladder, or 'stairway to heaven'.

Science is the child of the Magi, and from the point of view of the modern magus, is a distinguished branch of Magick. The scientist today, in general, would feel most uncomfortable with this, to say the least. But many of us think that the truly magical is inseparable from our existence as spiritual beings, as well as our existence as biological entities. I might fall in love with a spiritual being, I am unlikely to send flowers to a biological entity, though the behaviourists would have it so. All our love is so much 'evolutionary determinism'. Take away the poetry, the music, the living faith and spiritual knowledge, yea, even and especially the magick, and what would we have? Dr Johnson might say, "Why, sir, then you would have what you call the Modern World!"

Something is missing from the equation and this book represents part of my search to find out what that something is, and is not.

ACKNOWLEDGEMENTS

This book could not have been written without the facilities, inspiration and access to original documentation, books, incunabla and manuscripts provided by the *Bibliotheca Philosophica Hermetica* (J.R. Ritman Library, Amsterdam).

For a thorough understanding of the original creators of the Rose-Cross mythology, I am indebted to Dr Carlos Gilly of Basle. For a series of sparkling interviews on so many aspects of the gnostic tradition, I am indebted to Professors Hans Jonas, Gilles Quispel, Elaine Pagels, R.Mc.Lachlan Wilson and Dr. Kathleen Raine. The conversation and encouragement of the late Jean Gimpel has been invaluable in understanding the practical achievements of the Middle Ages.

Gratitude is due to the kindly and attentive staff of the Lichfield Record Office and the Stafford Record Office.

Maureen Archer is responsible for tireless labour, above and beyond the call of duty, on the typesetting.

I also want to thank Dr Christopher McIntosh, Columba Powell, Matthew Scanlan, Julian Jones, Sarah Miller, Victor and Patricia Churton (my parents), and Joanna (*née*) Edwards - who arrived in the (old) nick of time - for your love and patience.

The book is dedicated to the memory of Professor Jan Arvid Hellström, the late bishop of Växjö, Sweden, who first brought me to the Theology Faculty of Uppsala University to lecture on Gnosticism in 1990, so launching a collaboration cut cruelly short by his death in a car accident in 1994. We spoke often of a new thing – or really, a very old thing, that seemed new. We called it 'Stone Theology'. "He who trips on the stone shall be broken, but he on whom the stone falls shall be winnowed." I shall carry on, Jan Arvid.

This book is also dedicated to my darling wife, Joanna, and to our daughter, Mérovée Sophia, who, I hope, will read it, one day.

Introduction

Believe me, the only promise of a better future for our country
is to be looked for from those to whom her past is dear.
(Dean Inge. *Things New & Old*. 1933.)

The expression 'Hermetic Philosophy' has been discussed in academic coteries for many years. Is there a coherent Hermetic philosophy, or is it merely a convenient title for a mixed bag of late antique spiritual and moral philosophies, with only the figure of Hermes Trismegistus to lend a spurious unity to the collection? The most recent scholarship on the matter (Fowden, Mahé, Quispel, Edighoffer, Secret, Gilly, Van den Broek) has suggested that one can talk meaningfully of an Hermetic philosophy, even a spiritual 'way of Hermes' of Egyptian provenance (Van den Broek has even employed the term 'Hermetic lodge'), to which Hermetic authors have accreted sympathetic philosophical material, intuiting its inner consistency to the mainstream of their interest. This book accepts the expression Hermetic Philosophy in this sense, as a spiritual stream with its own special emphases.

When I wrote my first book, *The Gnostics*, in the middle of that (in retrospect) exciting decade, the 1980s, attention to the Hermetic philosophy in academic circles centred either on its place in the Gnosis of late antiquity (the children of Jonas and Nag Hammadi), or as a primary impulse in the Italian, French, German and English Renaissance (Yates, Walker, Faivre). There was very little linkage. Theologians didn't seem to speak to historians of art and Renaissance philosophy.

I hope the first part of this book fills some of the gaps and demonstrates that, in spite of appearances, the Hermetic Art is always one, at any time, and is a boon to all sacred traditions, be they ever so (apparently) distant. Infinity is Hermes' natural territory.

The Gnostics concentrated its Hermetic interest on the figures Pico della Mirandola and Giordano Bruno. We have the towering influence of the late Dame Frances Yates to thank for that. In this book, I have chosen to focus attention on the so-called 'Hermes' fool', Mercurio da Correggio, who dressed up as an hermetic messiah and entered Rome on an ass to tumultuous public interest the year before the Battle of Bosworth. He was not crucified, but went on to have an extraordinary impact on poet and Cabalist Lodovico Lazzarelli and thus on the wider

European cultural horizon. Looking at the untutored Mercurio, we find the message is the same, but somehow deeper, more personal, as if the spirit had glided down from the lofty heights of Ficino's abstractions, and nested in a single, receptive human heart. Ambrosia is stored in the catacombs of footnotes.

There are exceptions to this rule. Paracelsus is of course widely famous, especially on the continent. In Britain he has become a hero of homœopathy; recognised by history as a scientific giant, he should also be seen as a theological master.

Paracelsus' influence on those peculiar writings dubbed 'Rosicrucian manfestos' has long been regarded as seminal, but his influence on 16th and 17th century theological discourse – a revolution in attitude in fact – will come as much of a surprise to some readers as it did to me in the late eighties. Looking into the Paracelsian influence, we can see that the origins of Rosicrucianism should less hold the attention of conspiracy theorists than that of theologians, historians of science – and, of course, free spirits everywhere.

The true (as opposed to the mythological) story of the Rosicrucians is inspiring. How did it happen that a handful of brilliant men, working both alone and in concert, did create an enduring movement, firstly of spiritual and moral development, and secondly of scientific study?

The movement in question has been dubbed (by Dame Frances Yates in 1972), a movement of 'Rosicrucian Enlightenment'. However, as this book demonstrates, such nomenclature does not properly express the range of activities pursued by the movement's chief exponents, while its usage has had the unfortunate effect of confining the significance of the movement to the world of the esoteric : an idea which could not have been further from the mind of the movement's foremost progenitor, Johann Valentin Andreae (1586-1654). In fact, the movement described in this book resists simple classification, being part of an unfolding development of knowledge whose roots lay in the oriental world of the Middle Ages : the desire for operative knowledge of a natural creation, a natural creation, that is, deemed to be in essence magical : a world of spirit and matter combined. It is precisely in this combination of worlds that contemporary interest in this movement might lie, for purely materialist science has (since the 1920s) been touched by the suspicion that there's 'more to it than meets the eye'.

The movement in question came about chiefly because certain men - in particular, Johann Valentin Andreae, Tobias Hess (1568-1614) and

Christoph Besold (1577-1649) - believed that the lodestone of the ideal civilisation had been lost, and they set about finding it. Avoiding, as much as was possible, the contentions of Reformation theology, they sought their 'stone' through combined investigations of the worlds of spiritual alchemy, natural science (including mathematics) and pre-Reformation mysticism. In the period described, these areas of study constituted the greater part of the then-creditable (if sometimes disputed) endeavour of *magia naturalis* : natural magic.

In Part Two, the skin of history has been lifted to reveal a thriving world of advanced thought and culture, such as few could have imagined existed so long ago. We have much to learn from it, for contemporary civilisation is, in the opinion of the best minds of the age, at sea in a welter of foaming confusion; the problems stemming not so much from the want of a compass, but from the provision of too many of them, few of which can agree on the cardinal points. In this situation, anything that may give us knowledge of the original charts with which the *barca* of modern man set sail in the seventeenth century can fail to help us. Part Two contains the story of a boat which has come home, laden with riches and extraordinary tales - with a difference: these tales are true.

Part Three represents the fruit of a bond with the extraordinary figure of Elias Ashmole, a bond transcending more than three centuries. I believe Ashmole's significance to have been profoundly underrated. The effective demotion of Ashmole from the status of bright, even brightest, luminary of the 17th century English scientific renaissance to guarded appreciation as antiquarian and donor (see the catalogue for this year's exhibition on *Solomon's House in Oxford* held at the Museum of the History of Science, formerly the Old Ashmolean, for example), is disconcerting. Hermetic Philosophy has in the past been shunned as being at best pre-scientific (you can't measure spirits) and at worst, scandalous occultism (we don't want spirits anyway). I suppose exclusion brings its rewards. Poor Hermetism! Shunned by Science and Theology alike, some two millennia after having served as patron to both.

I think Ashmole himself – a grand character – would have been very much amused by this twist in the story of his reputation. He took the larger, cosmic view. *The stars rule mankind*, he believed – with all the paradox implicit in that statement. And things are changing. Amsterdam University has led the way by establishing a Professorship with a remit for pursuing the study of Hermetic Philosophy, an achievement which must owe much to Joost Ritman's epoch-marking

Bibliotheca Philosophica Hermetica, about which you can read in my book, *The Gnostics*.

Ashmole was an unashamed, majestic magus, competent astrologer, humble alchemist, discerning publisher, proud Hermetic philosopher, co-founder of the Royal Society, national star, "Mighty Good Man" – and Free Mason. I hope something of his golden, timeless gift comes over in the third part of this book, which concentrates on Ashmole's commitments to 17th century Free Masonry, a subject which has only lately attracted the attention of academe. Things *are* changing. Sheffield University now has a Chair for the study of Freemasonry, currently held by Andrew Prescott.

To approach this initially mysterious subject through Ashmole's life was illuminating. Its conclusions will be of interest to serious freemasons, but equally startling, I hope, to non-masons. After all, when Ashmole was a 'Free Mason' (as he styled his masonic identity), there was no Grand Lodge with rules an inch thick to tell the brothers what to say and do. There was a bright, strange, oddly comforting, imaginative vernacular tradition, a tradition capable of all but silently saving elements of a kingdom from chaos. Would that it were again, perhaps. Some masonic historians deny any influence or presence of Hermetic ideas on freemasonry. Perhaps this is partly because others have been all too keen to pose imaginative conspiracy scapes over history, dragging in every conceivable occult legend and every twistable fact in order to stimulate their readers and, especially, their sales. This book takes the sober path, believing that historical reality, as far as we may discern it, is quite stimulating enough. In this spirit of sobriety, it is worthwhile to give some signal of a number of the conclusions to be found elucidated in Part Three.

Forms of Free Masonry existed without centralised control before the establishment of Grand Lodge by four London lodges in 1717. That this is the case is well known to historians of freemasonry. However, the special definition of Grand and later (1813) United Grand Lodge has to a large extent consisted in a general assumption that its establishment marks the organised foundation of *speculative* and non-operative freemasonry. That a lodge of non-operative or *Accepted* Free Masons existed (if only very briefly) in 1646 (the date of Ashmole's initiation) of course subtracts from the force of this assumption, but the key word at issue here is 'speculative'. This term has become profoundly misleading from the historical point of view. As has been demonstrated by Professor David Stevenson (*The Origins of Freemasonry : Scotland's Century 1590-1710*. Cambridge. 1988), pre-1717 freemasonry already involved a symbolic, philosophical aspect which mitigates against the prejudice of seeing medieval craftsmen as simple, untutored souls, not much of a cut above the labourer in specialised knowledge.

Those varied masonic documents of the late 14th. and early 15th. centuries known collectively as the Old Charges clearly show that some English freemasons (at least) believed their craft to be linked to the figure of Hermes Trismegistus, a name familiar to scholars throughout the middle ages from translations of attributed texts from the Arabic language, and a name therein linked to cosmic philosophy (*scientia*), alchemy, architecture and magic. According to Professor Stevenson : "The mention of Hermes Trismegistus, the stress on the development of the craft in Egypt, and the identification of masonry and geometry were taken over by the masons from the medieval background of knowledge inherited from the ancient world, but they took on new significance and importance during the Renaissance." (*The Origins of Freemasonry.* p.24) This "new significance" was due to the elevation of the reputation of Hermes Trismegistus which followed on the first printed edition of the *Pymander* (or *Corpus Hermeticum*) in Treviso in 1471. Since Ashmole was by self-definition immersed in Hermetic studies (announcing himself to be the *Mercuriophilus Anglicus*), it is hardly surprising that he was fascinated by Free Masonry. Indeed, this confluence of Renaissance education and ancient craft freemasonry - coalescing about the figure of Hermes - may in part explain the attraction of gentlemen such as Ashmole (and his first wife's cousin, Col. Henry Mainwaring, who inherited a family-history littered with connections with late-medieval religious confraternities with which freemasons were associated) in becoming 'Accepted' Free Masons : that is, *accepted*, and not 'speculative' Free Masons.

Ashmole need only have looked at the ruins of the Cistercian houses at Croxden or Dieulacres in the Staffordshire moorlands - or simply gazed at the cathedral in which he sang as a boy (Lichfield) - to be filled with awe at the work of medieval freemasons. They were not 'medieval' to *him*. He was simply gazing at those religious structures which had survived the ravages of the English Reformation, and which were in his own time again under direct threat of demolition at the hands of radical Protestants.

As a natural antiquarian, Ashmole must have felt deeply the need to understand the provenance of both these structures and their inherent symbolism. That we know so little of the freemasonry which existed about the monasteries of pre-Reformation England, Wales, Scotland and Ireland may reasonably be accounted for on the basis that so very, very little of the monastic libraries survived what Ashmole himself called the "Great Deluge" of the Dissolution of religious houses in the century before his birth. He, like John Dee and others who lived through the calamitous events of the British Reformation, was keenly aware of the destruction of primary evidence involved in the despoiling of the monastic libraries. This was one of the reasons that inspired him to be a collector. Ashmole did not collect for the sake of it; he was looking for something. What that 'something' was we get a hint of in Part Three.

So who are these 'Golden Builders'? The title is taken from Blake's extraordinary poem and prophecy, *Jerusalem* (1804). Blake's 'Golden Builders' are building the city of Golgonooza, built from sacrifice of self (Golgotha) and the basic stuff and substance (ooze) that is visible life. From this confluence of the life-blood of man and the love of God that transcends self, the substantial city of Divine Imagination is built. This city has its citizens. Some few of them you can read about in this book. The author has found them to be excellent company in all conditions. I hope you find it likewise.

Tobias Churton
Lichfield July 2002

Part One

THE HERMETIC PHILOSOPHY

Chapter One

Hermes : Star of Alexandria

TAT : I will offer up the praise in my heart, as I pray to the end of the universe and the beginning of the beginning, to the object of man's quest, the immortal discovery, the begetter of life and truth, the sower of reason, the love of immortal life. No hidden word will be able to speak about thee, Lord. Therefore my mind wants to sing a hymn to you daily. I am the instrument of thy spirit. Mind is thy plectrum. And thy counsel plucks me. I see myself! I have received power from thee! For thy love has reached us.
HERMES : Right, O my son.

(Hermetic *Discourse on the Eighth & Ninth* between Hermes and his pupil. 2nd cent. AD. From the Gnostic Library of Nag Hammadi).

As each new dawn raised the sun over Egypt, the victory of the light was celebrated; darkness departed and visible life returned. For Hermes, it was business as usual, for he was a god both of the night and the day, as content with the moon and the powers invisible as he was with the merchant and the sunlit groves of morning.

The cult of Hermes was already established in the Greek-speaking world before Alexander the Great conquered Egypt and founded his city, Alexandria, in 331 BC. A century later, Greek settlers in that city had begun to apply the epithet *megistos kai megistos theos megas* to Hermes (roughly 'great and great the great god' Hermes). The settlers had doubtless derived this dignity from the epithet *two times great*, which, for as long as anyone could remember, had been applied to Hermes' Egyptian equivalent, the god Thoth. Thoth was a *mega megastar* : a popular god, the supreme master of trickery, magic, writing, the realm of the dead, the moon, medicine. The Graeco-Egyptian Thoth-Hermes stood - or flew - for the very spirit of inventiveness. Fleet of foot and quick of mind, Hermes was the divine messenger. A man who spoke with a message from the gods would be regarded as being in a sense possessed by Hermes. To be inspired by the *powers* of Hermes was to *become* Hermes. In this condition, one could write in his name. The name of the game was *communication*.

Sometime between the first century BC and the end of the first century AD[1], possibly under Jewish influence or perhaps to compete with other fashionable and venerated prophets and teachers, such as the long-since departed master-minds Zoroaster, Plato and Pythagoras, a new figure, Thrice Greatest Hermes (*Hermes Trismegistos*) began to appear in a series of knowledge-tracts. He appeared as an ancient patriarch of civilisation, a kind of relative of the exalted divinity, dwelling in a remote antiquity among the temples and pyramids of a pristine Egypt. Since many Greeks believed that their philosophy, especially in its spiritual aspect, derived in part from ancient Egypt, the ascendancy - or 'rediscovery' - of Hermes Trismegistos could be described as an astute enterprise by his literary progenitors. Having apparently overcome the test-of-time, the name Hermes could operate as a kind of intellectual designer-label.

The authority of Hermes Trismegistos was employed to dignify two main classes of writing. Firstly, a coterie of practical and theoretical lore relating to talismanic magic, astrology, astrological medicine and, notably, alchemy, and secondly, philosophical writings in dialogue-form. These latter tracts were concerned with the nature of God, man, and the cosmos. A veritable elixir, Hermes Trismegistos had an answer for everything.

Those works of Hermes which have always enjoyed the highest authority among their literary peers constitute the philosophical Hermetica, grouped together some time between c.AD 250-1050 into a body of writings now known as the *Corpus Hermeticum*. These texts seem to demonstrate an impatience with traditional philosophical methods and meet a hunger for a rational philosophy which could serve an essentially spiritual need. Going, they hoped, 'one better' than the philosophical schools, the 'ancient' teaching of Hermes Trismegistos was presented in the *Corpus Hermeticum* not as philosophical postulates in the traditional Greek sense, but as authentic *revelation* : ancient revelation which could be experienced by the student's identifying himself with Father Hermes' own experience, so acquiring *gnosis* or experiential knowledge of the spirit, making the student aware of his mind as a living fact. The texts were to operate like the Thrice Great Hermes' magical shoes : ready-made to follow in the divine footsteps - all the way to the mystical *One* : the journey fully vouchsafed and endorsed by centuries of assumed tradition.

> Once on a time, when I had begun to think about the things that are, and my thoughts had soared high aloft, while my bodily senses had been put under restraint by sleep, - yet not such sleep as that of men

weighed down by fullness of food or by bodily weariness, - methought there came to me a Being of vast and boundless magnitude, who called me by my name, and said to me, 'What do you wish to hear and see, and to learn and come to know by thought?' 'Who are you?' I said. 'I,' said he, 'am Poimandres, the sovereign *nous* [mind].' 'I would fain learn,' said I, 'the things that are, and understand their nature, and to know God. These,' I said, 'are the things of which I wish to hear.' He answered, 'I know what you wish, for indeed I am with you everywhere; keep in mind all that you desire to learn, and I will teach you."   (*Libellus* I. Iff. *The Poimandres*).

The Hermetic tradition was both moderate and flexible, offering a tolerant philosophical religion, a religion of the (omnipresent) mind, a purified perception of God, the cosmos, and the self, and much positive encouragement for the spiritual seeker, all of which the student could take anywhere. In modern parlance, much of the philosophy exposed in the tracts was 'psychedelic', that is to say, *soul-expanding*. The Hermetic experience was cosmopolitan, yet rooted in the dream of a romantic antiquity : the perfect intellectual and syncretistic cult for an Empire groping for new (and old) certainties. The Hermetic writings brought *gnosis* to those (perhaps youthful) pagans in search of a thoughtful and spiritual salvation from the world. For it was to Hermes, the texts informed the reader, that there had once come the 'giants' of a mythical past, in *their* youth, for instruction and initiation into the authentic, pristine cosmic philosophy. Their names were given as Tat, (King) Ammon and Asklepios. The understanding reader was invited to join the august host of that spiritual élite who had, they were led to believe, benefited from the master's authentic voice - the voice of "the authentic *Nous* [Mind]"- for century on imagined century.

TAT : O holy Gnosis, by thee am I illumined,
and through thee do I sing praise to the noetic Light.
...I rejoice in joy of mind;
rejoice with me all ye Powers.
..O God, thou art the Father;
  O Lord, thou art Mind.
HERMES : I rejoice, my son, that you are like to bring forth fruit. Out of the Truth will spring up in you the immortal generation of virtue; for by the working of mind you have come to know yourself and our Father.   (*Libellus* XIII.18. 21.22a)

The setting of Hermetic philosophical discourse is mostly one of teacher and pupil, and both Garth Fowden and Jean-Pierre Mahé[2] are convinced that this setting mirrors the situation in which the philosophical Hermetica were actually employed. That is to say that there may have existed in Egypt from about the late first century AD, schools of Hermetic discourse which aimed to take pupils to a direct experience of *gnosis*, combined with liturgical hymns and prayers. What inner voyager could fail to be, at least in part, seduced by the voice of a conception so abstract and timeless as the omnipresent and omniscient Mind?

Knowledge of the original pagan setting in which the texts were composed disappeared with the growth of Christianity in Egypt during the third century. From that time on, it would seem that the Hermetica represented a literary, spiritual path, divorced from the social and educational milieu of first and second century Alexandria. Anybody who could get hold of the texts could become a pupil of Hermes, or at least use his name and *logia* to endorse their own philosophical and religious 'products'. The texts simply became part of the *corpus* of ancient authorities in matters of antique spiritual and magical knowledge - and, as with all antiques, Hermes Trismegistos' reputation would grow again in direct proportion to the rarity of the texts which bore his name.

It was no great surprise to scholars of Gnosticism, such as Professor Hans Jonas, when our earliest manuscripts of the philosophical Hermetica, including a *Prayer of Thanksgiving*, were found among the documents of the now famous Nag Hammadi Library of 'Gnostic Gospels', buried in Upper Egypt by enthusiasts of Christian *gnosis* in the mid to late 4th Century. Jonas had long held that the Hermetica should be seen as integral to the phenomenon of Gnostic religion. Even Christian Gnostics had found these pagan writings congenial, and perhaps inspiring in the task of creating new gnostic documents. After all, if, as S.John's Gospel declared, Christ was the divine *Logos* - the creative mind or 'Word' of God, then it was a simple matter for Christian enthusiasts of the *gnosis* - particularly in Alexandria - to reach the conclusion that the Christian 'Word' and the Hermetic '*Nous*' were at the very least, similar in substance[3].

The Vision of Hermes

What is the principal message of the philosophical Hermetica? Firstly, the texts announce to the reader that in order to be saved from the ebb, flow, flux and corruption of material life, it is necessary to have perfectly pure vision. The stress is always on the state of mind of the pupil; the climax of spiritual growth is always accompanied by astonishingly increased powers of perception, breaking through from material to spiritual vision. The Hermetic teaching is to enable the pupil to see aright, and to 'see aright' is to have acquired what Catholic doctrine calls a 'sacramental vision' of the created order : the world manifests a visible experience which is the expression of far greater and more profound powers invisible to the organic eye but which are seizable by the enlightened eye of the mind - called the *nous*, a Greek word which can mean either 'mind' or 'spirit'.

While there is 'good news' for the Hermetic student within the tracts, the discourses are quite unlike the canonical gospels (with which the tracts perhaps competed), existing in a remote, yet 'clear' and timeless zone. There are no parables; there are repeated assertions of fundamental spiritual principles. There are no miracles; the cosmos is revealed as a continual miracle. There is no coercion; the pupil is free to choose the way of flesh or the way of *nous*. There is ultimately no master; the pupil must learn to become his own master. There is no end; it is an eternal life - the life of the *aeons* - which springs from the source of 'the All' (*Pan*).

The primary principle which the student of the texts is enjoined to understand is to "know thyself". What is the essential nature of man? The Hermetic doctrine is unequivocal :

> Man is a great miracle, O Asklepios, honour and reverence to such a being! Because he takes in the nature of a god as if he were himself a god; he has familiarity with the demon-kind, knowing that he issues from the same origin; he despises this part of his nature which is but human, because he puts his hope in the divinity of the other part. O what a privileged blend makes up the nature of man! He is united to the gods because he has the divinity pertaining to gods; the part of himself which is of the earth he despises in himself; all those other living things which he knows himself to be tied in the virtue of the celestial plan, he binds them by the tie of love. He raises his sights towards heaven. Such therefore is his privileged role as intermediary, loving the beings who are inferior to him and is loved by those above him. He takes the earth as his own, he blends himself with the elements by the speed of thought, by the sharpness of mind he descends to the

depths of the sea. Everything is accessible to him; heaven is not too high for him, for he measures it as if it were in his grasp by his ingenuity. What sight the spirit shows to him, no mist of the air can obscure; the earth is never so dense as to impede his work; the immensity of the sea's depths do not trouble his plunging view. He is at the same time everything as he is everywhere.
(*Asclepius* 6a. ff).

Here is an almost Edenic Man in all the fiery finery of his *potential* energy : airy, wise, loving, and free. The passage reads, and has been read, as a prophecy of a time when human-beings will throw off the shackle of their shadow and fear and take their place as bridges between the two worlds, seen and unseen. For the Hermetist, an intellectual appraisal of this vision of man is insufficient. One must see it for oneself; one must be reborn. The process involved here (*palingenesia*) purports to come from recognising, through an inner ascent experience, how far the passions of the world envelop the soul, like heavy coats of dull and dense material which hold the vision in darkness. These 'coats' or 'passions' are called "the irrational torments of matter". The passions keep man from *gnosis* of his true identity.

The twelve causes of "ignorance" (*agnosis*) are listed as follows : ignorance itself; grief; incontinence (obsession with sex); desire; injustice; covetousness; deceitfulness; envy; fraud; anger; rashness; malice. (*Libellus* XIII. 7bff.) Having risen above these in the *nous*, the pupil comes to a vision of the "Eighth and Ninth", beyond the control of the seven planetary spheres (which exist both within and without), and as the reborn Man - sharing in the vision of the original *Anthropos* (*Humanity* as pristine archetypal principle), who, according to *Libellus* I's account of the Fall into irrational Nature, fell into his reflection in the waters of the earth - the reborn one perceives "not with bodily eyesight, but by the energy of *nous*".

> HERMES : Even so it is, my son, when a man is born again; it is no longer body of three dimensions that he perceives, but the incorporeal.
> TAT : Father, now that I see in mind, I see myself to be the All. I am in heaven and in earth, in water and in air; I am in beasts and plants; I am a babe in the womb, and one that is not yet conceived, and one that has been born; I am present everywhere.
> (*Libellus* XIII. Treatise on Rebirth)

It should be understood that while this Hermetic vision of spiritual life combined with abundant nature was intended to have universal applications - and indeed has achieved this historically - there is a serious strain in the philosophical Hermetica of rooting the vision within the magical and devout land of Egypt herself. Egypt had a mystique to western antiquity which while undoubtedly dimming to the vaguest flicker of antique fire at the end of the Roman Empire, (when she was repeatedly invaded by hostile forces from the east), nonetheless returned with great vigour in the fifteenth century Renaissance and has never since left the European scene. In fact, the rebirth of the Egyptian mystique during the Renaissance was precisely due to the re-appearance in the west of once-lost Hermetic writings - the bulk of the *Corpus Hermeticum* - which were then joined to extant Latin translations such as this powerful lament for a disappearing world, composed between c.260 and 310 AD:

> Or are you ignorant, O Asklepios, that Egypt is the image of heaven? Moreover it is the dwelling place of heaven and all the forces that are in heaven. If it is proper for us to speak the truth, our land is the temple of the world. And it is proper for you not to be ignorant that a time will come when Egyptians will seem to have served the divinity in vain, and all their activity in their religion will be despised. For all divinity will leave Egypt and will flee upward to heaven. And Egypt will be widowed; it will be abandoned by the gods. For foreigners will come into Egypt and they will rule it. Egypt! Moreover, Egyptians will be prohibited from worshipping God. Furthermore, they will come into the ultimate punishment, especially whoever among them is found worshipping and honouring God.
>
> And in that day the country that was more pious than all countries will become impious. No longer will it be full of temples, but it will be full of tombs. Neither will it be full of gods, but it will be full of corpses. O Egypt! ...And the barbarian will be better than you, O Egyptian, in his religion, whether he is a Scythian, or the Hindus, or some other of this sort.
>
> ...And Egypt will be made a desert by the gods and the Egyptians. And as for you, O River, there will be a day when you will flow with blood more than water. And dead bodies will be stacked higher than the dams. And he who is dead will not be mourned as much as he who is alive.
>
> ...And in that day the world will not be marvelled at... it will be despised - the beautiful world of God, the incomparable work, the energy which possesses goodness, the many-formed vision, the abundance that does not envy, that is full of every vision. Darkness will be preferred to light and death will be preferred to life. No one will gaze into heaven. And the pious man will be counted as insane, and the impious man will be honoured as wise. The man who is afraid

will be considered as strong. And the good man will be punished like a criminal.

This speech motivated at least one Renaissance philosopher (Giordano Bruno, 1548-1600) to attempt to rebuild the vision of the imaginary Egypt described in the text. He hoped (mistakenly) to revive the essence of (Egyptian) magical religion within the Catholic Church: an eirenic exercise which he hoped would lead to the reuniting of Christendom about the principle of the Hermetic *One*. His beliefs would find a following in the Age of Reason - which, for a number of its (frequently masonic) exponents, was hoped to mean an Age of *Nous*.

The precise provenance of the philosophical Hermetica remains to a large extent a mystery. Certainly a number of disparate authors between the late first and third centuries were involved in the production of the texts, not all by any means of identical philosophic leanings; contradictions abound. The passage above seems to have been written by somebody with a deep reverence for Egypt as a place where pure philosophy had been taught and right worship had been offered to the gods since the beginnings of mankind, and is full of that hearty disdain for foreign cultures familiar to all those who had invaded Egypt in the past. However, the language of the texts is Greek (with no obvious intrinsic signs of having been a translation) and it may be wondered why a devout follower of Thoth-Hermes in Egypt should want non-Egyptians to know the philosophical lore of his country, if they were so unworthy of it. Furthermore, it is to be doubted whether the reader is in fact receiving such philosophic lore. The cosmic picture of the philosophical Hermetica conforms in the main to a number of doctrines familiar to students of Plato, the neo-Pythagoreans, the Stoics, the Septuagint and the Middle Platonists, while the underlying bid of the texts may be to the effect that the Greeks derived (imperfectly) their doctrines from the Egyptians in the first place. There is a want of technical Egyptian mythological, liturgical and sacerdotal knowledge in the texts. We really learn nothing about Egyptian religion, except in the most general terms, terms which would not stretch the vocabulary gained by the average reader of a tourist-guide to ancient Egypt today. In many ways we can see the philosophical Hermetica as having been 'made in Egypt for export' - and made almost certainly by highly Hellenized, but nonetheless rather peculiar Egyptians whose intellectual home was the great city of Alexandria.

However, there are characteristics within the philosophical Hermetica which are, at least in their combination, unique to the *corpus*. The first factor which strikes the modern reader is the imaginative power of many of the texts. We have an attractive array of similes, stories, and passages of poetic and rhetorical strength, whose inner consistency suggests the presence of clear and brilliantly communicative minds operating behind them. Particularly memorable are the opening of Hermes' mind to the "authentic *nous*" and subsequent vision in *libellus* I, the story of the herald and the *krater* (bowl) of *nous* in *libellus* IV, the discourse on rebirth in *libellus* XIII, the treatise on 'Man the Marvel' in *Asclepius* I, and the lament for a lost Egypt in *Asclepius* III. These passages, among others, have stimulated scholars, poets and religious teachers for nearly two millennia and cannot simply be written off as hodge-podges of contemporary philosophical commonplaces. Dr. Fowden[4] maintains that there was a distinct spiritual path taught in Roman Egypt which one could describe as a 'Way of Hermes', which might be undertaken either exclusively or as part of a broader religious and philosophical study. One might be able to talk of a culture of 'Hermetists', possibly pursuing their pagan (if philosophically, but not mythologically, monotheist) light in secret after the domination of Christianity in Egypt and the closure of pagan temples in the late fourth century. There can be little doubt that the texts could have been employed as part of a polemic to the effect of saying that the pagan intellectual had nothing serious to learn from Christian ideas of the goodness of God or his creative and redemptive power.[5] Certainly the texts survived in the few places where pagan philosophy survived after the fall of the western Roman Empire and even after the Islamic conquest of Egypt in the 630's, as we shall see. And here we come to another peculiarity of the Hermetic philosophical texts.

I have alluded earlier to the 'universal' quality of the *Corpus Hermeticum*. The Hermetica have been used by both Christian and Muslim scholars to support their contentions. Hermes has even been seen as a prophet of Christianity (for example, by the theologian Lactantius[6]) since Hermes' writings refer to God having a Son, and because Hermes was thought to have lived before Moses. The Hermetica are full of injunctions to be pious towards God, who is called the "Father" and the "Good" and other soubriquets consistent with the Christian revelation. God is incorporeal and contains all things within himself : "it is as thoughts which God thinks, that all things are contained in him." (*libellus* Xiii.20a). God is One : the maker and sustainer of all. The sin of mankind is that they fail to see things as they are, and are thus brought to stumbling, because they do not see what is around them. God gave the *nous* to man to enlighten him, but many forego its light because they prefer the things of the body of sense to the subtle world of the unseen. This doctrine would not be out of place in the Prologue to S.John's Gospel wherein we are told that the divine *logos* made the world, was in the world, but the world knew him not. The Hermetic writings set a very high store on the idea of knowledge, of *gnosis*. They are, after all, books of knowledge. The important thing is to know God, then all good and loving insights will follow and man will see himself as he really is, and how close to the source of All (*Pan*) he is. It is at this point perhaps that the Hermetic writings would suggest impiety to some orthodox, and especially unlearned, Christians.

The milieu of the Hermetic philosophical tractates is undoubtedly one informed by the intellectual (and in some cases anti-intellectual) revolution known (in Christian theology) as Gnosticism, which in various forms began to be accreted to the Church almost as soon as the Gospel left Palestine, and which was to proceed in the second century to flourish and luxuriate in the wildest imaginable forms of syncretistic magic. But the *gnosis* of the Hermetic writings is both pious and simple, devoid of the panoply of mythological baggage which haunted some of the numerous coteries of Christian Gnostics in the second century. The *gnosis* of the Hermetica is rooted in the most optimistic picture possible of human potential. One can almost describe its flavour as *innocent*, coming, as was believed, from a pristine past of unspoilt people :

> If then you do not make yourself equal to God, you cannot apprehend God; for like is known by like. Leap clear of all that is corporeal [ie : use your imagination], and make yourself grow to a like expanse with that greatness which is beyond all measure; rise above all time, and become eternal; then you will apprehend God. Think that for you too nothing is impossible; deem that you too are immortal, and that you are able to grasp all things in your thought, to know every craft and every science; find your home in the haunts of every living creature; make yourself higher than all heights, and lower than all depths; bring together in yourself all opposites of quality, heat and cold, dryness and fluidity; think that you are everywhere at once, on land, at sea, in heaven; think that you are not yet begotten, that you are in the womb, that you are young, that you are old, that you have died, that you are in the world beyond the grave; grasp in your thought all this at once, all times and places, all substances and qualities and magnitudes

12

together; then you can apprehend God. But if you shut up your soul in your body [or fail to use your imagination], and abase yourself, and say 'I know nothing, I can do nothing; I am afraid of earth and sea, I cannot mount to heaven; I know not what I was, nor what I shall be', then, what have you to do with God? Your thought can grasp nothing beautiful and good, if you cleave to the body, and are evil.

For it is the height of evil not to know God; but to be capable of knowing God, and to wish and hope to know him, is the road which leads straight to the Good; and it is an easy road to travel. Everywhere God will come to meet you, everywhere he will appear to you, at places and times at which you look not for it, in your waking hours and in your sleep, when you are journeying by water and by land, in the night-time and in the day-time, when you are speaking and when you are silent; for there is nothing in which God is not. And do you say 'God is invisible'? Speak not so. Who is more manifest than God? For this very purpose has he made all things, that through all things you may see him. This is God's goodness, that he manifests himself through all things. Nothing is invisible, not even an incorporeal thing; *nous* is seen in its thinking, and God in his working.

So far, thrice greatest one, [says *Nous*], I have shown you the truth. Think out all else in like manner for yourself, and you will not be misled.

(*Libellus* XIii. 20b-22b. *A discourse of Mind* [Nous] *to Hermes*).

It is still unclear as to what part, if any, Hermetic ideas played in the development of Christian Gnosticism, and such Christian philosophy as existed in Alexandria in the second and third centuries (though the works of Clement of Alexandria show some interpenetration of idea). It is also unknown as to what, if any, part was played by Christian doctrines in the formation of the philosophical Hermetica. While there are similarities of idea - especially as regards an aesthetic pantheism (see especially the *Gospel of Thomas*) and the need for *gnosis* of God - between the *Corpus Hermeticum* and the largely Christian Gnostic material of the Nag Hammadi Library, there is, overall, a marked difference in both tone and pitch. The *libelli* of Hermes Trismegistos are marked by a tranquil, genial tone of *gravitas* and contemplative ease, quite in contrast to the often hurried, intense, obscure, riddle-drenched barrage of pedantic and hieratic restlessness characteristic of some of the Christian Gnostic literary material. Eclectic Valentinian works such as the *Gospel of Philip*, for example, may appear to the unsympathetic as a parable gone mad. The Hermetic world, by contrast, is a good deal simpler, giving the impression of a time "when the world was a little younger." It is a charmed world. In retrospect, it is just as well that Hermetists and Christian Gnostics seem to have kept their distance. Had Christian Gnosticism entered into the Hermetic *corpus*, the chances are that we should have heard no more of its unique timbre after the fourth century AD. As it was, the words of Hermes - rare as they were - were destined to traverse the thoughts of scholars in both east and west for centuries to come, and though divorced from their original *sitz in leben*, continued to evoke an eternal fantasy-land of cool philosophy and spiritual awakening forever basking in the shadow of the inscrutable sphinx while the evergreen adept's feet dangled gently in an imaginary Nile.

Neoplatonism and the Hermetic tradition

It was the fate of the Hermetic philosophical writings to be regarded as ancient authorities : a kind of litmus-test to what was authentic (ie : ancient - and pristine) in philosophy. This usage of Hermes can first be glimpsed among certain writings emanating from the Neoplatonists. Schools of Neoplatonic thought flourished during and after the lifetime of the Egyptian philosopher Plotinus (b.204), and since Plotinus' followers took the Hermetic *corpus* to be of very ancient provenance, these writings would themselves add to Hermes' tremendous reputation among scholars in the Middle Ages, for a significant portion of the ancient philosophy available to the Middle Ages was in fact Neoplatonic - though sometimes attributed (incorrectly) to Aristotle or Plato. This situation came about largely because the origin of much of the western philosophical tradition (after the 9th century) was to be located in translation-houses based in Harran and Baghdad, preoccupied with scientific and (inseparably) magical knowledge; Neoplatonic philosophy provided the rational basis for much magical practice. And where there was magic, the enchanting reputation of Hermes was never far away.

While Plotinus, the chief progenitor of Neoplatonic philosophy, was critical of the value of magic in purifying the soul, we nevertheless read in Plotinus' pupil Porphyry's life of his master, an account of how the great man was subjected to a magical bewitchment at the hands of one Olympius. Olympius was, like both Plotinus and the great Christian theologian Origen, a pupil of the Alexandrian master Ammonius Saccas; he was not a vulgar sorcerer, and even though Porphyry's opinion of Olympius was low, the event testifies pointedly to the mélange of ideas and practices which surrounded the

14

Neoplatonic schools. We know that works found in the Nag Hammadi Gnostic Library were almost certainly read by associates of Plotinus, and doubtless with approval[7], an approval which led Plotinus to condemn the radical Gnostic notion of a violent rift between the natural and spiritual worlds. While Plotinus made it his business to 'cleanse' his philosophy of unharmonious elements, the attitude of Neoplatonists to magic was in truth ambivalent. Magic, Neoplatonic mysticism and *gnosis* were inextricably linked - though not at all points. The works of Plotinus' followers Porphyry, Iamblichus (c.250-335) and Proclus (410-485) show this mutual interpenetration of ideas very clearly.

In the very first line of Iamblichus' *de mysteriis*, the primacy of Hermetic wisdom is asserted directly :

> Hermes, the god who presides over learning, has for long been rightly regarded as common to all priests : he who presides over true knowledge [*gnosis*] about the gods is one and the same, whatever the circumstances. It was to him too that our ancestors dedicated the fruits of their wisdom, by placing all their own writings under his name.

Iamblichus claimed to have found his doctrine of passifying the demons of the soul (to neutralise the passions of the body) in the Hermetic books, where the liberation of the soul from the bonds of Fate, (that is : the star-demons), was many times described. Iamblichus was convinced that the Hermetic writings, while having been translated into Greek by those familiar with Greek philosophy, had their origins in the ancient Thoth (=Hermes) literature : the pristine wisdom of the East.

The late-antique Neoplatonists did have problems in dealing with the demonology or vulgar magic (*goetia*) of some Hermetic writings, an abiding problem which seems to have been due to the fact that magic in its intellectual phase bore within it essentially gnostic characteristics, and while it was the inherent *gnosis* of the Hermetica which appealed to the Neoplatonists, magic and *gnosis* were really inseparable. It is clear that gnostic theory in its primitive state derived much of its mythological and technical 'equipment' from the ancient magical theories of Egypt and Mesopotamia. Indeed, a *gnosis* without magical quality would be a pretty anaemic affair.

In spite of the magical context in which Neoplatonist and Hermetic works would often come to be received, the more philosophical texts were nonetheless devoid of obvious magical references, being pious, revealing a God beyond magic, a God to be worshipped in silence and thanksgiving, beyond Fate (the zodiacal *heimarmene* or 'night-cloak'). In *Corpus Hermeticum* XIII.8. and in the text called *The Ogdoad reveals the Ennead*, the access of the divine power, experienced as 'light', is immediately preceded by an embrace between master and pupil, a sign of divine love and mutual thanksgiving. This *gnosis* of God, according to the Hermetic tradition, enabled the aspirant to step onto the moving ladder which passed through the created cosmos directly to the life at its heart.

Iamblichus' idea of the practice of Theurgy - a set of rituals involving the pacification of the controlling demons of the material realm, also took from the Hermetists the cult practices of praying in the pure temple, praying at the setting and the rising of the sun, and the singing of hymns. Iamblichus also took the view from the Hermetic texts that once one had penetrated the seven spheres of Fate (the realm of astrology), magic ceased to be necessary : a compromise view which attempted to reconcile Theurgic magic with the pure philosophy of which Plotinus approved. Theurgic rites represented a preparation for eventual illumination, but were not to be identified with that illumination; man stood between two worlds, though these worlds were not in any way sundered : Theurgy was for the lower world; pure philosophy was for - and from - the higher. The classic sorcerer was seen as one addicted to the hidden powers of the lower world with little or no interest in the exalted spiritual philosophy. Herein lies the perennial ambivalence regarding the role of magic in western religion.

The beliefs of the Theurgists, handed over to the western Middle Ages by the Sabians of Harran and Baghdad, preserved the realisation that man could be a free agent within a divine cosmos, that he could engage directly with cosmic powers, that he shared in the being of the primal man, called *Phos* (=Light), that he was *in potentia* a being of light closed in a shell, and that man, like the gods which lived within him was endowed with immortality and the spark of *gnosis*, which if used properly could bring him out of a world of constraint and darkness into a world of freedom, love, light and truth. This optimistic picture was necessarily held discretely, not least since it stood in head-on collision with the Catholic Church's concept of original sin and purgatorial redemption. Hermes was an uncomfortable guest at the Church's festive board.

Chapter Two

Alchemy

Since the early Christian Era, the name of Hermes Trismegistos has been tied to one art above all arts : alchemy, the mysterious *fons* of modern chemistry. Hermes is, so to speak, the patron-saint of the art : the quick-change artist *par excellence*. The word alchemy is derived from the Arabic *al-kimiya*, preserving the tradition that the art was associated chiefly with Egypt, for the Arabic appears to be a transliteration from the Egyptian *kam-it* or *kem-it*, 'the black', referring to the dark soil of Egypt, following the Nile's annual inundation, an image also suggesting perhaps the alchemist's fascination for carbonised substance. For all that, we do not know when or where alchemy first began to be practised, though it is reasonable to assume that it had its technical beginnings among the mysteries of the smithy, the glass-maker and the jeweller, where the observer enjoyed ample opportunity to witness the startling transformations wrought by the action of fire, earth, air and water : the four essential elements of which, according to Aristotle - and to alchemical theory - the universe is composed. That theory can be broken down into three basic premisses:

1. All metals share a common essence, hidden within them, so transmutation from one to another is possible.
2. Gold is the purest metal, with silver next to it.
3. There is a substance capable of transforming base to pure metals, namely *the Stone*.

One name associated with our earliest historical knowledge of western alchemy is that of Bolus of Mendes (in the Nile Delta), a canny savant who wrote under the name of Democritus in *circa* 250 BC[8]. He made catalogues of the occult (hidden/invisible) properties of substances and organisms with notes as to their uses. His work *physika & mystika* shows that something like alchemy existed in the third century BC and already had a mystical and philosophical aspect worthy of separate mention, as well as a purely utilitarian one[9]. For example, the author attacks "those who, on an inconsidered and irrational impulse, want to prepare a remedy for the soul and a release from all suffering, and do not think of the harm they will come to." This is strongly suggestive of the known attempt (in third century AD

Neoplatonic circles) to isolate *spiritus* from matter in the form of a draught for imbibing, as a quick route to spiritual experience and transcendence of the body. It could also be a quick route to death. Bolus recorded the case of the Persian alchemist Ostanes who, in an attempt to separate the soul from (his) body, died : a victim of, or perhaps martyr to science, depending on your point of view. Ostanes' dates are uncertain (he is referred to by Gaius Plinius [AD 23-79] in his *Natural History*), but there is no doubt that Ostanes' reputation in the Art was well-established by the time of the Egyptian alchemist Zosimos of Panopolis (*circa* 300AD).

Zosimos, a great devotee of the Hermetic philosophical *corpus*, was familiar with the age-old alchemical interest in a transforming *stone* as both agent and goal of the alchemical work. In his *Concerning the Art and its Interpretation*, Zosimos quotes from a fascinating and suggestive passage which he attributes to Ostanes :

> Go to the waters of the Nile and there you will find a stone that has a spirit [*pneuma*]. Take this, divide it, thrust in your hand and draw out its heart : for its soul [*psyche*] is in its heart.[10]

The search for this stone - the famous *lapis philosophorum* - would occupy the time and practical resources of alchemists for at least 1500 years after the time of Zosimos.

The explosion of *Gnosis* in the second century AD made a definite and permanent impact on the development of alchemy. On the one hand, gnostic theories enriched and personalised it, but on the other, gnosticising the Art took it far from its experimental and utilitarian aspect. The Hermetic *Cyranides* explicitly states with reference to alchemy that the major *opus* is nothing less than the liberation of the 'soul' from 'body'. It is however never altogether clear in alchemical texts whether the operation of transmuting the lower metals, (*viz* : lead) to higher metals (silver and gold) might not simply be an analogy for a spiritual exercise or indeed *vice versa*. A mystical and a physical practice often seem to go hand in hand. For by the second century it was normal to think of metals as being composed of both a lifeless physical base (uniform for all metals), and an invigorating and distinguishable 'soul', (becoming visible through the action of fire). The 'soul' of the metal was thought to exist in varying degrees of purity, and this not only indicated the dignity of the metal but also provided analogies for the spiritual awareness of the alchemist. It also followed, according to the physics of the time, to see the 'soul' of the metal as subject to stellar influences, as people were thought to be. In this context it was logical to envision the possibility of transmuting the metal by influence upon the 'soul' of the metal. This explains why operations had to be undertaken according to appropriate astrological configurations. Each planet corresponded to a particular metal : Mercury with mercury; gold with the Sun; silver with the Moon; lead with Saturn; iron with Mars; copper with Venus and tin with Jupiter. The highest state of the soul was identification with God, and in alchemical language, this state was Gold : the Sun, the "visible god" of the Hermetists. The transmutation of the soul, as understood by the sages of Alexandria (where alchemy flourished), required the sympathy, in the deepest sense, of the alchemist with the work. If you wished to advance in alchemy, you had to advance in *gnosis*.

  The great question was how to arrive at the *Gold*, for which purpose it was necessary to know how to release the spirit (*pneuma*) or *mercurius* (principle of transformation - Mercury was of course the Latin form of Hermes), hidden or imprisoned within the chemical substance[11]. In order to effect the transformation, a system of more or less standard but polyvalent operations was employed, whereby higher substances impacted on lower ones in the belief that the *mercurius* of the superior substance would swallow the impurities of the lesser. Thus *mercurius* was frequently portrayed as a devouring serpent. As a symbol of the totality of the cosmos and its cyclic nature, we sometimes see the gnostic figure of the *ouroboros*, the serpent devouring its own tail, forming an unbroken process of transmutation : the cosmos. And since *mercurius* or philosophical (not chemical) mercury was thought to be the *quintessence* of the four elements, seventeenth century Christian alchemists were content to see the striking image of the serpent nailed to a crucifix (symbolizing the four elements) as Christ : the principle of the redemptive suffering of the metal's soul. Death and Resurrection are meaningful ways of interpreting the transformation of substances within the alchemical vase to the spiritual mind. By the sixteenth century, (in the works of Joseph Quercetanus[12], who drew on the medieval manuscript tradition), the processes associated with alchemy, forever watched over by the arch psychopomp Hermes Trismegistus, had been systematised as involving more or less the following stages :

1. Calcination.	7. Cibation
2. Solution.	8. Sublimation
3. Elementary separation	9. Fermentation

4. Conjunction.	10. Exaltation
5. Putrefaction	11. Augmentation
6. Coagulation.	12. Projection.

Note that last process, *projection* : a common enough term now in the argot of psychology, and taken from the esoteric jargon of alchemy. Indeed alchemy is full of processes we should now regard as interior psychological ones. For example, the annihilation of opposites through the *mysterium conionctionis*, sometimes represented in the image of the copulating couple, *Sol* and *Luna*. This drive to transcend duality has very clear parallels in gnostic philosophy. The gnostic conception within alchemy could not be expressed more clearly than it is in the prologue to the Hermetic *Cyranides* where the author quotes from Harpocration of Alexandria (mid-second century BC) who says he found the following inscription in Babylon "carved in Syrian characters" and which he had translated in Alexandria :

> O immortal soul, clothed in a mortal body, you are borne from on high by the evil bonds of Necessity, for God Himself declared that you would rule over mortal bodies and bear with the sinful, being the yarn spun by the fates and Necessity. For like a man who is imprisoned and in bondage, so you too are held by the harsh bonds of Necessity. But when you escape from the mortal and oppressive body, you will truly behold God ruling in the air and in the clouds. He who eternally brings upon the earth thunder and earthquakes, lightning and thunder-bolts, and moves the foundations of the earth and the waves of the sea. Such will be the eternal works of God the mother of all things. God has made known to mortals all things, and their opposites.

This account is reminiscent of the legend surrounding what is probably the most significant alchemical text of all time : the Emerald Tablet of Hermes Trismegistos, also known as the *Tabula Smaragdina*. This was variously thought to have been the only inscribed wisdom to survive the Great Flood, or to have been written on a tablet, found in the tomb of the Thrice Greatest himself. It was transmitted in Arabic texts from the eighth to the ninth centuries from a text of Syrian origin and was translated into Latin in the twelfth century and made subject to continuous commentary throughout the Middle Ages. The Emerald Tablet was almost certainly in existence in the fourth century AD, since it appears to have been paraphrased by the 'Gnostic Jesus' of the Nag Hammadi Library[13].

We find in the Emerald Tablet the quintessential doctrines of the

Hermetic Art of alchemy : the interaction of the microcosm and macrocosm - the two coming from a single source; the universe created out of the four Aristotelian elements; the universal power of the spirit to penetrate the macro and microcosm, and even the luminous couple of the Chemical Nuptials, *Sol* and *Luna* : the two opposed principles which must be united. The Emerald Tablet expresses the *Great Work* of the alchemist in a nutshell:

> It is true, without lie, certain and of all truth,
> That which is below is like that which is above,
> and that which is above is like that which is below,
> to work the miracle of the one thing.
> And as all things have been and came from one
> thus all things were born in this unique way by adaption.
> The sun is the Father,
> The moon is its mother,
> The wind carries it in his belly,
> The earth is its nourisher,
> The Father of all, the Will of the whole cosmos is here;
> Her power is complete if she is converted in earth.
> You will separate the earth from the fire, the subtle from the gross,
> carefully with great industry.
> It climbs from the earth to the sky, and then it descends in the earth,
> and it receives the power of the superior things and the inferior.
> You will have by this means all the glory of the world,
> and all obscurity is removed from you.
> This is the strong power of all power,
> because it will conquer everything subtle and everything solid.
> Thus the world has been created.
> From this will be and will follow the innumerable adaptions
> for which the medium is here.
> That is why I have been called Hermes Trismegistus,
> having the three parts of the philosophy of the world.
> That which I said on the operation of the sun is accomplished and
> perfected.[14]

Zosimos of Panopolis

From the fourth century onwards, the substantial name *mercurius* would be inseparably linked to Hermes or Mercurius Trismegistus. Instrumental in forging this link was the third to fourth century Egyptian alchemist Zosimos of Panopolis, (Akhmim), who operated in Alexandria, the heart of the gnostic world at that time. Zosimos is an extremely interesting figure. His dreams have been subjected to positive analysis by Carl Jung, while Garth Fowden writes of him in his excellent book *The Egyptian Hermes*: "Zosimos' spirituality is clearly the product of his contact with the philosophical Hermetica."

The vogue for timeless Hermetic study may have had something to do with the times. The century in which Zosimos was born has been described by Dean Inge as "an age of lengthening shadows and waning light. So we think; and so, on the whole, thought those who lived in it. 'The world has grown old.' 'This is indeed the *fin de siècle*' (*ipsa clausula saeculi*). 'Humanity is at its last gasp.' Pagans and Christians are equally pessimistic. To both alike, civilisation seemed to have no future. This feeling of hopelessness is intelligible. The government of the Empire had fallen into anarchy. There were seven puppet emperors, set up and deposed by the army, between 235 and 249.[15]" In spite of all this, Dean Inge asks the question, "May not political calamities actually liberate philosophy and religion, by compelling them to attend exclusively to their own business?" A good point, and one which may explain why we find Zosimos, obviously a brilliant individual, inspecting an alchemical furnace in a temple at Memphis fifty years after the period described.

While our inheritance of Zosimos' works is fragmentary, they nonetheless tell us a great deal about his inner life. Here was a man driven more by spiritual impulse than academic curiosity, a drive whose powerful urges found expression in his acquaintance with Platonism, Gnosticism, Judaism and the wisdom ascribed to Hermes and the oriental Zoroaster. "Like many men of his period, Zosimos reflected on how his soul might be freed from the world of flux and illusion; and his preoccupations occasionally invaded his sleeping hours, and gave rise to dreams and visions."[16] In one dream, Zosimos describes climbing steps towards a bowl-shaped altar, strongly reminiscent of the Hermetic bowl of *nous* (νους) described in *Corpus Hermeticum* IV. At the altar stood a priest who announced to Zosimos that he had :

> accomplished the descent of these fifteen steps of darkness and the ascent of the steps of light, and he who sacrifices is himself the sacrificial victim. Casting away the coarseness of the body, and consecrated priest by necessity, I am made perfect as a spirit...I am Aion, the priest of the sanctuaries, and I have submitted myself to an unendurable torment. For there came one in haste at early morning, who overpowered me and pierced me through with the sword, and dismembered me in

accordance with the rule of harmony. And he drew off the skin of my head with the sword which he was holding, and mingled the bones with the pieces of flesh, and caused them to be burned with the fire that he held in his hand [?], till I perceived by the transformation of the body that I had become spirit. And that is my unendurable torment.[17]

These archetypal dream-figures appear to embody or symbolise technical, alchemical processes. (Hence, for example, the 'steps' to be taken to the bowl/altar.) The dismembering, flaying, apparent death, resurrection and piercing would return in graphic form in seventeenth century Rosicrucian-inspired works such as *Atalanta Fugiens* (1618), by Count Michael Maier, to baffle the uninitiated.

Unlike modern science, which hopes to objectify the world through the disciplines of rational logic, alchemy, through meditation and imagination, brings the soul and the spirit directly into a vision of the creative process, creating an almost intermediate visionary plane of meaning, tending, adepts believe, towards psychic wholeness. This is why, among other reasons, Carl Jung (who saw himself as a kind of descendent of the Gnostics) took to alchemy with such passion and purpose. ("If you do not bring forth what is within you, what you do not bring forth will destroy you." says the gnostic *Gospel of Thomas* - and much of Jung's psychology has to do with this drawing-out process, though it should be added that Jung's psychological interpretation of alchemy is not shared by all scholars).

Zosimos held the magical view that the material and spiritual find their kinship in a universal pattern of powerful sympathetic links, with the corollary that spiritual experiences may be expressed in material metaphors and, more precisely, that disciplined understanding of the properties of matter is an indispensable aid for liberation of the soul from the 'body-tomb'. The paradox of the human experience, from this point of view, is that although the body is an expression of the soul, the body can become the prison of the soul. The tendency of man, according to the gnostic alchemical tradition, is to sink into what is, in the profoundest sense, his material projection. Our present plight, according to gnostic theory, represents the outflow of this fall. The spiritual alchemist, the divine operator, tries to redress the catastrophe.

Man's deepest problem, from the Hermetic point of view, is one of perception, ignorance : *a-gnosis*. For Zosimos, *gnosis* is linked to the image of the baptism in the Hermetic bowl of *nous* : mind or spirit, found in chapter IV of the *Corpus Hermeticum*. This chapter is mentioned by name in Zosimos' treatise, 'η τελευταια 'αποχη , (=he teleutaia apoche), a work devoted to the history of alchemical techniques in Egypt, and the primary role played by Hermes in their formulation. This work was addressed to a woman alchemist called Theosebia and contains a beautiful account of how to wait on God, and how to call Him :

> So do not allow yourself to be pulled back and forth like a woman, as I have already told you in my books *According to energy*. Do not roam about searching for God; but sit calmly at home, and God, who is everywhere, and not confined in the smallest place like the daemons, will come to you. And, being calm in body, calm also your passions, desire and pleasure and anger and grief and the twelve portions of death. In this way, taking control of yourself, you will summon the divine [to come] to you, and truly it will come, that which is everywhere and nowhere. And without being told, offer sacrifices to the daemons, but not offerings, nor [the sacrifices] which encourage and entice them, but rather the sacrifices that repel and destroy them, those of which Membres spoke to Solomon king of Jerusalem, and especially those that Solomon himself wrote as the product of his own wisdom. So doing, you will obtain the true and natural [tinctures] that are appropriate to certain times. Perform these things until your soul is perfected. When you realise that you have been perfected, and have found the natural [tinctures], spit on matter, and, hastening towards Poimenandres [*sic.* "the mind of the sovereignty"; possibly a word of Egyptian origin] and receiving baptism in the mixing-bowl [κρατηρ], hasten up towards your own race. [the race of perfected souls]

For Zosimos, conventional alchemy is a preparation for the subsequent purification and perfecting of the soul (cf : Iamblichus' Theurgy), information concerning which Zosimos takes wholesale from the Hermetica. *On apparatus and furnaces : authentic commentaries on the letter* Ω, is Zosimos's considered treatise on alchemy's spiritual aspect. The work is concerned to show the poverty of the fatalistic approach; the power of the stars can be transcended by fully realising man's spiritual dimension. Those who do not acknowledge this possibility are warned that : "Hermes calls such people mindless, only marchers swept along in the procession of fate." This is very similar to the plight of those who refuse to be baptized in the bath of *nous* in *Corpus Hermeticum* IV.4-5,7 :

just as processions pass into the crowd, unable to achieve anything themselves, but getting in the way of other people, so these men make their procession in the world, led astray as they are by the pleasures of the body.

Hermes divides humankind up into those who seek God and those who ignore Him. Zosimos follows Hermes and Zoroaster in believing those philosophers to be superior who are mastered neither by grief nor joy. He says that Zoroaster asserts that man can overcome fate by magic (possibly a reference to Neoplatonic Theurgy), but that Hermes declares magic to be unnecessary for the spiritual man. According to Zosimos, Hermes suggests a kind of cosmic quietism, reminiscent of the approach of the Zen Master : "nor must he [the spiritual man] use force upon necessity; but rather he should allow necessity to work in accordance with his own nature and judgement." Fate (the *heimarmene*, or 'night-cloak' of the stars), we are told, controls only the body, not the divine part of man. Man has the power to rise above the familiar sphere which is subject to zodiacal control. Hermetic man is forever breaking free.

Chapter Three

Hermes meets Islam

It is really no accident that our word for alchemy derives from the Arabic language, for it was to be in the lands conquered by the first four caliphs (between 632 and 661), that Hermes Trismegistos - and his Art - were to undergo a return to intellectual prominence in both the east and, subsequently, in the west as well.

In AD 830, the Abbasid caliph al-Ma'mún, (son of the illustrious Harun ar-Rashíd of *Arabian Nights* fame), was passing through Harran, about 40 miles south of Edessa. According to the Christian author Abú-Jusúf Abshaa'al-Qathíí[18], writing 70 years later, the caliph observed some men in unfamiliar costume :

> "To which of the peoples protected by law do you belong?"
> "We are Harranians."
> "Are you Christians?"
> "No."
> "Jews?"
> "No."
> "Magians?"[19]
> "No."
> "Have you a holy scripture or a prophet?"

The men offered an evasive answer. The caliph, running out of options, and patience, came to the inevitable point : "You are infidels and idolaters then, and it is permitted to shed your blood. If you have not, by the time when I return from my campaign [against the Byzantines], become either Moslems or adherents of one of the religions recognised in the Koran, I will kill you to a man."

On the departure of the caliph al-Ma'mún of Baghdad, these learned, pagan Harranians consulted with a lawyer as to a way of escape. The lawyer in turn consulted *Koran* II.59 which made it clear that Islam tolerated Christians, Jews - and *Sabians* :

> Surely they that believe, and those of Jewry, and the Christians, and those Sabians, whoso believe in God and the Last Day, and work righteousness - their wage awaits them with their Lord, and no fear shall be on them, neither shall they sorrow.

Fortunately for the Harranian pagans, nobody seems to have been too sure what the Prophet intended by the word 'Sabian'[20], so they took the name. However, the law also required a divinely recognised prophet and a book to support the new nomenclature. In this regard, the learned pagans of Harran settled on the Hermetica (in either Greek or Syriac versions) as their scripture, with Hermes as their prophet. This timely ruse was to bring Hermetic *gnosis* to the very heart of eastern and western intellectual, practical and spiritual experience : a momentous decision whose ramifications reverberate to this day.

Gnosis in Harran and Baghdad

By 898, a disinterested Arabic writer could describe the doctrine of the 'Sabians' (that is, Harranian pagans), as a philosophy taught by Hermes and *Agatho-daimon* (a patron deity of ancient Alexandria and a teacher of Hermes in the Hermetica). Since the Koran did not recognise these latter names as prophets, *Agatho-daimon* was identified with Seth, son of Adam, (an Egyptian Gnostic patriarch), while Hermes was identified as Idris, or Enoch, (a name identified with Jewish astrological gnosis). Justification came from Koran *sura* 19.57 and 21.85.

From 830 onwards, the Arabs got the greater part of their knowledge of Greek science and philosophy from the pagans of Harran. According to the philosopher-historian al-Farabi (d.950) : "Under Omar son of Abd-el-Aziz [AD 705-710] the chief seat of teaching was transferred from Alexandria to Antioch; and later on, in the reign of Mutawakkil, it was transferred to Harran." In about 856, al-Mutawakkil, in a reign characterised by a combination of rigidity and debauch, re-established the Baghdad library and and translation school. From that time to about 1050, the Harranian Hermetists played a conspicuous rôle in the intellectual life of Baghdad. This period produced a brilliant crop of Hermetic stars, the most renowned of whom must be the extraordinary sage, Thabit ibn Qurra (835-901).

Thabit

Thabit began his professional life as a money-changer, (a job familiar to cultural outsiders) but, fortunately for us, a quarrel with other Sabians led to his expulsion from Harran. Fortunately for Thabit, he found favour with the caliph of Baghdad, Muthadid, along with 500 dinars a year for his scientific work. Thabit even got the government to recognise himself and his companions as an independent and separate community of Sabians. The most learned Harranians followed him to Baghdad, a move which resulted in a kind of school of pagan Neoplatonism, the like of which had not been seen since the Christian Byzantine Emperor Justinian had closed down the Athens philosophy school 450 years previously; this time the Hermetica were regarded as master-texts.

Thabit certainly made his mark. It was said that he wrote 166 books in Syriac and Arabic. It was also said that "no-one would have been able to get any benefit from the philosophic writings of the Greeks, if they had not had Thabit's translations." He was a convinced and enlightened pagan, a conviction well underlined in the following quotation taken by Barhebraeus from Thabit's *Liber de confirmatione religionis ethnicorum*:

> We are the heirs and propagators of Paganism. Happy is he who, for the sake of Paganism, bears the burden [of persecution?] with firm hope. Who else have civilised the world, and built the cities, if not the nobles and kings of Paganism? Who else have set in order the harbours and the rivers? And who else have taught the hidden wisdom? To whom else has the Deity revealed itself, [quite an audacious statement to make under a Moslem government], given oracles, and told about the future, if not to the famous men among the Pagans? The Pagans have made known all this. They have discovered the art of healing the soul; they have also made known the art of healing the body. They have filled the earth with settled forms of government, and with wisdom, which is the highest good. Without Paganism the world would be empty and miserable.

Thabit's works include commentaries on Plato, Pythagoras, Proclus, Aristotle, Music, the Hermetica, works on local cultic practice and belief, astrology, mathematics, geometry, the occult sciences, and a treatise on the cryptic significance or magical efficacy of the alphabet. Thabit compiled a 'pandect' : a recapitulation of the whole of medicine in thirty-one scrupulously researched sections, in clear and succinct language. The Sabian master-mind also did pioneering work on the principles of balance, specific gravity, and the specific weight of alloys. He translated an *Introduction to Arithmetic* by Nichomachus, a work which also deals with music. Often regarded as the greatest Arab geometer, Thabit did science the service of translating into Arabic seven of the eight books of the conic sections of Appolonius, thus preserving three now lost in the original. His work on the shadows of the *gnomon* (sundial) is the earliest known on the subject.

Thabit made meticulous astronomical observations in Baghdad to determine the attitude of the sun and the length of the solar year. He not only elucidated ancient works on astronomy and geometry but also invented new propositions and contributed annotations to facilitate study. Nothing of scientific value appears to have been beyond his scope. He improved the translation of Euclid's *Elements* by Ishak b. Hunain, as well as the latter's weak translation of the *Almagest*. It was Thabit's work on Euclid which brought Gérard of Cremona (1114-1187) to Toledo in search of the *Almagest* over two hundred years later. Indeed, many of the Sabian works finally reached the minor-renaissance of the West in the 12th and 13th centuries in Latin translations, made at the Toledo school founded by Archbishop Raymond under Archdeacon Dominico Gundisalvi. Gérard of Cremona also translated other works by Thabit, including the *Liber Carastonis sive de Statera*, on the physics of balance, and it is by virtue of these transmissions that Gérard of Cremona became known as the "father of Arabism in Europe" : an influence which would later fortify the scientific aspect of the Renaissance. As late as the mid-sixteenth century, the great Elizabethan mathematician and magus, John Dee, when compiling his *Monas Hieroglyphica* (1564), used Thabit's *De imaginibus* : a treatise on planetary images, reflecting the talismanic type of Neoplatonic celestial magic. According to the late Professor Max Meyerhof : "Belonging to the pagan sect of the Sabians and at heart deeply attached to paganism, this scholar is one of the most eminent representatives in the Middle Ages of the tradition of classical culture."

Thabit ibn Qurra's son, Sinán, a physician of high repute, continued the family tradition. He was appointed head of the medical profession in Baghdad, fortifying his medicine with a thorough knowledge of mathematics, astronomy, logic, metaphysics, as well as Socrates, Plato and Aristotle. Sinán's generation also provided another influential Sabian : al Battáni (877-918), the famous astronomer and mathematician, born in Persia and known to medieval Europe as Albategnus. The *Zij* of al-Battáni was translated by Plato of Tivoli two and a half centuries later. According to Carra de Vaux[21], al-Battáni was "one of the most illustrious scholars of the East, perhaps the one whom Latin scholars of the Middle Ages and Renaissance most admired and eulogised." He compiled astronomical tables with more accurate computations regarding the first appearance of the new moon, the inclination of the ecliptic, the length of the tropic and sidereal year, lunar anomolies, eclipses, parallaxes, than had ever been seen before. His greatest claim to fame was that if he did not discover, then at the very least he popularised the first notions of trigonometrical ratios as used today. Al-Battáni substituted the *sine* for Ptolemy's clumsy chords; he used the tangent and co-tangent and was acquainted with two or three fundamental relations in trigonometry. His work on trigonometry and algebra brings us, according to de Vaux, "far beyond the point reached by the Greeks and really opens the era of modern science."

Perhaps the most obvious legacy of the Harranian Hermetists can be seen in the cathedrals and abbeys which have dignified the western catholic world from the time of the construction of the Abbey of Conques (c.1030-1080) onwards. Works translated by Thabit ibn Qurra were central to the understanding of forces and forms which made the Gothic explosion possible. According to the renowned medievalist Jean Gimpel[22]: "The remarkable Arab contribution to our culture is often underestimated, and yet it was this that made the full flowering of the Middle Ages possible. Without it, the Renaissance could barely have developed and the 20th century might still be technically and scientifically in the nineteenth." And at the very heart of the Arab contribution were the Hermetic Sabians of Baghdad.

It is, furthermore, difficult to escape the conclusion that Sabian influence in some way helped to shape the mythology of medieval freestone masons : originators of what we now call Freemasonry. The earliest masonic documents recognised by English Freemasons today, the so-called *Old Charges*, date from around the year 1400, and attribute the survival of the masonic sciences after the Flood to Hermes Trismegistus and to Euclid, operating in Egypt. Such knowledge of these two figures as existed in the western Middle Ages derived, as far as we know, from Harran and Baghdad. It is also recorded in the varied lore of the crusading years that some knights returned from the east with Saracen masons[23]. A learned mason from the Holy Land would almost certainly have obtained his Arabic translations of Greek technical works on geometry from the Sabian intellectuals of Harran and Baghdad.

It is curious that in the earliest extant copies of (late seventeenth/early eighteenth century) Scottish masonic catechisms[24], the master mason's secret word is given as *Mahabyn*, in association with the teaching of points of masonic fellowship. The origin of this word has always been a mystery to Freemasons. In the context of this study, it is not unreasonable to suppose that the word is derived from *mahabba*, the Arabic word for *love* used by Sufi brethren in greeting. The development of Sufic mysticism, or rather *gnosis*, is linked to the work and beliefs of the Baghdad Sabians.

Thabit and the Gral

It seems more than a mere possibility that the translation-work of Thabit has influenced one of the most significant works of European literature and spiritual mythology, and along the way has given us at least one key interpretation of that mysterious phenomenon known as the Holy Grail. The document in question is Wolfram von Eschenbach's (fictional) account of a celestial *Gral* guarded by 'templars' in his *Parzifal*, written between *circa* 1200 and 1220. Wolfram's account of how he received the Gral story for his *Parzifal* is undoubtedly intriguing, as there is the whiff of some historical actuality underlying the fantasy. Wolfram states that one of his sources, "the heathen Flegetanis", who left a document in Toledo (famous for its translation school), was an astronomer who was both Jewish and, on his father's side, a heathen (he "worshipped a calf as though it was his god") and that he had seen the *Gral*, its name spelled out in the stars, and left on earth by a "a troop" who then "rose high above the stars, if their innocence drew them back again". Wolfram states that the document of Flegetanis had been discovered by "the wise Master" Kyot of Provence, thus tying Wolfram's work into the vogue and status of the Languedoc troubadours for whom there was such a vogue in the courts of Germany. In spite of there having been a historical person called Gyot of Provins, a troubadour, the weight of scholarship falls against the idea that Wolfram is presenting a true story as regards his primary source.

Wolfram's sources, other than the highly catholic Arthurian stories of Chrétien de Troyes, are obscure[25]. Von Eschenbach was exceptionally well-read, and alchemical sources cannot be ruled out. For example, his account of the Gral bears little conceptual analogy to the idea of it being the cup in which Joseph of Arimathaea collected Christ's blood - as in Robert de Boron's *Joseph ou l'Estoire dou Graal* (c.1210). Wolfram's setting for his Gral account is almost wholly alchemical. The Gral is identified with the *Stone* :

31

'It is well known to me,' said his host, 'that many formidable fighting-men dwell at Munsalvaesche with the Gral. They are continually riding out on sorties in quest of adventure. Whether these same Templars reap trouble or renown, they bear it for their sins. A warlike company lives there. I will tell you how they are nourished. They live from a Stone whose essence is most pure. If you have never heard of it I shall name it for you here. It is called "Lapsit exillis"[26]. By virtue of this Stone the Phoenix is burned to ashes, in which he is reborn. - Thus does the Phoenix moult its feathers![27] Which done, it shines dazzling bright and lovely as before! Further : however ill a mortal may be, from the day on which he sees the Stone he cannot die for that week, nor does he lose his colour. ..Such powers does the Stone confer on mortal men that their flesh and bones are soon made young again. This Stone is called "The Gral".

'Today a Message alights upon the Gral governing its highest virtue, for today is Good Friday, when one can infallibly see a Dove wing its way down from Heaven. It brings a small white Wafer to the Stone and leaves it there. The Dove, all dazzling white, then flies up to Heaven again. Every Good Friday, as I say, the Dove brings it to the Stone, from which the Stone receives all that is good on earth of food and drink, of paradisal excellence - I mean whatever the earth yields. The Stone, furthermore, has to give them the flesh of all the wild things that live below the aether, whether they fly, run, or swim - such prebend does the Gral, thanks to its indwelling powers, bestow on the chivalric Brotherhood.

'As to those who are appointed to the Gral, hear how they are made known. Under the top edge of the Stone an inscription announces the name and lineage of the one summoned to make the glad journey. Whether it concerns girls or boys, there is no need to erase their names, for as soon as a name has been read it vanishes from sight! Those who are now full-grown all came here as children. Happy the mother of every child destined to serve there! Rich and poor alike rejoice if a child of theirs is summoned and they are bidden to send it to that Company! Such children are fetched from many countries and forever after are immune from the shame of sin and have a rich reward in Heaven. When they die here in this world, Paradise is theirs in the next[28].

'When Lucifer and the Trinity began to war with each other, those who did not take sides, worthy, noble angels, had to descend to earth to that Stone which is forever incorruptible.[29]
I do not know whether God forgave them or damned them in the end : for if it was His due He took them back. Since that time the Stone has been in the care of those whom God appointed to it and to whom He sent his angel. This, sir, is how matters stand regarding the Gral.'

'If knightly deeds with shield and lance can win fame for one's earthly self, yet also Paradise for one's soul, then the chivalric life has been my one desire!,' said Parzifal. 'I fought wherever fighting was to be had, so that my warlike hand has glory within its grasp. If God is any judge of fighting He will appoint me to that place so that the Company there know me as a knight who will never shun battle.' (From *Parzifal*, Chapt.9)

Had von Eschenbach's 'Flegetanis', (used here as a cover-name for some of Wolfram's alleged oriental sources), seen *Libellus* IV.25 of our present *Corpus Hermeticum*, he would have read there the story of a dish or bowl sent down to earth by God. This account, linking this mythical image directly to *gnosis*, was probably written in Greek in Alexandria (c.200-300AD), and is of course attributed to the mythic sage, Hermes Trismegistos.

> HERMES : ..it is man's function to contemplate the works of God; and for this purpose was he made, that he might view the universe with wondering awe, and come to know its Maker. ..Now speech, my son, God imparted to all men; but mind [*nous*] he did not impart to all.
> TAT : Tell me then father, why did God not impart mind [*nous*] to all men?
> HERMES : It was his will, my son, that mind should be placed in the midst as a prize that human souls may win.
> TAT : Where did he place it?
> HERMES : He filled a great bowl with *nous* [mind], and sent it down to earth; and he appointed a herald, and bade him make proclamation to the hearts of men : "Hearken, each human heart; baptize yourself in this bowl, if you can, recognising for what purpose you have been made, and believing that you shall ascend to Him who sent the bowl down." Now those who gave heed to the proclamation, and dipped themselves in the bath of mind, these men got a share of *gnosis*; they received mind, and so became complete men... as many as have partaken of the gift which God has sent, these, my son, in comparison with the others, are as immortal gods to mortal men. They embrace in their own mind all the things that are, the things on earth and the things in heaven, if there is aught above heaven; and raising themselves to that height, they see the Good.

This amusing account is plainly a gnostic allegory on the theme of free-will and spiritual predisposition. Acquaintance with the 'bowl' (Greek : κρατηρ = krater, origin of our 'crater') is a goal well worth seeking[30]. Are there any grounds for thinking von Eschenbach had access to Hermetic sources? Such access might be considered unlikely until the name of Thabit ibn Qurra emerges from Wolfram's text. Thabit ibn Qurra, the Sabian polymath who took Hermes as his prophet and the Hermetica as his holy book, is mentioned by name in chapter thirteen of *Parzifal* as a "philosopher" and one who "fathomed abstruse arts". When Wolfram has cause to list the planets, he gives their names in Arabic. Indeed, the whole of *Parzifal* is drenched in Germanicisations of oriental lore, which, we may surmise, was exactly what his readers wished to be stimulated by - and he makes it plain that the source for such information was Toledo, which indeed it was. Toledo was where Sabian translations of Greek and Syriac works into Arabic came to be translated into Latin.

The Sabian Inheritance in the West

This is a timely moment to look at what else came to the minds of western medieval scholars as a result of the Hermetic impulse in the east.

One very important magical text extant in the Middle Ages was that compendium known as *Picatrix*. This was a Latin version of the Arabic treatise *Ghayat al-hakim* (The Aim of the Sage), which appeared in Spain in the eleventh century and which was translated in about 1256. The work emanated from the Sabian school of Harran. *Picatrix* exercised an immense influence, being, according to Ernesto Garin, a major conduit of Neoplatonist thought from the Middle Ages to the Renaissance. In it we see a conflation of Hermetic, Jewish, Neoplatonic and vulgar magic, and through it we catch a glimpse of the mind which saw all these strands as related and conceptually inseparable.

Picatrix is a comprehensive treatise on sympathetic and astral magic with particular reference to the making of talismans. The work explains how to draw down the influences of the stars by establishing chains of correspondences with the celestial world. The author or authors perhaps recognised something which has only recently re-entered scientific speculation : that the universe may be considered as an 'holistic' system of interdependent activity where all things relate implicitly to all other things, that we isolate *things* for perceptual convenience by rationation. *Picatrix* maintains that the whole art of magic consists in "capturing" and guiding the influence of *spiritus*, (something like the souls of the celestial world, below *intellectus*, or the Greek *nous*) into *materia*. The method consisted in making talismans : images associated with the stars, inscribed on the correct materials at the most propitious times (astrology played a part), and in the right state of mind[31]. The practice demanded a deep knowledge of astronomy, mathematics, music and metaphysics, and formed a kind of mirror to the practice of alchemy. Talismanic magic aimed to get *spiritus* into material form, while alchemy aimed at extracting *spiritus* from matter in order to change the matter and the mind of the operator.

The book also contains an account of one of the first metropolitan utopias, the city of *Adocentyn*, (Arabic : *al-Asmunain*), built by Hermes and kept under good influences by astral magic. This idea was to re-appear in the ideal schemes of Thomas More in the 16th century and in the ideal visions of both Francis Bacon (*New Atlantis.* 1627) and the founder of the Rosicrucian idea, Johann Valentin Andreae's *Christianopolis* (1619), and is central to the history of European utopianism. Furthermore, *Picatrix* contained a description of an underground vault which may have influenced Johann Valentin Andreae's conception of the tomb of Christian Rosenkreuz in the *Fama Fraternitatis* (pub. 1614) :

> When I wished to bring to light the science of the mystery and nature of creation, I came upon a subterranean vault full of darkness and winds. I could see nothing because of the darkness, nor could I keep my lamp alight because of the many winds. Then a person appeared to me in my sleep in a form of the greatest beauty. He said to me : "Take a lamp and place it under a glass and shield it from the winds : then it will give thee light in spite of them. Then go into the vault; dig in its centre and from there bring forth a certain talismanic image, artfully made. When you have drawn out this image, the winds will cease to blow through the vault. Then dig in its four corners and you will bring to light the knowledge of the mysteries of creation, the causes of nature, the origins and qualities of things." At that I said to him : "Who art thou?" He replied : "I am thy Perfect Nature. If thou wishest to see me, call me by my name."[32]

From Baghdad *via* Spain came Thabit ibn Qurra's *De imaginibus* on talismanic, Neoplatonist celestial magic, and al-Kindi's important *De radiis* or *Theorica artium magicarum* : talismanic and liturgical magic in the context of a philosophy of causation based on the emanation of rays. The author, Abu Yusuf Ya'qub ibn Ishaq al-Kindi, (born in 850 in the southern Arabian peninsular and educated in Baghdad), also translated the "Theology" (*Uthulujiyya*) of Aristotle. This work was not by Aristotle but was in fact a commentary by Porphyry on books *iv* to *vi* of the *Enneads* of Plotinus, and was known in the west as the *Liber de causis* or Book of Causes. The book represents a kind of gnosticising of Plotinus, describing the descent of the soul, from the pure incorporeal realm of "intelligence" into the world of sense and corporeality. Very much like the second-century Gnostic Valentinian myth of the yearning *Sophia* (Wisdom), the soul *produces* the world of perception out of its pain and desire to give form to the ideal or intellectual forms which are present to it, and which derive from its origin in the *active intellect* of God the One. The soul or spirit (*intellectus* to the Latins in this context), creates reality. This gnostic theory of perception was to have great impact in the West for centuries and something like it is currently being revived in the world of quantum physics as well as in the continental philosophy of perception and optics. These ideas were directly to affect al-Kindi's work on light, rays, mirrors and the whole field of optics and were to colour that area of study for Latin scholars interested in the physics of light.

Al-Kindi's *de radiis* was highly influential on two medieval geniuses: Friar Roger Bacon (c.1214/20-c.1292) and Robert Grosseteste (1168/70-1253). It was particularly influential because it tried to explain through a natural philosophy that astral and other magical effects could be explained without demonology, through the propagation of astral and other 'natural' rays. In other words, it was a work of natural, not supernatural, science.

The theory of this 'natural magic' (there is of course no distinction between science and magic in this period) runs as follows. The nature and condition of a star is emitted as a ray. All terrestrial events are the product of a total harmony of rays in the heavens, a view which was often blended with both geometry and the more mystical *light metaphysics*, and served against the imputation of vulgar magic levelled at the 'scientist'. Robert Grosseteste interpreted al-Kindi's work as grounds for believing that the *essence* of light is the formative and structural principle of the universe. According to Grosseteste, in a striking conceptual premonition of Einstein's famous formula ($E=mc^2$), the universe is the result of the union of formless prime matter and 'light', of which visible light is only an aspect. Our word 'radiation' of course derives from the idea of astral rays. Grosseteste believed that a point of 'light' can produce a sphere of any size - again a striking premonition of the hidden potential within the atom - and that light formed the basis of spacial dimension and physical extension. Thus, man's essential being was *light* : a somewhat gnostic view. For Grosseteste, light was the principle and model for all natural operations, including the emanation of species and the virtues of things; as with light, all causes of natural effects operate by lines, angles and figures. The differences between phenomena depend on the laws of optics and perspective. Geometric optics thus became the basis for a mathematical philosophy of nature, affecting and effecting everything, including astrology. For example, a stellar virtue was understood to act more strongly when concentrated rather than when diffused through refraction or reflection, or when striking perpendicularly rather than obliquely, due to the numerically lower angles of incidence of those rays when reaching the earth. Astral influences were regarded not as occult forces or demonic powers but as rays which behaved as light. Thus, mathematics had become a divine science, or science of the divine. The full implications of this shift in perspective would have to wait until the seventeenth century for its fulfillment in the scientific revolution[33]. Nevertheless, Grosseteste's universe was still magical, but the magic was determined by an understanding of mathematical and physical laws. The deterministic power of the stars had been theoretically overcome by the illumination gained by knowledge of their mathematical nature. Hermetically-influenced manuscripts oversaw the birth of *Natural Magic* : the critical stage before the birth of modern science, the latter rejecting its mother in infancy.[34]

The Sabians lived on at Baghdad as a separate sect until about 1050, seeing out the decline of the Golden Age inaugurated by the great caliphs (al-Mansur, ar-Rashíd and al-Ma'mún). Shortly before 950, the Buwayhids took over the governance of Baghdad and a period of strictly enforced Islamic orthodoxy took place, lasting until the coming of the Seljuks in 1055. Explicit Hermetism went underground - or perhaps devotees simply changed their hierophant's name from Hermes to Muhammad.

It is certainly strange that at the very time the Sabians seem to disappear from Baghdad, the Hermetic documents known to us as the *Corpus Hermeticum* appear in Constantinople - after a 500 year interval - in the hands of the Platonic scholar, Psellus. As Walter Scott (d.1925), a translator of the Hermetica, wrote in his introduction to that work : "Is there not something more than chance in this?" What we now know as the *Corpus Hermeticum* may be no more than a chance collection of what was brought to Constantinople by a Sabian to escape destruction. Although conjectural, "there is nothing to prevent us from

37

supposing that it was the arrival in Constantinople of a few such Sabian Neoplatonists from Baghdad, and the writing which they brought with them, that first started the revival of Platonic study in which Psellus took the leading part." (Scott). Such an occurrence would certainly be strikingly similar to that by which the *Corpus Hermeticum* arrived in Florence from Macedonia with such epoch-marking momentousness in 1460, following the fall of Constantinople to the Turks in 1453 (see chapter four). And can it be complete external co-incidence that the disappearance of the Baghdad Sabians also co-incides with the appearance of the first great Sufi order, in Baghdad, in the form by which the *turuq* (paths) of Sufi mysticism are now known?

Alchemy in the Middle Ages

The alchemist known to medieval westerners as Geber has been identified as Jabir ibn Hayyan, called as-Sufi ('the Mystic'), but it is highly unlikely that much of the material which bears his name has anything to do with this eighth century sage. The works attributed to him are now thought to have been put together in the tenth century by some kind of secret society. There certainly was a Jabir, famous as the father of Arabic alchemy, born at Kufa and who practised as a physician to the family of the Barmecides, the viziers of Harun ar-Rashíd, caliph of Baghdad. Implicated in the downfall of the Barmecides, Jabir died in exile from Baghdad at Kufa in 803, where it is said his laboratory was discovered 200 years later.

There are about one hundred works of Jabir extant. Many are, in the words of Professor Max Meyerhof (no sympathiser with mysticism) "confused jumbles of puerile superstition". Others suggest the profound need for experiment, a unique trait of the Geber literature. His greatest fame lies in his practical scientific advances. He improved methods for evaporation, filtration, sublimation, melting, distillation and crystallisation. He described the preparation of, for example, cinnabar (sulphide of mercury), arsenious oxide and others. He knew how to obtain almost pure vitriols, alums, alkalis, sal-ammoniac, saltpetre, and 'liver' and 'milk' of sulphur by heating sulphur and alkali. He prepared fairly pure mercury oxide and sublimate, acetates of lead and other metals, sometimes crystalised. He obtained crude sulphuric and nitric acids as a mixture of them (*aqua regia*=kingly water), and explored the solubility of gold and silver in this acid. Several technical terms of alchemy were derived from Jabir's Arabic writings : *realgar* (red sulphide of arsenic), *tutia* (zinc oxide), *alkali*, *antimony* (Arabic : *ithmid*), *alembic* (for the upper) and *aludel* for the lower part of the distillation vessel. His *Book of the Seventy* was known from the Middle Ages in an inferior and incomplete Latin version, translated by Gérard of Cremona (d.1187). His *Book of the Composition of Alchemy* was translated by the Englishman Robert of Chester in 1144. Albertus Magnus (c.1206-1280), a thinker saturated in Neoplatonic learning, repeated Geber's teachings in his *De Mineralibus*, and Geber had a very pronounced influence on the encyclopaedic *Speculum Naturale* of Vincent of Beauvais. The large number of alchemical tracts ascribed to Arnald of Villanova and to Raymond (Ramon) Lull (c.1232-1315), the Majorcan mystic, are brimming with quotations from the works of Geber.

Geber's work also gave his followers clues as to the critical question of the state of mind of the alchemist when undergoing alchemical operations. Alchemy was a psychic experience for the successful operator. As Jung puts it : "what he was in reality experiencing was his own unconscious[35]." The making of the Stone transcends reason - as we should expect of a noetic, out of the 'body' (ego) experience. Geber's *Liber perfecti magisterii* demands that the operator, or *artifex*, be of a most subtle mind, with an adequate knowledge of metals and minerals. He must not have a coarse or rigid mind, nor should he be greedy or avaricious, irresolute or vacillating. He must not be hasty or vain. Firmness of purpose, perseverence, patience, mildness, a capacity for long-suffering, good-temper will be rewarded by God's enlightening the *artifex* and making Himself known. Morienus, said to have been the teacher of the Omayyad prince Khalid ibn-Jazid ibn-Muawiyah (635-706 AD), is quoted with approval : "This is the science that draws its master away from the suffering of this world and leads to the knowledge of future good."

Another Moslem who passed on the Greek and Graeco-Egyptian alchemical inheritance was al Rhazi, known to the west as Rhazes (c.865-925). His immediate sources were Christian and Sabian Syriac translations of Greek texts, made at the heyday of the Sabian presence in Baghdad. Al-Razi, a Persian Muslim born at Rayy near Teheran, is known as the greatest physician of the Islamic world, having studied alchemy as a youth. This connection between medicine and alchemy, noted also in respect of Jabir is a most significant one, and is central to the early seventeenth century conception of the 'Rosicrucian Brother' as a healer, using the divine powers hidden in nature for the good of humanity : an image partly based on the example of Paracelsus (d.1541) who followed, somewhat belatedly, these oriental sages in stressing the need for observation, experiment and sensible classification[37]. Although partly dependent on the same Greek sources as Jabir, al Razi excelled in exact classification of substances with clear descriptions of chemical processes and apparatus, consistently devoid of unnecessary mystical elements. This is demonstrated in his great *Book of the Art* (of alchemy) discovered in the library of an Indian prince in the 1920s. While Jabir and other Arabian alchemists divided mineral substances into 'Bodies' (gold, silver &c.), 'Souls', (sulphur, arsenic &c.), and 'Spirits' (mercury and sal-ammoniac), al Razi classified the alchemical substances as vegetable, animal or mineral - now a well-known division, and opened the way for a more objective chemistry. His classification did however allow for a restated concept of spirits and bodies. He divided minerals into spirits, bodies, stones, vitriols, boraxes, and salts, and distinguished volatile 'bodies' from non-volatile 'spirits', placing among the latter, sulphur, mercury, arsenic and salmiac.

The second half of the fifteenth century saw an explosion of interest in Europe in the newly printed works of Graeco-Arabic alchemy, but this movement had abated by 1550, partly as a result of the catastrophically divisive effects of the Reformation, (the dissolution of the greater and lesser monasteries in England in the 1530s may well have been injurious to the movement), and the growth of Aristotelian and Platonic classicism, along with a high-brow Ciceronian complacency and Averroistic scepticism.

One figure in particular stands at the twilight of the high Middle Ages, testifying to the power of medieval alchemy before Christendom finally broke apart. That figure was Sir George Ripley.

Sir George Ripley (c.1415-1490?)

Ripley was an Augustinian monk and sometime canon of Bridlington in Yorkshire, born at about the time of Agincourt. In 1471 he compiled the *Compound of Alchemie* and was also the author of the *Medulla Alchimiae* (1476). His works were collected into the *Opera omnia chemica*[38] (from which the quotations following have been taken), a work central to that of his pupil, the more famous Thomas Norton[39], author of the *Ordinall of Alchemy* (in English verse) which was to be included wholesale in Elias Ashmole's ground-breaking *Theatrum Chemicum Britannicum* (1652), and a work subject to the intense study of no less a personage than Isaac Newton, alchemical enthusiast.

It is highly significant that Ripley was part of the monastic system in England, for it is now clear that it was this system which provided the major conduit of Hermetic alchemical lore throughout the Middle Ages. The prime reason that this picture has taken so long to become clear is simply the criminal wastage of monastic libraries which took place during the Dissolution in England. According to J.C Dickinson, before the Dissolution "Some large monastic libraries had about 2000 manuscripts and many houses must have had several hundred. Hence it does not seem rash to estimate the total books in the 900 English monasteries existing in the opening of the sixteenth century as several hundred thousand. If this were so the surviving element [about 3600 works] cannot represent more than a very minute percentage - perhaps 5% would over-estimate it."[40] It is not uncommon to see the Dissolution of the Monasteries as a final (if cruelly brusque) clearing-away of the detritus of an age which had - as the vulgar phrase has it - 'passed its sell-by date'. The question is too great a one to be gone into in this particular work[41], but one thing is clear, that if Ripley's alchemical work is anything to go by, a flame of spiritual inspiration was still bright at least in some quarters of the English monastic world as that age (later) called medieval passed into that period posthumously called the Renaissance[42].

Ripley's work seems to bear out the modern view, first established by Professor Carl Jung,[43] that while transformation as a principle was the chief aim of the alchemist, it was transformation of the 'wet', earth-bound soul into spirit which was held in greatest esteem by those 'chymists' who so fervently distinguished themselves from the vain seekers of "vulgar gold" : spiritual gold was their primary aim; material benefits were regarded as *parergons* or by-products of the spiritual *opus*.[44] Again, one must bear in mind the *sitz in leben* of the spiritual alchemist : the cloistered, sacral life.

The alchemist projects his purified mind (imagination) into the natural world : "The aerial soul is the secret fire of our philosophy, our oil, our mystic water."[45] Into the vision of the natural world - and in particular into the world of chemical change - the alchemist actualised the contents of his unconscious - the archetypal world 'outside' of nature - which are constellated on seeing analagous processes in the chemical vase. Of course, the alchemists did not use concepts such as the 'unconscious' and as a result held their perceptions as emanating from a divine source. Ripley was aware that he was employing imagery, that is the imaginative life : the creative principle of the mind. He says that all his secrets are formed from an "image" (*imago*) [46]. The alchemist begins the operation with the 'first matter' or *prima materia* : something of the world - the first 'stone' of the work (recall Ostanes' stone of the Nile in chapter 2). This 'stone' can be found everywhere; it passes unnoticed by worldly eyes : "The philosophers tell the inquirer that birds and fishes bring us the *lapis* [stone], every man has it, it is in every place, in you, in me, in everything, in time and space."[47] "It offers itself in lowly form. From it there springs our eternal water [*aqua permanens*]."[48]

The implicit identification of the stone's mercurial secret with Christ is clear enough. Christ the lowly messenger was "in the world, and the world was made by him, and the world knew him not." (*John* I.10). By taking the alchemical root to spiritual awareness, Ripley automatically found himself (though probably unbeknownst to himself) in the gnostic territory where the "living Jesus" is actualised in himself. The Nag Hammadi *Gospel of Thomas* (unknown to Ripley of course) elucidates this mysterious territory with remarkable clarity:

> From Me did the All come forth, and unto Me did the All extend. Split a piece of wood, and I am there. Lift up the stone, and you will find Me there. (46.25)

> It [the Kingdom of the Father] will not come by waiting for it. It will not be a matter of saying 'Here it is' or 'There it is.' Rather, the Kingdom of the Father is spread out upon the earth, and men do not see it. (50.14ff.)

According to Jung, "Ripley belonged to an age when God and his mysteries still dwelt in nature, when the mystery of redemption was at work on every level of existence, therefore unconscious happenings still lived in untroubled, paradisal participation with matter and could be experienced there."[49]

Ripley was content to use Christian typology for the alchemical work in a way which when seen by uncomprehending eyes would certainly have appeared blasphemous : one of several reasons why the alchemist worked in secret.

> Christ said : "If I be lifted up, I will draw all men unto me." From that time forward, when both parts, having been crucified and exanimated [souls separated], are betrothed to one another man and wife shall be

buried together and afterward quickened again by the spirit of life. Then must they be raised to heaven, so that body and soul may be there transfigured and enthroned on the clouds; then they will draw all bodies to their own high estate. (*Opera omnia chemica.* p. 81).

The life and passion of Christ is clearly taken here as the archetypal alchemical process : something to be enacted both by and *within* the being of the *artifex* himself. Substances could be 'redeemed' through transformation of their inner life. That inner life was normally called the *mercurius*, a word not necessarily denoting the chemical of that name (mercury) but the animating spirit which alchemists believed to be diffused throughout nature. In the words of the alchemist Paracelsus (who was born when Ripley was in his sixties) "There are as many mercuries as there are things." *Mercurius* is usually the penetrating agent of the transformative work : the spirit which acts upon the 'souls' of lesser substances.

This concept of the alchemical *mercurius*[50] is directly linked to the ancient Egyptian god Thoth who as the communicative, transformative and binding deity was worshipped by the ancients in his Roman form of Mercury and Greek form as Hermes at particular geographical features such as hills, streams, wells, springs and groves. These were the places where the unhappy wanderer might experience *panic,* that is to say an experience of the god *Pan* : the *All* - Nature as an immeasurable and overwhelming immensity. Such a place could put 'the fear of god' into the uninitiated[51]. When Hermes Trismegistos in *Libellus I* of the *Corpus Hermeticum* encounters the "authentic *Nous*", this being (called *Poimandres*) is described as "a Being of vast and boundless magnitude." The gnostic faculty of *nous* (mind or spirit) is thus identified with the substance of the All : in Ripley's alchemy the source of the "All" is clearly identified with Christ, to whom "all bodies" are drawn (cf : "from Me did the All come forth, and unto me did the All extend." - *Gospel of Thomas*).

It is remarkable how the essence of gnostic psychology was so well preserved within the polyvalent traditions of Hermetic alchemy, without the benefit of the explicitly Gnostic texts now known to us.

--------- *Chapter Four* ---------

The Hermetic Renaissance

1484 : one year before the battle of Bosworth will end the English Wars of the Roses. In Florence : the Neo-neoplatonists Giovanni Pico della Mirandola and Marsilio Ficino are actively re-asserting the value of Hermes Trismegistus, Plato, Plotinus, Porphyry, Proclus. They believe they are reaching back to the *One*, to the pristine theology (*prisca theologia*).

A new spirit is in the air. Printing has arrived. From the model of Gutenberg's press in Mainz, moveable metal type has spread to Paris (1470), London (1477) and Stockholm (1483). The art of printing has now been established in Italy for nineteen years. Among the first and most popular works to become available in print : the Latin *Asclepius*, a dialogue between Hermes Trismegistus and his disciple, the work which would give Pico della Mirandola's revolutionary *Oratio*[52] its primary text : *A great miracle, O Asclepius, is man*. Printed in 1469, it was followed two years later by the publication of Ficino's translation into Latin of the Hermetic *Pimander* at Treviso : the first fourteen books of the *Corpus Hermeticum*, a revolutionary publication which would appear in at least sixteen editions before the year 1500.

Kept alive by the Harranian and Baghdad 'Sabians' from the collapse of the Roman Empire to the mid-eleventh century, and then passed on to safety in Constantinople, the Hermetic books had been brought to Cosimo dei' Medici from a Macedonian monastery in 1460 by Cosimo's agent Leonardo da Pistoia, seven years after the fall of Constantinople to the Turks. As far as Cosimo, Ficino and Pico are concerned, the works of Hermes contain the principal prophetic message of the century.

Palm Sunday (11 April) 1484, in the Papal reign of Sixtus IV. A man, thirty-three years old, stops by the banks of the river Manara outside Rome with a group of excited followers. He puts on a pair of winged shoes and then a crown of thorns. Above the crown is a crescent moon on which is written : *This is my son Poimandres whom I have chosen*. He then mounts a white ass and makes a speech in which he announces himself as the "angel of Wisdom, Poimandres, in the most sublime manifestation of the Lord Jesus Christ." He says that he has descended from heaven. He then rides the ass into the streets of Rome, preaching to the people, while his followers distribute papers to the throng : papers whose subject is *Rebirth*, regeneration, or in French, *renaissance*. He performs a number of symbolic rites and then makes his way to the Vatican to deposit a number of objects on the throne of S.Peter. His work accomplished, he returns home to Bologna, to his wife and sons. This man is Giovanni Mercurio da Correggio : a footnote in history, a man almost completely forgotten.

> 'Who are you?' I [Hermes] said. 'I,' said he, am Poimandres, the authentic Mind [*Nous*].' 'I want to know,' said I, 'the things that are, and understand their nature, and get knowledge [*gnosis*] of God. These,' I said, 'are the things of which I want to hear.' He answered, 'I know what you wish, for indeed I am with you everywhere; keep in mind all that you will to learn, and I will teach you.
> (*Libellus* I. *Corpus Hermeticum* : Hermes encounters *Nous*.)

The Mercurial Spirit

The historian H.A.L. Fisher in his *History of Europe* (1935) wrote of how "The soul of a people will never be greatly stirred by the religion of the artist or the savant. Philosophy, erudition, the critical examination of texts, the passionate pursuit of art for art's sake, these activities will always be confined to a small intellectual minority of the human race. So it is now, so it was then. If the humanist of the Renaissance elevated taste, he also enlarged the distance between man and man." It is rarely considered that a reverse operation might take place. What when the humanist takes his religion from a 'man of the people'?

Giovanni Mercurio da Correggio was one such man, a man of no oratorical or academic learning but one who nevertheless 'turned around' the soul of an Italian humanist. The name of the humanist was Lodovico Lazzarelli, a poet and scholar who, he claimed, owed his salvation and *rebirth* to this Giovanni Mercurio, a man who claimed to be a manifestation of the "authentic *Nous*", and a living embodiment of the Hermetic principle. Were it not for the fact that Mercurio gained this humanist for a disciple, and stirred the interest of one other 'respectable' humanist, we should never have known that he even existed. Giovanni Mercurio, with the freedom which stems from inspiration unspoilt by too much learning, actually carried out in himself that which the humanist scholars, for all their brilliance, largely only wrote about. In the case of minor humanist Lodovico Lazzarelli, even his biographer (a certain Lancilotti, writing in c.1700) omits to mention any contact between his subject and Giovanni, the Hermetic messiah. Furthermore, more famous scholars who used Lazzarelli's works on the Hermetic writings took no interest at all in the fact that they were dedicated to "my father" *Ioannes Mercurius de Corigio*.

What little we do know of Mercurio we owe largely to some chance discoveries made by the 20th Century Renaissance scholar Paul Oskar Kristeller[53] in the 1930s, discoveries made when he was investigating the vogue for Hermetism among Neapolitan and Florentine humanists at the Community Library of Viterbo, seventy miles north-west of Rome. The account of Mercurio's appearance in Rome in 1484 was found by Kristeller in a unique work, the *Epistola Enoch* : "The Epistle of Enoch concerning the wonderful and portentous apparition of the new and divine prophet to the whole human race." The Epistle consists of the account given in outline above, and is prefaced by a sermon to humanity in which people are exhorted, in highly convincing terms, to accomplish *regeneration* in order to bring the soul to the true *gnosis* of God. The author, 'Enoch', makes it clear that he owes his own regeneration from secular poetry to sacred studies, practice and consciousness to *Ioannes Mercurius*.

The name Enoch is a special name, presumably given to Lazzarelli by Mercurio as a sign of his new sonship. It may be a reference to the patriarchal Enoch of the Book of *Genesis* under whose name an apocryphal and apocalyptic work was circulating privately. The *Book of Enoch* was held in reverence by some Hermetic scholars. However, it should also be mentioned that Enoch was a name given to Hermes Trismegistus by the Harranian and Baghdad Sabians, to tie their prophet into the realm of acceptable figures from the Koran (19.57; 21.85). The name would thus intend to put Lazzarelli under the spiritual guidance of the Thrice Greatest Hermes himself.

Other than from Lazzarelli, the only other account of the historic figure Giovanni Mercurio da Correggio comes from the pen of another humanist scholar, Carlo Sosenna di Ferrara[54] who wrote a commentary on a sonnet attributed to Mercurio. Sosenna appears from 1489-1491 among the teachers of the great University of Ferrara, famous for his prophecies and for his magic arts, as well as his humanist poetry.

Mercurio's sonnet is attributed to "Hermes the younger, who disputed and preached publically marvellous and new things above nature, recently joined by a great following in Rome." It was apparently composed on the occasion of this preaching, during which it seems that Mercurio approached Pope Alexander VI. This must have been an occasion subsequent to that described by Lazzarelli, (indicated as taking place in the reign of Sixtus IV), and Kristeller dates this new appearance of Mercurio to 1492, based on his knowledge of Sosenna's activities during that decade. This may have been the same occasion wherein, according to Lazzarelli's *Epistola Enoch,* Mercurio presented himself before the College of Cardinals[55]. Mercurio's strategy seems to have been to make intermittent public appearances, when the spirit led him to do so. We also know that he appeared in the same Hermetic rig in Florence in 1496, a year after Savonarola had welcomed the French army of Charles VIII to that city as liberators who would purify the abuses of the Church, and not long after the French king's retreat. Perhaps inspired by the potential for a French-led Hermetic Renaissance, Mercurio later appeared in Lyons. We know absolutely nothing more about his historic activities.

What Mercurio stood for can be gleaned from Carlo Sosenna's commentary on Mercurio's sonnet, and from other works by Lodovico Lazzarelli. According to Carlo Sosenna di Ferrara, Mercurio's sonnet stated that :

> Above the first heaven lies a sphere which, motionless, governs us and revolves, making some happy, others breathe : the happy place of the true Mind. Here, the highest Good has its throne; here no one unworthy can enter[56]; here the great Creator draws us but rules over our erring good with His; and in the lowest centre of the earth is that enemy of the human-race who controls the wandering spirits in the wind. Whence, my son, happy is the man who repents of all sin committed, abasing himself before God, rejecting all vain goodness from the mind, turning away from the human and mortal veil to possess that heaven which is above the sky.

This constitutes a fairly pious rendering of the Hermetic message in the thought-forms of the time. The true Mind (*Poimandres* in *Corpus Hermeticum* I) is accessible to the purified mind which has, in effect, separated itself from earthly attachment. This doctrine is more or less in tune with Marsilio Ficino's quintessence of the ancient Hermetic doctrine, a doctrine which influenced all his work subsequent to his translation of the first fourteen books of the *Corpus Hermeticum* in 1463. Since Ficino believed Plato had derived his wisdom from Hermes Trismegistus - through the esoteric traditions of Orpheus, Aglaophemus, Pythagoras and Philolaus - the Hermetic conception also informs his *Theologia Platonica* (1468). For Ficino, as for Carlo Sosenna and Lazzarelli, the Hermetic revelation encouraged him to leave behind the concerns of the body, (Ficino's "love of the flesh"), to embrace the "contemplative" (gnostic) life. ('Contemplation' is Ficino's regular translation of *gnosis*). According to Ficino (whom Lazzarelli had read and held in high esteem) the human soul, through its link to the body, is submitted to the evils and errors of the world along with the vagaries of the stars; but to those few who know how to free themselves through the art of inner ascension, they can find the way open to a truer and more perfect existence. This existence is man's origin and destiny, and ordinary men do not know it. Ficino takes his idea of the final purpose of earthly existence from the *Corpus Hermeticum* : γνωσις του θεου (*gnosis tou theou*), knowledge of God : Ficino's *contemplatio Dei*, which, along with Love is the essential task of man. From the Hermetic writings Ficino also takes the view of the transcendent potential of man : Man is an earthly god with a special link to the highest God. For man, the evil and imperfection of earthly life, the sickness of the human soul is due to *agnosis* - literally : without gnosis.

Sosenna is pressed by the sonnet to distinguish between man's *Will* (his inmost soul), and his animal appetite which, while it cannot be ignored in this life, must needs be subjected to the inner divine Will. Sosenna interprets the Earth allegorically (and alchemically) as *prima materia* : the 'first matter' of alchemical transmutation or regeneration, of itself the fount of evil and the "mortal veil" over the spirit, which stands between body and soul, and through cognizance of which the soul is regenerated, arising as the alchemical phoenix rises from the ashes of the world, to head beyond the control and influence of the stars. Here we have, as an underground movement with a public face, led by a common man (or uncommon man) with no theological expertise, but with an open ear to inspiration, an authentic attempt to link an esoteric Christianity to an ancient *gnosis*, a regenerative experience which, according to Lazzarelli, has been forgotten for centuries and which can now flower again, to recover the glory of humanity and to effect the transformation of the world.

Mercurio promised initiation to his disciples. He had come in a conscious parallel to Christ's entry into Jerusalem; he had been greeted by the people and had headed for the 'Temple' of Rome, the Vatican, to announce a new dispensation and divine revelation. He had also actively demonstrated something few would dare to do - at least in the open. He had identified the Mind (*Poimandres*) which had opened to Hermes Trismegistus with Christ, and made that identity itself open to all who dared to be reborn in the *gnosis*[57].

Lodovico Lazzarelli - Born-again gnostic

According to the antiquarian Lancillotti, who made a study of Lazzarelli in about 1700, Lodovico Lazzarelli, a "minor humanist" was born in 1450 in Sanseverino in the Marche province, north-east of Rome and part of the Papal lands. He was taught by Eligio Calenzio and Merula. Hebrew, Greek, mathematics and astrology were his best subjects. He was crowned a poet in 1469 by Federico III, king of Naples and went on to work as secretary to Matteo Acquaviva at Atri; for Campano at Teramo, for Guilio Cesare Varano at Camerino and for the Patriarch of Antioch, Lorenzo Zane in Rome. He remained in contact with Neapolitan humanist circles and with those in Rome but, interestingly, there is no evidence that he ever had any contact with the exalted atmosphere of the Florentine Platonists, patronised in the 1480s by Lorenzo the Magnificent, grandson of Cosimo dei'Medici. While Lancillotti does not refer to Lazzarelli's conversion from humanist poetry to Hermetism, he does tell us that he was known to drive out evil spirits and sickness at the sign of the cross, and that perverse men suspected him of being interested in magic arts. Lazzarelli is certainly notable for his Hebraic interests, quoting Hebrew authors repeatedly in his *Crater Hermetis* and displaying a knowledge of Qabalistic literature normally regarded in this period as the speciality of Giovanni Pico della Mirandola. Lazzarelli is recorded as having debated with the Jewish scholar Vitalis Hebraeus while a resident of Teramo.

Lancillotti, without stating the provenance of Lazzarelli's interest, does refer to the latter's unique translation of *libellus* XVI of the *Corpus Hermeticum*, the original of which did not appear in Marsilio Ficino's 1463 translation, nor subsequent editions of his *Pymander* published that century. This work, the epistle of Asclepius to King Ammon (ὅροι Ασκληπιου προς Αμμονα Βασιλεα =*horoi Asklepiou pros Ammona Basilea*) was rendered by Lazzarelli into the Latin composition entitled *Definitiones Asclepii*, and featured in the discoveries made by Paul Oskar Kristeller while exploring the Community Library of Viterbo[58]. These discoveries tell us quite a lot about the relationship between Lazzarelli and his spiritual father, Mercurio.

The codex consists of a small and very delicate collection of manuscripts dating from the late fifteenth century. Ninety-two pages long with beautiful titles in red, blue and gold with illuminated initials, this exquisite collection is not only the earliest example of a Latin humanist volume re-uniting the entire Hermetic tradition but was assembled as a presentation from Lazzarelli to Mercurio da Correggio - a fitting act of homage from disciple to master. The codex contains three works : two of which are prefaced in prose and one in verse, addressed to 'Ioannes Mercurius de Corigio' and written by 'Ludovicus Enoch Lazarellus'. The three works are as follows : Ficino's translation of the first fourteen treatises of the *Corpus Hermeticum*, the Latin *Asclepius* (whose translation was attributed wrongly to Apuleius of Madaura) and the *Definitiones Asclepii*, translated by Lazzarelli himself.

In the preface to the *Pymander*[59], Lazzarelli pays tribute to Marsilio Ficino but takes the opportunity to correct the latter's dating of Hermes. Ficino had dated Hermes as having lived very shortly after Moses. Lazzarelli claims the classical author Diodorus Siculus[60] as his authority for believing Hermes to have been senior to Moses. By the values of the time, this was tantamount to saying that Moses' wisdom derived from the tradition of Hermes. It is however interesting in this context that Lazzarelli does not mention the Harranian Sabian identification of Hermes with Enoch (which had appeared in the West in pseudo-Hermetic alchemical works since the twelth century). This would have afforded him plenteous ammunition for ascribing a date for Hermes way back in the hoariest antiquity, for in *Genesis* chapter V we learn that Enoch was the great, great, great grandson of Seth, Adam's son, and father of Methuselah (who we are told lived for 969 years and was the grand-father of Noah). We may thus suppose that Lazzarelli was himself ignorant of the Enoch-Hermes identification. Was Mercurio so when he (presumably) gave the new name to Lodovico?

> And Enoch walked with God : and he was not; for God took him.
> (*Gen.* V.24).

God took him. As a regenerated man, fostered by his spiritual father, Lazzarelli was granted the privilege of ascending to the highest. In Lazzarelli's account of his adoption and rebirth, the gnostic mood is perhaps more definitely pronounced than in any other document of the Renaissance.

Lazzarelli's prefaces to each of the three collected works are drenched in the sacred and solemn tone of the true initiate. Great accent is placed on doctrines of a secret or even sectarian character, in particular the idea that the Hermetic rebirth which he has experienced is exactly analgous to Christ's gift of the Holy Spirit to His disciples.

Those who have experienced the *palingenesia* (=rebirth) are set aside from ordinary humanity. So deep is Lazzarelli's conflation of antique Hermetism with the origin of Christianity that he even interprets the famous idol-making passage in the Latin *Asclepius* as being a *type* for the appearance of the flames of spirit above the heads of the disciples in the *Acts of the Apostles*, the act whereby (according to Lazzarelli) Christ made those closest to Him gods. The passage in question, *Asclepius* III.37 tells of how :

> Our ancestors were at first far astray from the truth about the gods; they had no belief in them, and gave no heed to worship and religion. But afterwards, they invented the art of making gods out of some material substance suited for the purpose. And to this invention they added a supernatural force whereby the images might have power to work good or hurt, and combined it with the material substance; that is to say, being unable to make souls, they invoked the souls of daemons, and implanted them in the statues by means of certain holy and sacred rites.

This passage was rejected throughout the next century by religious Hermetists (with notable exceptions such as Giordano Bruno), as having been either a). an insertion of the 'translator' Apuleius of Madaura, or b). as simply being incompatible with Christianity altogether, its being tainted with demonic magic. Lazzarelli was in no doubt that his conversion from secular poetry to sacred studies was a real rebirth, exactly on the lines of *Corpus Hermeticum* XIII. Through it, Lazzarelli was convinced that he had been brought to a higher perception of life and reality :

> TAT: Father, God has made me a new being, and I perceive things now, not with bodily eyesight, but by the working of *nous* [mind].
> HERMES : Even so it is, my son, when a man is born again; it is no longer body of three dimensions that he perceives, but the incorporeal.
> TAT : Father, now that I see in mind, I see myself to be the All. I am in heaven and in earth, in water and in air; I am in beasts and plants; I am a babe in the womb, and one that is not yet conceived, and one that has been born; I am present everywhere.
> HERMES : Now, my son, you know what the Rebirth is.
> (*Corpus Hermeticum* XIII.11-12).

Lazzarelli contrasts the old life and the new. While sacred writing offers the enticements of the angels, the water of eternal life, the fruits of the Tree of Life and the joy of Paradise; profane verse offers merely the baiting of Tantalus, the waters of Lethe, the wicked fruits of the Tree of Knowledge of Good and Evil, (dialectical or dualistic consciousness, mundane awareness), and the deadly allurements of Tartarus (hell). According to Lazzarelli, whoever knows how to taste the fruit of the Tree of Life can free himself from material attachment and ascend above the celestial realms to the kingdom of angels; while those devoted to the Tree of Knowledge of Good and Evil fall from their native dignity into the *heimarmene* (ε'ιμαρμηνη = 'the night-cloak': destiny/fate/the governance of the stars) and become the slaves of death. This true *gnosis*, declares Lazzarelli, he owes to the illiterate Giovanni Mercurio, his initiator and spiritual master. Lazzarelli as Enoch is Mercurio's faithful disciple and he offers his work to him. Mercurio, who knows all the mysteries of Christ and of Hermes - mysteries reserved for the few - has fostered the spiritual regeneration of Lazzarelli, secretly communicating his wisdom to him. Mercurio is the spiritual son of Hermes Trismegistus. Enoch is his grandson : "Thus he is called to communicate his wisdom to all men, being the salvation and hope of his century."

The inward consistency of what Lazzarelli has gained from Mercurio and from the Hermetic writings with the better-known position of the famous Pico della Mirandola (1463-1494), Lazzarelli's brilliant contemporary, is immensely striking. Take for example, the following quotations from Pico's epoch-marking *Oratio de dignitatis homini* (1486):

> Think on how Origen the theologian, asserts that Jesus Christ, the Teacher of Life, made many revelations to his disciples, which they were unwilling to write down lest they should become commonplaces to the rabble. This is in the highest degree confirmed by Dionysius the Areopagite who says that the occult mysteries were conveyed by the founders of religion, from mind to mind, without writing, through the medium of speech.

> We shall fly up with winged feet, like earthly Mercuries, to the embraces of our blessed mother and enjoy that wished-for peace, most holy peace, indivisible bond, of one accord in the friendship through which all rational souls not only shall come into harmony with the one mind which is above all minds, but shall in some ineffable way become altogether one. This is that friendship which the Pythagoreans say is the end of all philosophy. This is that peace which God creates in his heavens, which the angels descending to earth proclaimed to men of good will, that through it men might ascend to heaven and become angels. Let us wish this peace for our friends, for our century.

Consistency of thought, yes, but one can only speculate as to what Pico would have thought if he had known that authentic Hermetic regeneration practices were available in the Italy of his time. For all the likeness of viewpoint, there is yet a very different flavour between the writings of the two men. Pico did not see himself as being a privileged insider in the same way as Lazzarelli did; as a revealer of mysteries, yes, but not in the strictly initiatic sense. In spite of Pico's evident mysticism, he was very much a man of books. However, it is hard to imagine that Pico would not have known about Giovanni Mercurio da Correggio. Was there a certain snobbery which might have prevented him from making contact? We must suspect that to Pico, Mercurio probably looked ridiculous. The issue does highlight the fact that at the very time of the eruption of serious religious Hermetism into Europe, there were at least two ways of taking the matter. For Pico and Ficino, and many churchmen who followed these two Florentines in whole or in part, the Hermetic revelation was regarded as a confirmation of Christianity, a basis for unifying the disparate philosophies of Averroes, Aristotle and Plato; a major insight into the *religio mentis* (the religion of the mind), the contemplative life : an epoch-marking spur to scientific endeavour, since the Hermetica stressed man's freedom and potential dominance of the natural order, and a remarkable vision of the original theology from which all thought was thought to have been derived.

The other stream, and one can see that this stream might already have predated even the translation of Ficino's *Pymander* in 1463, was to see Hermetism as a magical religion of itself, into which one could happily place Christian elements on the basis that the revealer of *gnosis*, be he Hermes or Asclepius, or even 'Enoch', had been inspired by Christ. Even Pope Alexander VI approved of Hermes. The Egyptian hierophant did not seem in any way to threaten the Church. Besides, Pico had all but Catholicised the ancient mystagogue. However, there were others (among whom we must include Giordano Bruno 1548-1600, author of an epoch-marking work on the infinitude of the universe) whose intention may have been rather to *Hermeticise* the Church : a different matter altogether - and one feels strongly that Lazzarelli is somehow among them, if in fact he is not a progenitor of this impulse. It may be that southern Italian humanists, living under the thrall of a frequently erratic and ever-present politicised Papacy, favoured the latter view. Magic and surviving pagan practices were particularly rife in the south, (looked down on by Florentines and Venetians), as was the ubiquitous threat of punishment for heresy, when it suited the Papal state. It does seem to me that there is something in this atmosphere that may bind the most determined religious Hermetists of the fifteenth and sixteenth centuries : Lazzarelli, Giordano Bruno and Tommaso Campanella - every one had very strong southern Italian connections.

At the Hermetic Bowl

One scholar who was hot on the Hermetic trail was the Frenchman, Lefèvre d'Étaples, known to Latin readers as *Jacobus Faber Stapulensis*. In 1494, while Mercurio and Lazzarelli were active in Italy, Lefèvre had the University of Paris publish his edition of Ficino's *Pymander*. Lefèvre made a number of trips to Italy and certainly met Ficino and Pico della Mirandola. In 1505, a most significant work appeared in Paris bearing Lefèvre's name and dedicated to Guillaume Briçonnet, bishop of Lodève in the Languedoc. This exciting publication not only joined the *Pymander* and the Latin *Asclepius* in print for the first time, but its appearance also marked the beginning of a momentous importation of Hermetic ideas into France and the French Renaissance. His commentary on the *Asclepius* even came to be printed along with Ficino's collected works, and was long mistaken for Ficino's own work. But most importantly for our purposes, this book also contained another Hermetic work : the *Crater Hermetis*, written by Lodovico Lazzarelli and dedicated to *Ioannes Mercurio de Corigio*.

It is not unlikely that Lefèvre d'Étaples had encountered Lazzarelli on his travels around Italy. The impression which Lazzarelli's work - if not his person - made upon the Frenchman must have been great, for Lazzarelli to have his own work linked in print to the key works of Renaissance Hermetism was a tremendous privilege; his work was being linked to what was regarded as the very origin of religious thought, thereby promising his vision of the Hermetic message a very wide currency indeed. Again, one can only speculate on how it was that Lefèvre came upon Lazzarelli's manuscript. Was it recommended to him by Florentine Platonists? Had he heard of Mercurio through his friend Symphonien Champier who lived in Lyons, where we know Mercurio made an appearance at some time in the 1490s? We can only guess, and wonder at the extraordinary co-incidence of interests which Lefèvre d'Étaples' publication signifies.

Crater Hermetis means the "Hermetic bowl (or vessel)", and the work is a kind of meditation on the meaning of the fourth treatise of the

Corpus Hermeticum[61]. Lazzarelli sees the description in the fourth treatise as symbolic of the transformative relationship between Hermetic master and pupil :

> TAT : I too, father, much want to be baptized in that bowl.
> HERMES : If you do not first hate your body, my son, you cannot love yourself; but if you love your [true] self, you will have mind; and having mind, you will partake of gnosis also. ...In these things, my son, I have drawn a likeness of God for you, so far as that is possible; and if you gaze upon this likeness with the eyes of your heart, then, my son, believe me, you will find the upward path; or rather, the sight itself will guide you on your way. For the Good has a power peculiar to itself; it takes possession of those who have attained to the sight of it, and draws them upward, even as men say the loadstone draws the iron.

Lazzarelli's meditation takes the form of a dialogue between the author and the old King of Naples, Ferrante d'Aragona. The dialogue is permeated by ecstatic hymns - very much in tune with the flavour of the original Hermetic discourses, (one such hymn was discovered among the codices of the Nag Hammadi Library) - and exhortations wherein the king asked him not to speak of his quality as a poet, but of what he has seen happening on Mount Sion. Sion is linked to the inspirational mountain of Parnassus and clearly symbolises that which is seen when the soul ascends towards the Father. There is a long eulogy to Hermes Trismegistus as precursor and master of Moses. *Poimandres*, (possibly Greek transliteration of 'the knowledge of Re'), is explicitly identified as Christ, teacher of Hermes. Thus, we see the Gnostic Christ emerging as a cultural force four and a half centuries before the discovery of the Nag Hammadi Gnostic Library (1945).

Lazzarelli poses the question : what is the way to happiness? - to which the response is that of the Oracle of Delphi : *nosce te ipsum* : Know Yourself. Knowledge of ourselves is necessarily linked to the love of God, for man was made in God's image. We cannot know the substance of God. God created the All for his love of mankind, and by means of man is brought to perfection all that the world itself could not do. God cultivates the soul; man brings nature into culture. The human soul is "the light of God", and by this link, we can come down from knowledge of God to knowledge of ourselves. There then follows a 'hymn of contemplation' wherein the Hermetic mystery is expressed thus : as God, like man, is fertile, we may expect fruitfulness in intellect (*nous*), as well as in body - not only in the sciences and the arts, but in the *syngenea mentis generatio*, through which "mind generates mind". This generation of a new mind by the agency of a divinely illuminated mind is then expressed in the "hymn of divine generation". As God created the angels and true man, He produces divine souls which live with humans, (cf : the Qabalistic *sefiroth*), and who bring cares and fears, supplying aid, guidance and providence. These beings are God's servants and through them God gives man a mind and the gift of language, so that men might generate other gods.

The king, somewhat set back by all this abstruse theology, asks Lazzarelli for his authority. In reply, Lazzarelli cites Hermes Trismegistus, *Asclepius,* the *Book of Enoch*, a certain Abraam, and the example of Christ. The dialogue concludes with a *Prayer of Thanksgiving* - again, very much in the proper Hermetic mode. (A *Prayer of Thanksgiving* emerged from the Nag Hammadi Library discovery also). By divine generation, the "true man" is capable of regenerating souls, and such a one is elevated to the *gnosis* of God. The God-like souls created by him become the servants of God, accomplishing supernatural deeds and through their regeneration, rise to even greater heights of divine existence so that they receive the faculty of prophecy and the ability to work miracles. The process of generation is seen as strictly subsisting within the relation of master and pupil - books are apparently insufficient. There must be an actual transmission of *mind to mind*. Mercurio da Correggio is of course credited with this gift, so Lazzarelli feels he can speak with authority.

Lazzarelli, the Hebrew scholar, cites 'Abraam' as a source for his theory and practice. In particular, Abraam's work *Zepher izira* - clearly a reference to the ancient *Sefer Yetsirah*, or 'Book of Creation'. (*circa* 3rd-6th century AD). This Jewish Gnostic work of no more than 1600 words is the earliest extant 'speculative' work in Hebrew. The *Book of Creation* concerns the elements of the world : the ten *sefiroth*, (numerical projections of the divine Name), and the twenty-two letters of the Hebrew alphabet, combining to form the "thirty-two secret paths of wisdom". Perhaps it is Lazzarelli's "divine souls which live with humans" which form the link with the Qabalah of the *Sefer Yetsirah*. The guiding servants of Lazzarelli's Hermetic vision may have been linked in his mind to the *hayoth* who support the Throne (or Chariot) of God (the *Merkabah*) in *Merkabah* mysticism : the "living beings" described by Ezekiel in his vision of the heavenly throng. (*viz* : Ezekiel I.26). These beings are identified in the *Sefer Yetsirah* with the "living numerical beings" of the *Sefiroth* whose *"appearance is like a flash of lightning and their goal is without end; His word is in them when they come forth [from Him] and when they return; at His bidding do they proceed swiftly as a whirlwind, and before His throne they prostrate themselves."* (cf the "heavenly science" which leads men to the "throne of God" in the masonic Third Degree.)

It may be inferred from the deep contents of the *Crater Hermetis* that Lazzarelli has himself been taken on a journey of inner ascent with, presumably, Mercurio as his spiritual helmsman, and has seen with the "eyes of the heart" the living *Anthropos*, the cosmic Man who has appeared in gnostic revelation literature through the ages, guaranteeing to the eyes of the seer at least, the fundamental conception that man is in essence a spiritual being. In a fascinating parallel to the language of alchemy, Lazzarelli compares the making of the 'new' or 'true' man from the regenerative mind to the making of Adam from the "red earth", the alchemical *prima materia* (in this context). Little wonder then that Lazzarelli grew to regard his merely artistic gifts of verse as barely skimming the surface of reality. That what men consider to be 'good', or even 'high art' is not the same as the Divine Good, is a consistently re-iterated message of Lazzarelli, and, one suspects, of Mercurio as well. Mercurio, as far as Lazzarelli is concerned, is a 'natural', performing in deed that which the scholar had previously, only read about: the Hermetic rebirth, with visionary gifts as the parergon of that experience. This was spiritual magic of a high order.

Frances Yates in her influential book *Giordano Bruno and the Hermetic Tradition* (1964), described the *Crater Hermetis* as "a work which is something like a magical interpretation of the psychology of religious experience", and suggested that it may have influenced the mind of that wild genius of cosmology and psychology, Giordano Bruno. Bruno was one of the very first men to imagine that the universe was infinite and thoroughly populated with life (though perhaps of kinds we cannot readily recognise) - and he *was* deeply interested in the idol-making passage in *Asclepius*, regarding this ability as a fundamental distinction of the high level of magical awareness and spiritual technology achieved by his ideal culture, that of Ancient Egypt. He wished to re-apply these Hermetic principles to a renewal of the Catholic Church based on the cosmic, magical religion of his (fictional) Hermetic Egypt, combined with his epoch-marking pan**en**theist concept of the infinite universe. According to an authority on Renaissance Magic[62], the experience described in the *Crater Hermetis* "is somewhat like a magical operation by which the master provided his disciple with a good daemon [his 'true Self'], and is analagous to the introduction of daemons into idols described in the *Asclepius*." It is certain that Lazzarelli saw the parallel, and it is hard to imagine that Bruno's voracious intellectual appetite would have passed over the *Crater*, especially since he was such an avid enthusiast of the *Asclepius*. Frances Yates went so far as to suggest that Bruno may have in some way modelled his own sense of destiny and importance on the authority of the regenerative or divinizing experience described in the *Crater Hermetis*. Professor Yates made the following judgement of Bruno : "People like Giordano Bruno are immunized from a sense of danger by their sense of mission, or their megalomania, or the state bordering on insanity in which they constantly live. 'Although I cannot see your soul,' he makes an English admirer say of him, 'from the ray which it diffuses I perceive that within you is a sun or perhaps some greater luminary.'[63] Hermetism, with its belief in a divinizing experience, is conducive to religious mania of this kind." Clearly Bruno irritated contemporaries by his 'not of this world' demeanour, but Bruno was trying to change the world, indeed was part of that change. He needed to get 'above' things. He saw further and deeper than ordinary men and he really *needed* to be 'immunized' from day-to-day pressure. He was not a cloistered, academic type, so it seems to this author that to call his condition a "mania", with all that that implies, (*viz* : 'he should be put away') is unkind to say the least. He *was* 'put away' - permanently his enemies might have thought - burned at the stake for his beliefs in 1600. If an element of Bruno's courageous stance can be laid at the door of Mercurio and Lazzarelli - at least in the dimension of encouraging Bruno to believe in himself, (against tremendous odds) - then surely some credit is due to the (officially) unlearned Mercurio da Correggio.

In the Sun

Another French scholar who helped to promote the Hermetic vision into the very centre of European cultural life was Symphonien Champier of Lyons. He was the leading apostle of Neoplatonism in France and a profound admirer of Ficino and his circle. In fact he modelled his *De Quadruplici Vita* (Lyons,1507) on Ficino's work on the relationship between the soul and the cosmos. This book is also remarkable because it contains a kind of response to Lefèvre's Hermetic publication of 1505, which had contained Lazzarelli's *Crater Hermetis*. Champier not only dedicates his book to Lefèvre d'Étaples, but also adds to its contents the first-ever printed version of Lazzarelli's *Definitiones Asclepii*, which we last encountered in the community library of Viterbo in manuscript form, dedicated to *Ioannes Mercurio de Corigio*. By including Lazzarelli's Latin translation of treatise XVI of the *Corpus Hermeticum* (the Letter from Asclepius to King Ammon), Champier completed the printed availability of the classic Hermetic works begun in 1469 with the publication of the Latin *Asclepius*. The inclusion of Lazzarelli's work was also intended to complement the work of Lefèvre d'Étaples. It is again remarkable to see Lazzarelli's work finding centre-place among the great works of the Renaissance Hermetic *corpus*. Furthermore, *libellus* XVI of the *Corpus Hermeticum*, short as it is, was, in conjunction with the gathering momentum of interest around the other Hermetic works, to have far-reaching effects on Renaissance thought.

The *Letter of Asclepius to King Ammon* (which Lazzarelli translated and prefaced) takes as its chief subject the nature of the sun. There is a stunning description of the sun surrounded by a veritable choir of daemons[64]. Treatise XVI reinforced the gathering interest in the sun as the key star in the planetary system, (still not yet called the 'solar' system), based on Plato's view of the sun as the chief image for the world of *Ideas* which project their nature into the world, and which, (according to the Neoplatonic scheme), lose a quantity of their purely spiritual nature as they become expressed in the natural, organic world. This view gained even more support from the system of *Divine Hierarchies* attributed to Dionysius the Areopagite where the sun is seen as the image for the origin of spiritual light, a kind of living metaphor.

When Copernicus came to write his work *On the Revolutions of the Celestial Orbs*[65], proposing the heliocentric system, he justified the philosophical soundness of his mathematical conclusions by quoting Hermes Trismegistus; that the sun is a "second God", most suitable to be venerated as the spiritual centrepiece for a divine cosmic system. One gets the impression that Copernicus is saying : *the truth of the matter was already there, but went unseen because we judged things from an earthly perspective. But Hermes, at the beginning of science, he saw it.* Treatise XVI, brought to the public attention by Lodovico Lazzarelli provided the fullest expression then available on the dignity of the sun as seen by Hermes :

the Demiurgus (that is, the Sun) [identified in *libellus* I as 'Mind the Maker'] brings together heaven and earth, sending down true being from above, and raising up matter from below,...and if there is such a thing as a substance not perceptible to sense [intelligible substance=mind], the light of the sun must be the recepticle of that substance...God does not manifest himself to us; we cannot see him, and it is only by conjecture, and with hard effort, that we can apprehend him by thought. But it is not by conjecture that we contemplate the sun; we see him with our very eyes. ...for he is stationed in the midst and wears the *kosmos* as a wreath around him.

Next, in startling prescience to such theories as photosynthesis we are told of how:

the light is shed downward, and illuminates all the sphere of water, earth, and air; he puts life into the things in this region of the *kosmos*, and stirs them up to birth, and by successive changes remakes the living creatures and trasforms them...For the permanence of every kind of body is maintained by change.. And as the light of the sun is poured forth continuously, so his production of life also is continuous and without intermission.

The intelligible *kosmos* then is dependent on God; and the Sun receives from God, through the intelligible *kosmos*, the influx of good (that is, of life giving energy), with which he is supplied. ...God then is the Father of all; the Sun is the Demiurgus; and the *kosmos* is the instrument by means of which the Demiurgus works. ...Therefore in making all things, God makes himself. And it is impossible that he should ever cease from making; for God himself can never cease to be.

It is perhaps hard for us today to imagine the effect of these words on an early sixteenth century mind, a mind seeing what were being regarded more and more as the primal thoughts of intelligent, divinely illuminated man, linked directly to the power of the spiritual sun.

Respect for Hermes Trismegistus grew apace. He was quoted throughout the sixteenth century as an authority on an almost equal level to that of the Bible and, as far as real Hermetic enthusiasts were concerned, he could even be seen in some senses as *superior* to the Bible, insofar as his works were (wrongly) considered to predate Moses. The influence of Lazzarelli's work was subtle, unspoken. The *Crater Hermetis* appeared again in 1549 in a French translation of the *Hermetica*, dedicated to Cardinal Charles de Lorraine. Hermes was even being considered as a basis for transcending religious differences between Catholics and Protestants (after 1517), and members of the Lorraine family privately encouraged this. Wherever the *Hermetica* were studied, religious toleration and cosmic understanding grew. This dynamic is seen in a parallel movement regarding the dating of Hermes Trismegistus. In 1554, Turnebus published Ficino's *Pymander* along with the *Definitiones Asclepii*, (translated by Lazzarelli). This highly influential edition, appearing 103 years after the birth of Mercurio da Correggio, followed Lazzarelli's dating; that is to say, Moses derived his wisdom from the sage of pristine *gnosis*, Hermes Trismegistus. As Frances Yates has expressed it : "There seems to be a tendency by which the holier and more Christian Hermes Trismegistus becomes, the more his date is pushed back." (The *Hermetica* were not properly dated until 1614).

The call for Rebirth - and the successful realization of that call (accomplished in Lodovico Lazzarelli) - perhaps represents the abiding value of the fifteenth century Hermetic effort. There is something uncanny and mysterious about Mercurio's 'operation' : a great symbolic public showing, demanding attention, getting it - and then withdrawing into obscurity. Meanwhile, he attracts an unlikely 'fisher of men', a disappointed scholar who found that academic honours, for all their glitter, mattered not too much at all. Crowned a poet, he threw the crown away, preferring the sight of Mercurio da Correggio's crown of thorns and ridiculous crescent : *This is my son Poimandres whom I have chosen...*

There is reason for considering that Jesus' entry into Jerusalem "to fulfill the prophecies" and to set a storm raging in the Temple was conceived deliberately as a symbolic drama, organised by a faithful following. In a sense, Mercurio, whether he knew exactly what he was doing or not, *did* dramatise the beginning of a new age. He called for a rebirth and a new hope. He brought at least one man closer to God, and there can be no doubt that Lazzarelli, the deep, obscure scholar, passed on the torch.

Chapter Five

The Hermetic Background to the first Rosicrucians

While Lazzarelli contemplated his signal rebirth, printed books on alchemy continued to proliferate about the centres of learning in Europe. The theories and promise of what would later be termed "magical panvitalism" vouchsafed in translations from Arabic alchemical texts would profoundly affect the thought of Renaissance philosophers and contribute greatly to the impetus for scientific development in the seventeenth century, when a major revival of alchemy co-incided and interpenetrated with movements which would culminate not least in the founding of the Royal Society in 1661. Elias Ashmole, Robert Boyle and Isaac Newton - to name but a few - were fascinated and inspired by the alchemical enterprise, an enterprise which quietly gained in strength and sophistication throughout the middle ages. Nor should it be forgotten that Pico della Mirandola's famous *Oratio* on the Dignity of Man (1486) - the "manifesto of the Renaissance" according to Ernesto Garin[66] - begins with the words :

> I have read in the records of the Arabians, reverend fathers, that there is nothing to be seen more wonderful than man. In agreement with this opinion are the words of Hermes Trismegistus : 'A great miracle, O Asclepius, is man.'

141 years later, one of the geniuses behind the Rosicrucian Fraternity, Johann Valentin Andreae, the inventor of the hero Christian Rozenkreuz, will put the following words into the mouth of his dramatic figure, Christianus, in a dialogue featured in his attack on the decline and corruption of learning, *Menippus* (1617) :

> There is no limit to my amazement when I see that in our age - although it will forever be known as a very happy and erudite one - there are so few people who investigate our creator's wisdom in his creations and the structure of his wonderful machine, - as only a few generations ago men like Pico della Mirandola, Reuchlin, Cardanus and others pioneered in this field.

In many respects, the Rosicrucian enterprise, as conceived by its initiators, was an attempt to re-instate the kind of open-ended, open-minded, and, above all, spiritually uplifting approach to nature as shown by the oriental and Alexandrian alchemists. The Islamic sciences had declined in the twelth century due to the same kind of intolerance for authority-challenging investigation which the learning institutions of Europe were suffering from, following the initial strides forward characterised as the Renaissance. The 'Rosicrucians' wished to rekindle the true spirit of this movement and institute a *second Reformation*: a reformation of learning and, more importantly given the fissures which were splitting Europe apart, a reformation of the heart as well. Alchemy, with its ample exposition of such themes as the soul regenerated from its blackened state, the purification of the 'metal' through the fire of devotion and suffering, the central significance of meditation (dialogue with God within), combined with the mighty power of the creative imagination and culminating in the ecstatic release of the spirit, provided the essential imagery and formulae for this gigantic undertaking.

> The Light is the true Light of nature, which illuminates all the God-loving Philosophers who come into this world. It is in the World and the whole edifice of the World is beautifully adorned and will be naturally preserved by it until the last and great day of the Lord, but the World knows it not. Above all it is the subject of the Catholic and Great Stone of the Philosophers, which the whole world has before its eyes yet knows not.
> (*Von hylealischen Chaos*. pp 71ff. Heinrich Khunrath. (1520-1605).

> Imagination is the star in man, the celestial or supercelestial body.
> (Martin Ruland's *Lexicon alchemiae*. 14th cent.)

> Because men do not perfectly believe and imagine, the result is that arts are uncertain when they might be wholly certain. Resolute imagination is the beginning of all magical operations. (Paracelsus*)

The key document of the first 'Rosicrucians', the *Fama Fraternitatis*[67] has been called the "Gospel according to Paracelsus" by the French scholar Roland Edighoffer[68]. Indeed the consonance of the *Fama* with so many of the ideas cherished by Paracelsus' intricate underground of continental disciples accounts for much of the amazingly widespread influence of the *Fama's* magical message. Paracelsus was an alchemist - with a difference. Not content with healing himself, he sought to heal the whole world.

---

* Quotations from Paracelsus (pp. 63, 65, 66) taken from his *magnum opus*, *Archidoxa Medicinae* (Johann Huser, 1589). English translations appear in Spence, Lewis, *The Encyclopaedia of Occultism* (US, 1920).

Paracelsus (1483-1541)

God is in everything from the angel to the spider.
(Meister Eckhart c.1260-1328)

Aureolus Philippus Theophrastus Bombastus von Hohenheim was born near Zurich in 1483. Fortunately he shortened his name - while simultaneously increasing its power - to Paracelsus, meaning, *greater than Celsus*, Celsus (c.20BC-c.35AD) being an ancient medical authority. This kind of contempt for authority, combined with a big - and generous - personality, made Paracelsus' life a constant struggle, but it also ensured that he stuck to his path : *don't believe what you read in books just because they're old; get out there and experiment for yourself!* This was his message.

Paracelsus lived a life of perpetual challenge to all academic authority. He also lived his life to the full, trying everything for himself and travelling widely. It is said that he toured the East, but while this is disputed, his reputation is certainly one model ingredient in the composite make-up of Christian Rosenkreuz, the ideal hero of the *Fama Fraternitatis*. Wherever it was that Paracelsus had travelled to, we know that he returned home to Switzerland in 1524, settling in Basle and opening his career with a fracas at the university. We are speaking of a time when it was customary for an academic physician to stand at a comfortable distance from a sick person's bed, reading from some ancient tome while the assistant did as he was told. Paracelsus preferred the hands-on approach. It gave him a thousand insights, including the first diagnosis of an industrial disease. Paracelsus is also credited as the father of modern medicine, being the first man to introduce chemistry into his practice, happy to employ drugs such as *laudanum* which he discovered, and anything else he found useful from herbal lore or well-tried rustic practices. He held diagnosis to be central to the practice of the physician. He liked to roll up his sleeves and get involved with the patient : "There can be no physician who is not also a surgeon. Where the physician is not also a surgeon, he is an idol that is nothing but a painted monkey." This is the kind of 'excessive' language which got him into trouble with the authorities, ever anxious for their status and pockets. In 1527, he threw a copy of Avicenna's vast *Canon* onto a traditional student bonfire and created a storm. He was kicked out of Basle, as he was out of many towns, notwithstanding his amazingly successful record in healing people - a small matter for the medical authorities.

> I considered with myself, that if there were no teacher of medicine in the world, how would I set about to learn the art? No otherwise than in the great open *Book of Nature*, written with the finger of God.

The "Book of Nature" is an expression which appears in the *Fama Fraternitatis*, and alerts us at once to the Hermetic character of many of Paracelsus' medical theories. For the Hermetist, *the world is the image of God (mundus imago dei)*. God's 'hand' is to be found all over it, or rather within it, in what Paracelsus calls the *divine signatures*. It is the task of the physician to trace them and to see where they lead. Strong gnostic characteristics can be discerned throughout his writings[69]. For Paracelsus, the soul which invigorates the physical body is the expression of an *astral body* which is the 'frame' in which the life of the organism takes place. The astral body is effectively the bridge or link between spirit and matter, according to a whole range of traditional correspondences between the stars, plants, minerals, and the individual organs of the body. The root of the soul is the timeless *pneuma*, the spirit. Healing, in principle, consists of clearing obstructions between *pneuma* and soul, by opening up the channels from spirit to body. In gnostic terms, this means tracing the soul back to its source, its divine origin, thus freeing it from that which binds it to earth. This is also the *type* for the alchemical operation, and in Paracelsus' thought, alchemical, spiritual and medical terminology cohere freely.

Paracelsus followed Pico's friend Marsilio Ficino's 'natural magic'[70] in his tripartition of the human microcosm. Paracelsus' elementary body, astral body and heavenly body correspond to Ficino's *corpus, spiritus* and *mens* (mind or *nous*=divine intelligence : the gnostic faculty). This triad is also expressed in alchemical terms in Paracelsus' salt (matter), sulphur (soul) and mercury (spirit). It is in fact the descendent of the classic Gnostic division of consciousness into the *hylic* (material), *psychic* (soul), and *pneumatic* (spiritual). Another classic Gnostic term, that of the *archon* or cosmic ruler, and related to the intermediary position of medium between divine and material, appears in Paracelsus' system as the *Archeus* : the creative principle implicate in Nature, defining individuality, and responding to the spirit - or in Paracelsus' terminology the *mercurius* : the essence of transformation, or resurrection. The *Archeus* can both join the sparks of divine light with matter and it can separate them from matter. Hence Paracelsus calls the *archeus*, the "inner alchemist" (*cf* : DNA control systems).

The great alchemist, master of mercury - or Mercury in human (if mythic) form - is of course Hermes Trismegistos, the great mystagogue of the Hermetic Art. We find him not only in Paracelsus but in Johann Valentin Andreae's *Chymical Wedding of Christian Rosenkreutz*[71] the first version of which was written by Andreae as a teenager some time between 1603 and 1605. On the fourth day of Christian's voyage of alchemical self-discovery, he comes across a lion, holding an ancient tablet :

> I, Hermes the Prince,
> After so much injury
> Done to the human race,
> Through Divine Council
> and the help of the arts
> Made into wholesome medicine
> Flow here.
> Drink from me who can :
> wash in me who likes :
> trouble me who dares
> Drink, brothers and live.

According to Paracelsus' mercury theory, should the 'mercury' (not the chemical of that name) or *quinta-essentia* be drawn from every animal, plant and mineral, the result would equal the *anima mundi* or Soul of the World, while a draught of the same, (the *elixir*) would renew vigour. Paracelsus obtained *laudanum* from the poppy as its *quintessence*. This came to him and his patients as an unequivocal gift of God.

> I have shown in my book of 'Elements' that the quintessence is the same thing as mercury. There is in mercury whatever wise men seek. There are as many mercuries as there are things.

'Mercury' then is a metaphysical principle without which nature could not be sustained. It should then be no surpise to find that the dominant alchemical symbol of the British astrologer and Hermetic philosopher, John Dee's *Monas Hieroglyphica* (1564) is mercury, the very crux of the cosmos. 'Mercury' is diffused at every level of nature, enabling one aspect to be transformed into a higher aspect.

For Christian theologians with an interest in alchemy such as Johann Valentin Andreae (born in 1586), and for mystical alchemists, the highest product of alchemy was the 'stone' (*lapis*) : the Medicine of Medicines, cleansing the wounded world and purifying the soul so that higher spiritual evolution may take place. Nature is not to be despised; she is the first-matter. Alone she is sorrow, but transformed by the Stone, she gives pure joy. Paracelsus' alchemy suggests the on-going process of an implicate apocalypse : the old world burned away to reveal the spirit, or in the words of the apocryphal, and highly influential II *Esdras* :

> *Then shall they be known, who are my chosen; and they shall be tried as the gold in the fire.*

What could be more like the 'coming of Christ' (usually associated with the 'Last Times') than the appearance within the alchemist's psyche of the *Stone*?

The Amphitheatre of Eternal Wisdom

In 1598, the magus John Dee is reported to have met the aged German alchemist Heinrich Khunrath[72] in Bremen. What may have passed between them is not recorded, but almost certainly conversation would have involved discussion of Khunrath's huge illustrated work, the *Amphitheatrum Sapientiae Aeternae* (Amphitheatre of Eternal Wisdom), published in that year by permission of the Emperor Rudolf II. Khunrath's extraordinarily vivid work offers ways for the adept to enter into a mystical brotherhood. The book contains an illustration of a cave entrance which opens into the earth - Nature - while within the cave are steps which lead upwards to the source of light : a neat paradox on the theme of the apparent darkness of matter. The door into the Amphitheatre of Eternal Wisdom reveals seven laws for those who would enter :

1. We are cleansed of the world. Be ye!
2. YHWH the one maker of all. Let the other powers be your ministers.
3. Make your vows and prayers to the First One, your hymns to those below.
4. Even if perchance your prayer has gone to the powers below, your purpose in so doing should only be to acquire help delegated from God.
5. Let reverence and fear be the messengers flitting to and fro between us and YHWH.
6. Following the customary trial be joyfully obedient towards them.
7. Let the holy matters, which you came here to engage upon, be upon the worthy and closed to the unworthy.

This work undoubtedly helped to frame the way onlookers would regard the claims of the Brotherhood of the Rosy-Cross as revealed in the *Fama Fraternitatis*, published sixteen years later. Indeed, Khunrath's work would come to be seen as a work issuing from the same mysterious source[73]. The reason for this is quite obvious. Notwithstanding the fact that the Paracelsian Benedictus Figulus helped Khunrath prepare the second edition of the *Amphitheatrum*, (a man who would later have advance access to the manuscript *Fama*[74]), the book itself is full of suggestions that Khunrath had attained to an inner brotherhood of *Christo-Cabalistic Divine Magic*, (the phrase is Khunrath's), seeing himself as a being apart from the mass of humanity, communing directly with the Truth :

> ..when ye my contemporaries were idly dozing, I was watching and at work, meditating earnestly day and night on what I had seen and learned, sitting, standing, recumbent, by sunshine, by moonshine, by banks, in meadows, streams, woods and mountains.
> (From Khunrath's *Confessio* in the *Amphitheatrum*)

"Do not think yourself successful unless the masses laugh at you." he wrote in his *Confessio*. While the masses jeered, Khunrath came to what was for him a conclusion of tremendous import. For Khunrath, "the Perfect Stone is attained through Christ." He is made 'flesh' in the womb of the outer world. The "College of the Mysteries" is *Nature*. The universe in its inward aspect is a perpetual apocalypse of the coming of God. Long hinted at through generations of alchemical literature, Khunrath's identification of the Stone with Christ had tremendous ramifications for those who followed him. Meditation and science had become a single path to God. *Put purely intellectual theology aside : seek the revelation of God in Nature - reconcile man to the cosmos, man to himself, man to his fellow, and man to God. Seek the Stone!* is the essence of Khunrath's message.

In his laying out of the inner process and path to the Philosopher's Stone, Khunrath depends on a mystical Christian and quite radical interpretation of the micro-macrocosmic theory, revealing a gnostic sense of man's capacity to know God.

> a. Purification of the personal part, that we may come to see God.
> b. Closing of the avenues of sense, stillness of soul, sanctification, illumination, tincture by the divine fire.
> c. Here is the path of attainment for the Stone of the Philosophers,
> d. which stone is the living spirit of the Elohim, and

e. the entreating of Jehovah the divine power, the Word of God in nature.

f. That Word is made flesh, so to speak in the virginal womb of the greater world and

g. is manifested in Jesus, in the virginal womb of Mary, but also

h. in the soul of man in a light super-added to that of Nature; hereby the knowledge of God and His Christ is communicated.

And then, in 1614, Wilhelm Wessel of Cassel in Hessen printed a mysterious document. The document's anonymous authors announced themselves as members of a secret Brotherhood, a holy Fraternity with knowledge of the Philosopher's Stone at their daily disposal, and who called for new brothers to share in the mighty task initiated by their founder, Christian Rosenkreuz[75]. Here, it was declared, lay the golden key to Europe's rebirth from the ashes of religious strife.

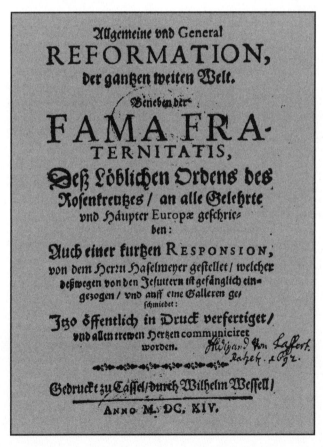

Notes to Part One

1 According to Garth Fowden (*The Egyptian Hermes*. Cambridge University Press. 1986) the first unambiguous testimony to literary 'Hermetica' probably comes from the first century BC Antiochus of Athens who, according to Gundel (*Weltbild und Astrologie in den griechischen Zauberpapyri*. Munich. 1968), probably spent some time in Alexandria. Antiochus refers to an earlier interpreter of Hermes called *Timaeus*, though this could be a reference to Plato's work of that name. Plato twice refers to the Egyptian god Thoth, without equating him with Hermes. Festugière (*La Révélation d'Hermès Trismegiste* (4 vols. 1944-54) was convinced that some astrological Hermetica were of Ptolemaic origin. Astrological and iatromathematical (astrological medicine) Hermetica were widely read by the first century AD.

2 Jean Pierre Mahé, *Hermès en Haute-Égypte*. Les Presses de l'Université Laval, Québec, Canada. Tomes I-II. 1978.1982.

3 See *Libellus* I.6. (Scott translation) : "'That Light,' he [Poimandres] said, 'is I, even Mind, the first God, who was before the watery substance which appeared out of the darkness; and the Word [*logos*] which came forth from the Light is son of God. ...They are not separate from one another; for life is the union of word and mind." Speculation on the nature of the divine Logos had been a feature of Alexandrian intellectual life since at least the time of the Jewish philosopher, Philo of Alexandria (c.25BC-c.50AD), a contemporary of Jesus. Indeed, Philonic *logos* speculation breathes through much of the first book, commonly called *Poimandres*, of the *Corpus Hermeticum*. For example, Philo calls the Logos "first-begotten Son of the uncreated Father", "second God" - and even "the man of God" (*de confusione linguarum* 41; 62; 146).

4 *The Egyptian Hermes. A historical approach to the late pagan mind*. Cambridge. 1986.

5 There is only vague evidence that the philosophical Hermetica were employed by the emperor Julian the Apostate (acceded 361) in his polemical justification of the sufficiency of paganism and the destructiveness of Christianity in his *Contra Galilaeos*. However, Cyril of Alexandria (d.444), when attacking Julian's work, regarded the late emperor as one of Hermes' leading spiritual disciples. Cyril could certainly see how Hermes could be used to produce a kind of Christianity without Christ, but was able to turn the philosophical Hermetica to his own advantage, using it to justify the Christian doctrine of the Logos. The false dating of the Hermetic writings worked against their anti-Christian use in this instance, simply because no-one could blame the antique Hermes for not knowing yet about Christ - and, since many of his ideas chimed in with the revelation of Jesus, did it not prove the antecedent truthfulness of Christianity? Thus, Hermes became a prophet of the Church, and remained so until the seventeenth century when Isaac Casaubon dated the Hermetica more or less correctly in a work published in 1614.

6 See *De divinis institionibus*. (Venetiis, Johannes de Colonia & Johannes Manthen. 1478). The Church Father L. Caecilius Firmianus Lactantius (3rd. cent.) regarded Hermes Trismegistus as one of the most significant non-Christian prophets to anticipate Christianity. Lactantius was struck by references in *Poimandres* and *Asclepius* to the creative Word that is Son of God, and the designation of God as Father. In his *De divinis institutionibus*, IV.6, Lactantius took the following idea from the lost Greek original of *Asclepius* 8 : "The Lord and creator of all things, whom we call God, made a second God, visible and tangible (...) The latter was beautiful in his eyes and full of what is good; and He worshipped him and loved him as his own Son." Lactantius was to be much favoured by Renaissance philosophers addicted to Hermetic wisdom, especially since in his *De ira Dei*, Lactantius maintained that Hermes Trismegistus was much older than Pythagoras and Plato.

7 *viz* : *Zostrianos; Allogenes*.

8 *De arte magna*. (pseudo-) Democritus. (Dominico Pizimentio interprete. Pativii, Simone Galigmani. 1573).

9 The text of *physika kai mystika* also contains interpolations from the first century. Bolus/Democritus asserts himself as an Hellenistic prophet, sent to teach man to rise above confused matter. The text of recipes is punctuated by an alchemical formula which refers to the sympathetic and antithetical principles which set the dynamic *physika* (matter) in motion : "a nature rejoices in another nature, and a nature defeats another nature, and a nature dominates another nature." A Latin translation from a Greek manuscript appeared in 1572 in Padua under the title *De arte magna*, and was reprinted a year later with a longer text by the 7th century alchemist Stephanos of Alexandria. Stephanos' work, more poetic and mystical than Democritus forms an important link between Greek and Arabic alchemy. He used lost texts of Hermes as a basis and spoke about nature in paradoxical terms : "O nature that defeats another nature, nature that rises above itself, nature that fills the All, unity and reunited separation (...) O immaterial matter that holds matter together, nature that defeats another nature, heavenly nature that arouses the spiritual, O bodyless body that makes other natures unphysical." See J.Lindsay *The Origins of Alchemy in Graeco-Roman Egypt*. (London 1979) and *The Alchemical works of Stephanos of Alexandria*, by F. Sherwood Taylor in *Ambix* I (1937),pp.116-139; 2 (1938), pp.38-49).

10 cf : *Luke*. XX. 17-18 for a possible analogy with alchemical transforming-stone symbolism in the first century AD.

11 References to 'mercury' in alchemical texts rarely indicate the chemical substance of that name. Mercury was thought as the living quintessence, the quicksilver principle which enabled the essence of the metal to be transformed: its spirit, or portion of the divine mind.

12 *De ortu et causis metallorum* (1576) in *Theatrum Chemicum*, II, pp. 198ff. (*Theatrum Chemicum, praecipuos selectorum auctorum tractatus...continens*. Ursel., 1602. 3 vols.).

13 *The Gospel of Philip* 67. 30-35. (*The Nag Hammadi Library in English*. Ed. James M.Robinson. E.J. Brill. Leiden. 1977). "[The Lord] said, "I came to make

71

[the things below] like the things [above, and the things] outside like those [inside. I came to unite] them in that place." It would be hard to deny that the author of the gospel's conception of 'Jesus' in this passage is influenced by Hermetic philosophy.

14   cf : the *Cooke MS.* familiar to historians of Freemasonry. This English document, of c.1420, was in use by a guild of freestone masons and refers to an ancient science which was said to have survived the Flood and been transmitted by Pythagoras and Hermes. Pythagoras in the middle ages was a name associated with an esoteric system of ritual purity and of secret numerology : the confluence of alchemy and numerology lies in the mythology of ancient architecture. The mason/sculptor draws out the hidden power of stone : the secret of the craft.

15   *Mysticism in Religion.* W.R.Inge. (undated edition c.1946).

16   Garth Fowden : *The Egyptian Hermes* (Cambridge University Press. 1986)

17   Quotations from Zosimos from *Alchimistes grecs* (M.Berthelot. Paris 1893).

18   Reported in *Die Ssabier und der Ssabismus* (*The Sabians and Sabianism*), by D. Chwolsohn (St.Petersburg 1856. 2 vols). And subsequently in *Avicenne* by Carra de Vaux (1900) & *Hermetica*, (p.98, n.1, n.2) edited and translated by Walter Scott (Reprinted by Shambhala, Boston 1985).

19   Zarathushtrians.

20   The name 'Sabian' had become associated with the Mandaeans, (from the root *mandâ*, meaning *gnosis*) : gnostics who were to be found in the marshlands between Baghdad and Basra, as well as in the Iranian province of Khuzistan, in Ahwaz and Shustar - and still are, as far as we know. 'Sabian' may come from a Semitic word meaning 'those who wash themselves'. Full-immersion baptism is a very pronounced feature of Mandaean initiation rites. Indeed, they constructed their own pools, (called *Jordans*), by redirecting irrigation channels. The water had to be 'living', that is : flowing, and was held to have sacred properties.

The Mandaeans owe knowledge of their origin to a work entitled the *Diwan of the Great Revelation, called 'Inner Haran'*, (the *Haran Guwaita*). The work tells of their heretical Jewish origins, (reminiscent of the more famous sectaries of Khirbet Qumran). The Mandaeans believe their ancestors were persecuted by the priestly community of Jerusalem and maintain it was their ancestors' condemnation of that community which led to the Holy City's destruction - most likely the conflagration of AD 70 which saw the destruction of the Herodian Temple. Perhaps it was John the Baptist's attack on the morals of the Herodians which earned that prophet the Mandaean title of him as "envoy of the kingdom of light" (cf *Gospel of John* I,6,8-9). John the Baptist is seen by Mandaeans as the adversary of "Christ the Roman". Claiming a direct link to the Light beyond the "Sabbaoth" or seven planetary spheres, the Mandaeans called themselves the "elect of righteousness", "Nasoreans" : guardians or possessors of secret rites and knowledge. The *Haran Guwaita* scroll reports that during the reign of the Parthian king Artabanus, a coterie of "Nasoreans" fled the Jewish authorities for the "inner Haran" territory or the "Median hill country". According to Kurt Rudolph (*Gnosis.* 1985), the "reference is clearly to the penetration by the community, or part of it, of the north-western Iranian territory between Harran and Nisibis or Media during the period of the later Arsacids (1st or 2nd century AD)." According to the *Haran Guwaita,* a community was established in Baghdad where Mandaeans became regional governors. These good times apparently came to an end with the consolidation of Shapur I's neo-Zarathushtrian state (AD241-272) and the destruction of Mandaean temples. We know that in the same period, Mandaeans had contact with the Gnostic prophet Mani, whose followers were also persecuted by the old guard of the Zarathushtrian priesthood. By the ninth century, the Mandaeans of Harran and Baghdad had apparently been forgotten. Perhaps they had moved, or some had moved to the Arabian peninsular (Hejaz and Sheba - the modern Yemen), where the Prophet Muhammad may have encountered them and found them worthy of divine recognition. ('Sabian' could then come from 'Saba', the biblical 'Sheba'). It would appear then that up to AD 830 'Sabian' indicated a Mandaean. Between 830 and c.1000 the term referred to the Harranian learned pagans, and afterwards to pagans generally. However, Arabic writers were not on the whole aware of the distinctions, so we can never be sure in which of the above senses they mean the term 'Sabian'. (Scott. *Hermetica.* p.99. n.1. Shambhala Press. 1985).

21   *The Legacy of Islam* (Ed. Arnold. Guillaume. Oxford. 1931).

22   *The Cathedral Builders* by Jean Gimpel. (Michael Russell. 1983).

23   Such as Ormus le Guidon, lord of Biddulph, Staffordshire, whose name is linked in stone to the extraordinary carvings in an oriental style which still grace the church of S.Chad's in Stafford, constructed in the mid-twelth century when Ormus le Guidon flourished. The inscription on the chancel column reads : ORM VOCATUR QUI ME CONDIDIT, appearing opposite a carving of what appears to be the goddess Ishtar.

24   See Prof. David Stevenson's *The Origins of Freemasonry : Scotland's century 1590-1710.* Cambridge University Press. 1988. p.135ff.

25   Spurious connections between the Gral and Catharism are explored in a scholarly and thorough fashion in Michel Roquebert's exhaustive work *Les Cathares et le Graal.* (Éditions Privat. 1994) Roquebert makes it plain that the major accounts of the Holy Grail in the period of flourishing Catharism (c.1160-1256) owe their Christological background to Catholic eucharistic doctrines (the holy cup of sacramental wine/blood), whatever the sources of the Grail or 'Gral' image might be. Visionary mysticism was not the prerogative of heretical movements, whether gnostic or of any other kind. Anyone can use a symbol for their own purposes, and there is no evidence that the Cathars had any interest in the Gral symbology - and even if they did, and the evidence has yet to come to light - they would certainly not have linked it to the eucharistic cup in the way that Chrétien de Troyes does, since Cathars found the transubstantiation concept of the eucharist abhorrent in any form. Chrétien de Troye's patron, Philippe d'Alsace, count of Flanders - who commissioned *Perceval the Gaul or the story of the Graal,* when he came to Troyes in 1182, hoping to marry Marie of Champagne, daughter of king Louis VII of France - was a determined persecutor of all heretics, including the Cathars.

26   According to Professor Hatto (*Parzifal*. Penguin. 1980. p.431ff.), Wolfram has apparently taken the word from a work (which he knew and used in *Parzifal*) called *Alexander*, written in early German, wherein we hear of a miraculous Stone which a Latin translator calls the *lapis exilis*, the 'small or slight stone'. Subsequent versions of Wolfram's work have apparently repeated a mistake by an early copyist, unless Wolfram was indulging in an obscure pun. The small or uncomely Stone is of course completely consistent with traditional alchemy's assessment of the stone as being something unnoticed or invisible to the eyes of the world, deriving from what Jung calls the "psychic non-ego" or "unconscious" : a direct link to the spiritual world.

27   The Phoenix which emerges from alchemical fire is a staple symbol in medieval alchemy and beyond for *resurrection*, and in the polyvalent world that is alchemy is furthermore related to the peacock, and to Christ who, from a Christian reading of the medieval Arabic *tractatus aureus*, can be identified with the Stone. It is from the Stone that the knights ride out in quest of adventure. The mountain itself is also a polyvalent alchemical symbol. The Stone is generally both the start and the *goal* of the alchemical *opus* of transformation.

28   It is significant that access to the Stone can be achieved in this world.

29   We have already learned from Flegetanis that a "troop" of angels left the Stone on earth in the first place. The mythology behind this story is strongly reminiscent of the account in the *Book of Enoch* (c. 1st cent.BC) wherein Enoch is told that the secrets of heaven were brought illegitimately to men by the "Watchers", stellar angels who rebelled against the "Lord of Spirits". Rebel angels having brought the Stone, neutral angels had to descend to earth in what is apparently a punishment, to make contact with the Stone. From the psychological point of view, this myth is highly suggestive.

30   The Egyptian alchemist Zosimos of Panopolis (c.300 AD) had recognised the Hermetic *krater* as being directly linked to the spiritual alchemical *opus* 900 years before.

31   Perhaps the conceptual origin of Photography : 'light-writing', from the Greek *photos*=light and *graphe*=writing; making an impression.

32   According to Henry Corbin's *The Man of Light in Iranian Sufism*, (Shambhala. 1981), *The Aim of the Sage* was circulated among a Middle Eastern Sufi sect called the Ihwan al Saafa (the Pure Brethren) which, according to Dr Christopher McIntosh (*The Rosicrucians*. Weiser. 1997) "would have been active around the time that Christian Rosenkreuz was supposed to have made his journey to that region [late 14th cent.]." (p.25).

33   Announced by the so-called *Rosicrucian Manifestos* (1610-1616).

34   See Brian Stock, *Myth and Science in the Twelfth Century*, (Princeton U.P. 1972). For Neoplatonism in the school of Chartres, consult H.Waddell's *The Wandering Scholars*.

35   *Psychology & Alchemy*. Trans. F.C. Hull (Routledge & Kegan Paul) p.245.

36   *Allgemeine und General Reformation der gantzen weiten Welt. Beneben der Fama Fraternitatis, Dess Löblichen Ordens des Rosenkreutzes, an alle Gelehrte und Häupter Europae geschrieben. &c.* (Kassel, Wilhelm Wessel. 1614).

37   Advanced herbalism and drug manufacture today mirrors the alchemical approach to medicine, reinforced so powerfully by Paracelsus. Manufacturers today "separate the subtle from the gross" by extracting rare healing agents from obscure plants. Paracelsus, the practical gnostic, discovered and isolated *laudanum*, meaning : "We praise" (God) - so beneficial it was to the relief of the pain of humankind. Paracelsus found the work of God in Nature, through his quest for the "divine signatures" diffused throughout the natural realm.

38   *Opera omnia chemica*. Kassel. 1649.

39   Norton was M.P for Bristol in 1436 and became a member of Edward IV's Privy Chamber. He was employed on embassies and was a member of the London Grocer's Company. He died in 1477.

40   *Monastic Life in Medieval England*. (A&C Black. London. 1961.)

41   On 15 January 1556, the magus, alchemist and antiquarian scholar John Dee (1527-1608) sent a supplication to Queen Mary begging for the "Recovery and Preservation of Ancient Writers and Monuments" (British Museum, Cotton MS. Vitellius. C. VII, art..6). He writes that "Among the exceeding many most lamentable displeasures, that have of late happened unto this realm, through the subverting of religious houses, and the dissolution of other assemblies of godly and learned men, it has been, and for ever, among all learned students, shall be judged, not the least calamity, the spoile and destruction of so many and so notable libraries, wherein lay the treasures of all Antiquity, and the everlasting seeds of continual excellency in this your Grace's realm." Dee's hope that if "speedy diligence be shewed" a great deal could still be preserved by the establishment of a royal library, fell on deaf ears. In 1536 the antiquary John Leland had similarly begged Henry VIII to preserve the monastic libraries - again, in vain. Thirteen years later John Bale (*The Laboryouse Journey*. 1549) also wrote of the need for preservation, remarking that the precious manuscripts and ancient tomes were being used to wrap food, scour candlesticks, clean boots, and other commercial uses wherein literacy was not required, adding that "Yea, the universities of this realm, are not all clear in this detestable fact." (See Francis Wormald's and C.E. Wright's *The English Library before 1700*. London. 1958. pp.152-153). Dee himself collected as many books and manuscripts as he could, thus acquiring England's largest library. In the following century the antiquary Elias Ashmole (1617-1692) made extensive efforts to recover as much of Dee's collection as he possibly could : efforts which indirectly led both to his collection of medieval English alchemy (*Theatrum Chemicum Britannicum*. 1652) and to England's first chemical laboratory to be sited in a university. Ashmole was one of the 114 founder-members of the Royal Society.

42 No historian to my knowledge has fully recognised the incompatibility of the 'monasticism-is-medieval' idea with the fact that at least two key 'Renaissance' figures, namely Pico della Mirandola (1463-1494) and Giordano Bruno (1548-1600) were both products of monastic environments.

43 *Psychology & Alchemy*. C.G. Jung. Collected Works Vol. 12. Ed : Sir Herbert Read. Routledge & Kegan Paul. 1953.

44   See the *Ripley Scrowle* (1588. British Museum MS. Add. 5025) wherein can be found an illustration depicting the three manifestations of the *Anthropos* during transformation from body to soul and from soul to spirit. Below this sequence squats a toad next to a dragon : the mysterious powers of the wet earth. This tripartite division of man is a staple of Alexandrian Gnosis.

45   *Opera omnia chemica*. Kassel. 1649. p.62.

46   Ibid. p.9.

47   Ibid. p.10.

48   Ibid. p.130.

49   *Psychology & Alchemy*. p.412.

50   Paracelsus made the epoch-marking discovery of the pain-reliever *laudanum* as the *mercurius* of the poppy.

51   According to Ripley the *prima materia* is water : the material principle of all bodies (*Opera*. p.369) including mercury (p.427). It is the *hyle* (matter) which the divine act of creation brought forth from the dark chaos in the form of a dark sphere (p.9). The chaos is a *massa confusa* (cf : the darkness of the unconscious, according to Jung) which gives birth to the stone. The hylical water contains a hidden elemental fire which was believed to permeate all things (a pre-Socratic doctrine identified with Heraklitos). The alchemist must at certain stages of the work, bring this fire forth through chemical combination and sublimation. In the illustrated manuscript *Ripley Scrowle*, compiled in 1588 (British Museum, MS. Add. 5025), the sphere is represented with dragon wings. The use of dragon symbology is itself highly significant and occurs again in another illustration from the *Ripley Scrowle* where, within a sphere subdivided into the zodiac, two dragons bite each others' tail in a cyclic image of the common gnostic-alchemical *ouroboros* (usually two serpents symbolizsing the totality of the cosmos or nature's infinite rebirth-process), while girding the alchemical *sol* and *luna* while the sun's rays extend to the zodiac. Entwined dragons have been found on stone monuments throughout Britain (*viz*: the churches at Overchurch and Prestbury in Cheshire) and are associated with sacred sites and the (by some) perceived lines within the earth which link them. These *loci* and links between *loci* were described by the alchemist genius Paracelsus as the *divine signatures*, (*Compendium*. Leo Suavius (=Jacques Gohory). Basileae, Petrus Perna, 1568) and could be found diffused throughout nature and in all the four Aristotelian elements. If the cosmos was, as it were, drawn with 'the finger of God', the "divine signatures" could be regarded as his evidential fingerprints. Such phenomena were regarded as guides to help the wise discover, principally, the healing powers within nature herself. Thus the alchemist sought to separate the potent *mercurius* from the 'body' of a substance through alchemical 'crucifixion' of a substance into the four elements. The alchemical 'dragon' therefore bore the *mercurius* within it as a body is bound together in health by veins and arteries. Interestingly, this theory ties in with the ancient pagan and Christianised pagan folklore of these islands. Where the dragon reared its head, so to speak, Celtic wise men (the *Ovates*) are thought to have erected stone markers or added carvings to sacred sites dedicated to the the deity equivalent to Hermes

(sometimes called Baal, for whom fires were lit in May). While the dragon was held not unnaturally by medieval theologians to have been a dangerous pagan superstition, it is curious how medieval freemasons (workers in 'free stone') chose to carve representatives of the dragon both without and within churches. A very splendid example is that carved opposite the profile of a Green Man, so forming a frame for the holy-water (note) basin at the largely fourteenth century church of Cawston in Norfolk. On many formerly pagan sites in England the Church dedicated their structures to the 'dragon-slayers' S.Michael or S.George, regarding the gods of such places as demonic and in need of plugging-up. One such church is S.Michael's Lichfield which stands on a Green Hill once sacred to pagan Celts. (A fertility rite is still enacted every year in May which processes a 'Bower Queen' in state through the city). While such folklore presents many problems of attribution to the scholar, there can be little doubt that alchemists made their projections from imaginations linked into images of the divine energies known throughout the ancient pagan world - not least of whom was Hermes himself.

52   The 'Oration on the Dignity of Man', 1486. According to Ernesto Garin, Pico della Mirandola's *Oratio* is "the manifesto of the Renaissance".

53   Kristeller : *Marsilio Ficino e Lodovico Lazzarelli*, first published as an article in 1938 and expanded in *Studies*, pp.221-47; *Ancora per Giovanni Mercurio da Correggio*, Studies, pp. 249-57; *Lodovico Lazzarelli e Giovanni da Corregio* in *Biblioteca degli Ardenti della Città di Viterbo*, 1961.

54   Sessorian Codex 413; Vittorio Emmanuele National Library, Rome.

55   It should be held in mind that in this period Hermes Trismegistus was held by some informed ecclesiastical authorities to have been a largely respectable prophet of Christianity, a contemporary of Moses, mentioned with some approval by S.Augustine in *Civitas Dei*, and enthusiastically by the Christian theologian Lactantius, *circa* 400.

56   Compare with François Rabelais' 'Abbey of Thelema' in *Gargantua & Pantagruel* (1535).

57   Frances Yates has called Mercurio "a kind of Hermes Fool", while Edgar Wind has described Lazzarelli's devotion to him as "notorious". Neither of these statements is in my opinion adequate to this unique case.

58   Viterbo Codex IID 14 (No.199).

50   The figure of *Poimandres* (hence 'Pymander') only appears in the first treatise of the *Corpus Hermeticum*, but Ficino took it to be the title for the whole.

60   *Bibliotheca Historica* 1,13sqq.

61   The symbol of the baptismal bowl in which willing initiates are bathed in order to soak in and attain *nous*, has analogies to the mythology surrounding the Holy Grail. Joseph Campbell was fond of the analogy and asserted the connection as fact to his students. (Canadian Broadcasting Corporation. *The Holy Grail* by C. Bisaillon. 1995).

62   Prof. D.P. Walker. *The prisca theologia in France*. &c. Also *Spiritual and demonic magic from Ficino to Campanella* (London. 1958).

63   *De l'infinito universo e mondi* Dialogue I. 1583.

64   That is, spiritual creatures, not 'devils' in the vulgar sense, ie : in the Renaissance, one could describe one's 'genius' as one's *daemon*.

65   Written 1507-1530 and held back so as not to offend the Church; published in 1543.

66   *La 'Dignitas hominis' e la letteratura patristica*, in *La Rinascita* (Florence, 1938), IV, pp.102-146.

67   Meaning the 'Fame of the Fraternity' : the formerly hidden fraternity of the Rosy-Cross.

68   *Rose-Croix et Société Idéale*. (Roland Edighoffer)

69   Mostly published after his death by admirers, works such as the *Compendium* (*Basileae*, Petrus Perna. 1568), and the great *Archidoxorum* (*Basileae*, Petrus Perna. 1570)

70   *De vita coelitus comparanda* (How to attain Life from heaven) by Marsilio Ficino, the third book of his *Libri de vita* (*Bononiae*, Benedictus Hectoris, 1501. First published : 1489).

71   Published by Lazarus Zetzner in Strasbourg, 1616. The author was also responsible for the *Fama Fraternitatis*.

72   Heinrich Khunrath. Born Leipzig 1520.d.1605.

73   In fact, Johann Valentin Andreae regarded Khunrath as an obscurantist and a "mystagogue", and his followers victims of the 'demon of the savants' : *curiositas*. Andreae would play with the myth of the secret fraternity in order to generate a *genuine and open* fraternity.

74   Much to the chagrin of its author. Andreae called Figulus "an adventurer and a charlatan".

75   Called in Andreae's *Chymische Hochzeit* (1616) a "Knight of the Golden Stone."

Part Two

THE TRUE STORY OF THE ROSICRUCIANS

Wir Die Brüder Der Fraternitet deß R:
C. Entpieten allen und Jeden so dise unsere Fa=
mam christlicher meinung lesen, unsern gruß
liebe und gebet.   Nach dem der allein weise
und Gnädige Gott In den letzten dagen sein gnad
und güte so reichlig über das mennschlige gesschlecht
auß gossen, daß sich die Erkantnus beydes Sei=
nes Sohns und der Natur Je mehr und mehr er=
weitert, und wir uns billig einer glückseliger Zeit
rühmen mögen, Daher Er dan nit allein die das
halbe thail der Unbekanten und verborgenen Welt
erfunden, viel wunderlige und zuvor nie gesche=
hene werck und geschöpf der natur, uns Zu führen
und dann hocherlauchte Ingenia erst stehen lassen
die zum thail die vermeinigte und unvolkomne
künst raidanim Zu recht brechten, domit doch endlich
der mensch seinen Adel und herrligkeit verstünde,
wellcher gestalt der Microcosmus, und wie weit sich
sein künst In der Natur erstrecke. Ob wol nun aug
hiermit der Unbesünnemen Welt wenig gedient,
und daß lestern, lachen und gespött Immer mehr Zu
auf diß den gelarten die stolz und abgeitz so hoch
daß sie nit mögen Zusammen dretten, und außal=
len so wol In unsern Seculo richlig mitgethail
Em Librum Naturæ oder Regulam aller künsten
samlen machten, Sundern Je ein thail dem Andern
zu raider thut, Bleibt man doch bey den Alten lehren
und muß

Manuscript c. 1610-1612
Fama Fraternitatis

Chapter Six

The Fame of the Fraternity

Sit Jessica. Look how this floor of heaven
Is thick inlaid with patens of bright gold;
There's not the smallest orb which thou behold'st
But in his motion like an angel sings,
Still quiring to the young-eyed cherubins.
Such harmony is in immortal souls.
But whilst this muddy vesture of decay,
Doth grossly close it in, we cannot hear it.
(*The Merchant of Venice*. Act V. scene 1)

An innocent trip from Heilegenkreuz in the Tyrol to Innsbruck in the autumn of 1612 brought an unpleasant surprise to Adam Haslmayr, musician, theosopher, medical celebrity and notary public to the Archduke Maximilian. On the orders of the Jesuit inquisitor Hypolyt Guarinoni, Haslmayr was arrested and sentenced to slavery on the Mediterranean galleys.

Why?

In March, Haslmayr had published his answer to the *Fama Fraternitatis* – the Fame of the Fraternity – a manuscript which had been privately distributed to persons with an interest in the advancement of science and religion in a corrupt society. Was Haslmayr's ill-fortune a result of his interest in this document? What was so extraordinary about the *Fama Fraternitatis*?

The Fama

Seeing the only wise and merciful God in these latter days hath poured out so richly his mercy and goodness to mankind, whereby we do attain more and more to the perfect knowledge of his Son Jesus Christ and Nature, that justly we may boast of the happy time, wherein there is discovered unto us the half part of the world, which heretofore was unknown and hidden, but he hath also made manifest unto us many wonderful, and never heretofore seen, works and creatures of Nature, and moreover hath raised men, imbued with great wisdom, who might partly renew and reduce all arts (in this our age spotted and imperfect) to perfection; so that finally man might thereby understand his own nobleness and worth, and why he is called *Microcosmus*, and how far his knowledge extendeth into Nature.

This elegant speech serves to usher the reader into the *Fama Fraternitatis*: a 'god's-eye' view of Europe in the first decade of the 17th century. A massive expansion of knowledge has taken place. Galileo has brought the craters of the moon into telescopic focus[1]. The Americas have been discovered and partly colonised. The globe has been circumnavigated. Copernicus has revolutionised the conception of the universe with his solar system. Giordano Bruno, burnt at the stake only a decade ago has declared the universe to be infinite.

All of this, implies the *Fama*, is no accident. A certain mentality has been at work; a spiritual endeavour is afoot. It is God, the *Fama* declares, who has revealed Himself through Nature to the "men of great wisdom", and through an allegory, the *Fama* will show what has *really* been going on, and why it is necessary to deepen and enlarge on what has been achieved.

The second paragraph makes explicit the criticism of the present "spotted and imperfect" age. There is more to come, but certain vices must be overcome: "*the pride and covetousness of the learned is so great, it will not suffer them to agree together; but were they united...*" This is the main issue to which the *Fama* addresses itself: unity, co-operation. The learned could, if they would, "collect *Librum Naturae*, or a perfect method of all arts: but such is their opposition, that they still keep, and are loth to leave the old course..." We are then led swiftly into the main allegory - so obviously an allegory, but one which has for over three centuries (due largely to the nature of the circles in which the *Fama* has been transmitted) been seen erroneously as a statement of more or less historic fact.

> To such an intent of a general reformation, the most godly and highly illuminated father, our brother, C.R. a German, the chief and original of our Fraternity, hath much and long time laboured..

The Myth of Christian Rosenkreuz

At age five, brother C.R. (Christian Rosenkreuz) is put into a cloister to learn (indifferently[2]) Latin and Greek. At the first opportunity he escapes the monastery to journey to the Holy Land with Brother P.A.L. P.A.L. dies in Cyprus, whereupon C.R. heads for Damascus to find favour, due to his knowledge of medicine, with some wise men from Damcar in Arabia, where next he goes. Aged sixteen, Brother C.R.

arrives in Damcar to be received "not as a stranger, but as one whom they had long expected." - a marvellous touch, echoing the arrival of the 'Thief Abu' in the *1001 Nights* who finds himself among "the relics of a Golden Age: *golden because gold was nothing*". The wise men teach Christian Arabic. C.R. is thus able to translate the "Book M".

> This is the place where he did learn his physic, and his mathematics, whereof the world hath just cause to rejoice, if there were more love, and less envy.

He next goes to Egypt, observing its plants and creatures, and then moves on to Fez, as instructed by his Arabian teachers.

> And it is a great shame unto us, that wise men, so far remote the one from the other, should not only be of one opinion, hating all contentious writings, but also be so willing and ready under the seal of secrecy to impart their secrets to others. Every year the Arabians and Africans do send one to another, enquiring of one another out of their arts, if happily they had found out some better things, or if experience had weakened their reasons. Yearly there came something to light, whereby the mathematics, physic and magic (for in those are they of Fez most skilful) were amended. As there is nowadays in Germany no want of learned men, magicians, Cabalists, physicians, and philosophers, were there but more love and kindness among them, or that the most part of them would not keep their secrets close only to themselves.

At Fez, brother C.R. makes acquaintance with the "Elementary Inhabitants": the spirits of earth, air, water and fire, who reveal secrets of the inner nature of Nature to C.R[3]. C.R. finds the *magia* of Fez somewhat impure (demonic), and their cabala restricted by their faith (Islam), but he nonetheless intends to make use of the knowledge acquired; Rosenkreuz is no bigot. The knowledge is *agreeable with the harmony of the whole world*: a characteristically Renaissance Neoplatonic and Hermetic concept. Truth is truth and agrees with itself :

> might one examine all and several persons upon the earth, he should find that which is good and right, is always agreeing with itself; but all the rest is spotted with a thousand erroneous conceits.

From Fez C.R. departs for Spain, expecting widespread rejoicing at his discoveries, discoveries which will henceforth lead to a firm foundation for all scientific endeavour :

He showed them new growths, new fruits, and beasts, which did concord with old philosophy, and prescribed them new *Axiomata*, whereby all things might fully be restored. But it was to them a laughing matter; and being a new thing unto them, they feared that their great name should be lessened, if they should now again begin to learn and acknowledge their many errors, to which they were accustomed, and wherewith they had gained them enough.

This great theme of the perversion of knowledge is never lost sight of throughout the *Fama*. It is the keynote.

C.R., much to his innocent surprise, finds the reaction to his discoveries everywhere the same. No one wants to know. So he dreams of "a Society in Europe", fully endowed with sufficient wealth to provide solid guidance for the good governance of the continent.

Meanwhile Brother C.R. returns to Germany and looks forward to a reformation. He could have bragged of the transmutation of metals but instead "did esteem more Heaven, and the citizens thereof, Man, than all vain glory and pomp." His view of Man is transcendental and universalist: Hermetic Man is the *Great Miracle* who has fallen into darkness. Five years of ruminations, mathematics and construction of fine instruments follow until he decides again to attempt the "wished-for reformation": the return to first principles and the harmonious unity of the cosmos. He recruits three brothers from his "first cloister" whom he carefully instructs in the necessary arts: Brothers G.V., J.A. and J.O. Thus begins the Fraternity of the Rose Cross.

In the House of the Holy Spirit

The Brothers set about compiling a dictionary of the "magical language" (Cabala?), producing the first part of *Book M* and constructing their house, called "Holy Spirit". The work is hard and further constrained by the huge numbers of sick people who come to be treated, so more members are recruited - "all bachelors and of vowed virginity" until they number eight. They produce a book "of all that which man can desire, wish, or hope for." Having ordered things and learned fully the *Axiomata* of the Fraternity, the brothers spread out into many countries to secretly impart their learning and to correct errors from as many divers sources as possible, and to communicate their discoveries one to another. They have six rules:

1. They must cure the sick *gratis*.
2. They should dress in the fashion of the place where they live.
3. They should meet once a year or write a note explaining their absence.
4. Each should find a worthy successor.
5. The letters *C.R.* should be their mark and seal.
6. The Fraternity should remain secret for one hundred years.

C.R. remains with two brothers, hoping for the cleansing of the Church and thinking of her with "longing desire", while every year they meet "with joy". They tell of all the inventions of the world and all the new revelations of His world that God has delivered to men's minds.

> Everyone may hold it out for certain, that such persons as were sent, and joined together by God, and the heavens, and chosen out of the wisest of men, as have lived in many ages, did live together above all others in highest unity, greatest secrecy, and most kindness one towards another.

The first brother to die is J.O., much learned in Cabala and a resident in England where he was much known and famed for curing a young Earl of Norfolk of leprosy. The Fraternity no longer knows where some of the brothers are buried but each did, we are told, find a fit successor. There follows a reference to a document to come, the *Confession* wherein readers may learn 37 reasons why the Fraternity has decided to open itself to the worthy.

> Also we do promise more gold than both the Indies bring to the King of Spain; for Europe is with child and will bring forth a strong child, who shall stand in need of a great godfather's gift.

Meanwhile, time has passed and the present brothers no longer know when brother C.R. died or where he is buried, or even if they have the entirety of the original wisdom. We are next informed of how the "high illuminated man of God, *Fra.* C.R.C." was found.

The death of Brother A in *Gallia Narbonensis* (Languedoc) makes way for his successor N.N., an architect, who in the course of renovations to his 'building' uncovers a memorial tablet inscribed with the names of the original brethren. In the tablet is a nail which when pulled out dislodges some of the masonry behind it, revealing a hidden door on which is written *POST ANNOS 120 PATEBO*, prophesying the precise time of the discovery of Father Christian

Rosenkreuz. ("I shall be revealed after 120 years"[4])

From information given in the succeeding *Confession*, we can put a date to this 'event' as being 1604. (C.R. having been born, according to the *Confessio Fraternitatis*, in 1378 - the Year of the Great Schism of the Church - and having died in 1484). The allegory continues:

> For like as our door was after so many years wonderfully discovered, also there shall be opened a door to Europe (when the wall is removed) which already doth begin to appear, and with great desire is expected of many.

The next morning, a small band of brothers open the door. Their efforts reveal an extraordinary vault of seven sides: five feet broad and eight feet high. The vault is illuminated by an *inner sun* "situated in the upper part of the centre of the ceiling". In the middle is a round altar covered with a brass plate declaring, "This compendium of the universe I made in my lifetime to be my tomb." In a circle is written : *Jesus mihi omnia* : Jesus, all things to me. In the middle of the plate, four figures in circles are inscribed with the words:

1. A Vacuum exists nowhere.
2. The Yoke of the Law.
3. The Liberty of the Gospel.
4. The Whole Glory of God.

The whole design is a quite stunning array of geometrical symmetry of mystical import whose exact nature will be revealed only to those found worthy of joining the society. The floor, for example, is divided into triangles which describe the powers of the "inferior governors" (the stars). Against each wall is a chest containing books, the first of which to be mentioned is the *Vocabular* of Paracelsus[5]. Another chest contains looking-glasses, bells, burning lamps and sufficient things by which the principles of the Order might be reconstructed, should the Order's labour come to nothing.

Removing the altar, the brothers find the body of Christian Rosenkreuz "whole and unconsumed", grasping to his chest the *Book I*, and a Bible: "our greatest treasure." They read in Latin a concise *eulogium* of R.C.'s life :

A grain buried in the breast of Jesus. C.Ros.C. sprung from the noble and renowned German family of R.C.; a man admitted into the mysteries and secrets of heaven and earth through the divine revelations, subtle cogitations and unwearied toil of his life. In his journey through Arabia and Africa he collected a treasure surpassing that of Kings and Emperors; but finding it not suitable for his times, he kept it guarded for posterity to uncover, and appointed loyal and faithful heirs of his arts and also of his name. He constructed a microcosm corresponding in all motions to the macrocosm and finally drew up this compendium of things past, present and to come.

After a list of the first and second "circles" of brethren, come the words, *We are born of God, we die in Jesus, we live again through the Holy Spirit.*

And so we do expect the answer and judgement of the learned, or unlearned. Howbeit, we know after a time there will now be a general reformation, both of divine and human things, according to our desire, and the expectation of others. For it is fitting, that before the rising of the sun, there should appear and break forth *Aurora*, or some clearness, or divine light in the sky.

This must be a reference to the appearance of new stars in the constellations of *Serpentarius* and *Cygnus* in the year 1604, written about by the astronomer Kepler in the year in which the exhumation of C.R. is said to have taken place: a definitive sign that the New Age had at last come.

The *Fama* is concluded by a series of exhortations concerning the unity and agreement of genuine knowledge, as well as warnings against "the ungodly and accursed gold-making" (materialist alchemy) which has become so popular, and which the author or authors regard as a perversion of the real thing. The making of gold, the 'purest' metal, incorruptible and analagous to the divine is, according to the *Fama,* merely a *parergon*: a by-product of the main work that is *spiritual transformation*. Readers are warned against false books of alchemy which promise what they cannot deliver and lead men[6] to dismal fates.

At last comes the final invitation for outsiders to join the Fraternity. It is clearly stated that the Brothers will inwardly and spiritually know which enquirers are genuine or not, however they might try to make contact with the Order. The false cannot hurt the Order: "our building (although one hundred thousand people had very near seen and beheld the same) shall for ever remain untouched, undestroyed, and hidden to the wicked world." The Fraternity lives under the protection of Jehova's wings : *SUB UMBRA TUARUM JEHOVA*. This is a spiritual Order. Those who share its aims and spirit are, in a sense already part of it, but the spiritual body must begin to manifest its works and illuminations in the material world.

So this was that *Fama* which made such a fateful impression upon Adam Haslmayr. What particularly struck him was its consistency with the ideas of his idol Paracelsus (1493-1541), the "German Trismegistus", greatest and most controversial medical doctor of the age. Although, according to the *Fama*, Paracelsus was "none of our fraternity," he did look over the *Book M* (which most likely stands for *mundus* since Paracelsus is famous for taking his ideas directly from the natural world), and while the *Fama's* author was well aware of Paracelsus' subversive reputation as a vulgar critic of his opponents, the author takes a sympathetic view: "in his writing he rather mocked these busybodies, and doth not show them altogether what he was."

Paracelsus had introduced chemistry to medicine, believed in the virtue of experiment, had more faith in the 'book of nature' than received paper authority, got his hands dirty and tirelessly fulminated against those who could spout but could not cure. Such is well known. What is far less known is that Paracelsus, inspired by the Hermetic tradition, wrote reams on the subject of religion. Kept secret in his lifetime these writings would become time-bombs after his death.

Paracelsus held to a gnostic cosmogony: Man was a *microcosm* of the universe, but the spirit that giveth life was generally trapped in gross matter. The result: spiritual and bodily sickness. This prognosis applied as much to the churches as to the body. Paracelsus had no time for the "mauerkirche", the external church of stone, but believed in the church of spirit, the inner Word. As his follower Haslmayr put it, God does not need bishops or professors to tell him where to go, what to do, or to whom He should speak. Paracelsus regarded Catholic and Protestant disputants alike as liars. Paracelsus' own middle name, *Theophrastus*, means God-speaker or God-expounder, and he lived up to it. Followers such as Haslmayr took it as the name for a 'new' religion, the *Theophrastia Sancta* or religion of the two lights: the light of grace and the light of nature.

Follow the 'divine signatures' in Nature and a harmony invisible to the disharmonious mind would appear. The priest was doctor; the doctor scientist; the scientist priest. Paracelsus prophesied the coming Golden Age of Grace. The magi were returning.

What Haslmayr read in the *Fama* chimed in with the Paracelsian bell, and in his printed *Antwort* of March 1612 he thanked the Brethren of the Rose Cross for their *divine gift and Theophrastiam*. Haslmayr's open letter to the Brotherhood also refers to a number of apocalyptic prophecies.

In 1605 a French prophecy, falsely attributed to Paracelsus[7], appeared in Germany. A double catastrophe of political and religious import was predicted. The prophecy spoke of a hidden treasure that a group of initiates would discover and use for the benefit of humanity. A group of faithful elect would appear: men who had resisted the lies of the world, led by a messenger and mystagogue who would destroy the Antichrist and give good things to all.

Three treasures were mentioned in the prophecy, one of which was hidden in Germany. The German treasure would provide enough funds to feed a dozen kingdoms. Furthermore, rare books would reveal the Great Art of alchemical transmutation to make a drinkable gold according to the virtue of the *philosopher's stone* and the procedures of Paracelsus. When the treasure was found, a yellow lion would oppose the eagle, resulting in war and revolution.

Haslmayr begs for help for the renovation of the world, for "a new heaven and a new earth". The treasures within the vault of Christian Rosenkreuz are linked by Haslmayr to the three treasures of the "Lion of septentrion", waiting until the arrival of "Elias the Artist" (Elijah the prophet, whose coming was predicted by magus Tommaso Campanella for 1604) to be opened; when everything hidden would come to light and, according to Paracelsus' *De Tinctura physicorum*, the Golden Age of Grace would commence.

For the Adam Haslmayr of 1612, the end of time was approaching. The Judges would appear in 1613 and the Great Judgement would take place in 1614. Spurred on by his enthusiasm and sense of imminent expectation, Haslmayr compared the Brotherhood of the Rose-Cross to the Jesuits and asserted that it was the Fraternity of Christian Rosenkreuz that was the *true* Society of Jesus. He wrote to his employer, the Archduke Maximilian (for whom Haslmayr was a notary) for permission to go to Montpellier to search for the Rosicrucian Brotherhood. The choice of Montpellier was presumably the result of seeing the reference in the *Fama* to Brother N.N ("the architect") from *Gallia Narbonensis*.

Unfortunately for Adam Haslmayr, Haslmayr's intentions came to the attention of Inquisitor Hippolyt Guarinoni. Guarinoni was a Jesuit and fervently anti-Paracelsian[8]. Haslmayr was tricked into an arrest at Innsbruck, force-marched to Genoa and made a galley slave between that port and Messina[9].

Haslmayr was not alone in his enthusiasm for Paracelsus. During the 1980s, Spanish scholar Dr Carlos Gilly discovered correspondence between Prince Augustus of Anhalt and the Augsburg city physician Carl Widemann. For many years Widemann had been collecting the red-hot theological writings of Paracelsus as well as those of the sympathetic radical reformers Caspar Schwenckfeld (1489-1561), Sebastian Franck (1499-1542) and Valentin Weigel (1533-1588). These works of alchemico-spiritual Christosophy scandalised the closed worlds of *all* the proponents of authoritarian religion in the 16th century.

Widemann had also been secretary to English alchemist Edward Kelley in Prague 1587-88, during the tail end of the latter's engagement as seer to British Magus John Dee. This experience was doubtless of interest to Augustus von Anhalt, a man in search of the philosopher's stone[10].

In 1611 Widemann became acquainted with Haslmayr, sharing Haslmayr's understanding of the *Theophrastia Sancta* as "a sort of perpetual religion, which since the days of the apostles had been practised in concealment until the time when the German Trismegistus, Philippus Theophrastus [Paracelsus] began publicly to expound its meaning." (Gilly). He had no hesitation in recommending Haslmayr's alchemical and compositional prowess to Augustus.

In December 1611 the officially Calvinist Prince Augustus von Anhalt, based at Schloss Plötzkau near Magdeburg, received a new year's present from Haslmayr – copies of both the *Fama* and his response to it. Prince Augustus "read it [the *Fama*] and re-read it again" (letter of Augustus-Widemann, January 1612). Deeply hooked, he asked Widemann how he might obtain the *Fama*'s promised follow-up, the *Confessio*.

Widemann was aware that the manuscript of the *Fama* had been disseminated from the house of one Tobias Hess in Tübingen, Württemburg. Enquiries, however, yielded nothing.

In the summer of that year, Augustus gave Haslmayr the task of assembling 'Theophrastian' texts for his secret printing press at Plötzkau, a plan which came to a halt after Haslmayr wrote to the Archduke Maximilian of the Tyrol in August 1612, asking for permission to go to Montpellier to search for the *Fratres R.C.* Thanks to the inquisitor Guarinoni, Halsmayr's stony path would take him not to Languedoc, but to the galleys of the Habsburgs, wherein he would languish for five terrible years.

Meanwhile, Haslmayr's manuscripts - including a copy of the *Fama* - had been entrusted to the Paracelsian alchemist Benedictus Figulus. Figulus was soon made subject to an arrest-warrant in Freiburg and left that city to travel 150 miles north to friends in the city of Marburg in Hesse-Cassel.

Hesse-Cassel was governed by the Landgrave Moritz von Hessen, alchemically minded Calvinist and friend of Augustus von Anhalt (they would later establish their own *Societas Hermetica*). In Marburg lived Raphael Eglin and Johann Hartmann, two alchemists patronised by Moritz von Hessen. Arriving in Marburg, Figulus deposited Haslmayr's manuscripts[11] at the home of Raphael Eglin. Eglin's manuscripts, including those formerly belonging to Adam Haslmayr are now in Cassel, formerly the home of Moritz von Hessen. Cassel was also the base of the printer Wilhelm Wessel.

In 1614 Eglin wrote a letter of complaint to his patron Moritz von Hessen. He complained that he had sent his work to Wessel two months before Wessel had received the *Fama*, but still his work had not been printed. Who could have given the *Fama* to the printer? Was it Eglin? Augustus? Moritz von Hessen? Could it have been Figulus? We do not know as yet. *Somebody* it seems wanted to bring the Fraternity of the Rose-Cross out into the open.

Wilhelm Wessel of Cassel printed the *Fama Fraternitatis* in 1614, along with a piece called *The general Reformation of the whole wide world*: an extract from Trajano Boccalini's satirical *News from Parnassus*, hot from the liberal (and politically threatened) Republic of Venice. As a result, the *Fama* was immediately linked to an itinerary of worldwide Reformation. The Wessel edition also included Adam Haslmayr's *Antwort*, with an account of Haslmayr's unfortunate incarceration at the hands of the Jesuits - a highly political inclusion. *The Reformation of the whole wide world...*

The timing was extraordinary. Publication of the *Fama* provided the proverbial spark in the powder-keg. What had begun as an imaginative experiment in communication was very soon to become one of the most virulent intellectual hurricanes ever to hit Europe. The "greatest publicity-stunt of all time"[12] had begun.

Chapter Seven

The New Age

The *Fama* was powerful stuff - all the more powerful because its dense contents succeeded in triggering off a set of highly charged associations. In order to understand fully the excitement generated by the *Fama*, it is necessary to look at those associations and their origins.

First of all, the manuscript *Fama* and subsequently the (almost certainly unintended) printed version, were taken by many readers as a definitive sign for the inauguration of a New Age. The idea of the 'New Age' is nothing new. It is not uncommon for human-beings to believe they are living in the 'last times', or even the worst times; to look back to a golden age before the rot set in. The corollary of this outlook is to see a better world as imminent, if only one was endowed with the eyes to see the requisite signs. The idea is usually linked to the concept of judgement, of righting wrongs, punishing the guilty and rewarding the faithful with the fulfillment of their best dreams. The idea is also related to the acquisition of new knowledge and new liberties.

Apocalyptic

As far as we know, the literary roots of this belief lie in Jewish apocalyptic writings. Dire warnings of divine judgement to recompense the evils done among His Children go back at least to the eighth century BC, to the time of the prophets Amos and Hosea. Nevertheless, 'apocalyptic' as a specific type of literature did not emerge until after the return of the Jews from the Babylonian Exile in the sixth century BC, when in spite of attempts to rebuild the Temple after the edict of Cyrus, the king of Persia (559-530BC) which authorised this undertaking, the Jews who returned to their homeland continued to languish amid various miseries as a minor component of a Persian satrarpy. The glorious return and elevation of the Jewish people prophesied by men such as the prophet Isaiah failed to materialise, and in spite of attempts to rationalise the situation, faith was put under extreme challenge.

The defeat of the Persians by Alexander the Great in 333 BC did nothing, as far as the Jews were concerned, to remedy the situation, and the challenges to faith grew in intensity. Furthermore, vital elements of the Jewish faith had undergone change. Whereas the pre-Exilic faith stressed the communal dimension of God's covenant with Israel, the development of a pan-oriental Wisdom movement in the sixth century BC (Gautama in India, Zarathushtra in Persia and the 'pre-Socratics' such as Heraklitos, in Greece) laid greater stress on the position, *vis à vis* eternity, of the *individual*. What of the individual's 'right' to a just reward for a life well lived? In the Jewish writings we find this question put directly in the *Book of Job*. Unfortunately, experience appeared to be indifferent to such a 'right', and a longing for divine intervention intensified. Suspicion of the world under the dominance of devouring Time lies at the roots of the development of *Gnosis*, the aim of which was to uncover the transcendent within the finite.

While the full flowering of *Gnosis* would have to wait until the apocalyptic hope of the Maccabaean revolts of the second century BC and the Jewish Wars of the first and early second centuries AD had been exhausted, the seeds of *Gnosis* were already sown within the apocalyptic scheme.

Apocalyptic literature linked the old prophetic format of eventual judgement and salvation to the personal access of the prophet to the very secrets of God's determinations for His People : timetables for deliverance, combined with explanations for the alleged delay in enacting them. The *forth-telling* of the early prophets had become the *foretelling* of apocalyptic. Elements of Persian astrology played a part along with the emphasis on signs : an interplay of heavenly deliberations with earthly and political changes, mediated through the correct interpretations of the stars, and the messages of angels, or messengers of God. The seer now had privileged access to the divine books in which human history was prefigured *already*. This knowledge of the divine intention and secret angelic activity was then inscribed in books such as the *Book of Daniel* in the Old Testament and the *Apocalypse* of S.John in the New, as well as the ubiquitous *Book of Enoch*. Books played a big rôle in apocalyptic theory.

It was almost certainly the failure of hope in an external historical deliverance from the pressing contradictions and waywardness of earthly life that encouraged some of the earliest explicit Gnostics to *internalise* the apocalyptic process as a description of the destiny of the transmundane spirit. Certain features of apocalyptic nonetheless remained constant :

1. The Coming of the Divine Child after a period of chastening and

purification - only this time, (in the Gnostic scheme) as an inner experience in the revelation of the Divine Self to the mundane self-awareness.

2. The belief in special books as vehicles of divine knowledge.

3. The position of the stars as intermediaries between the material and spiritual worlds.

4. The possibility of making contact with angels.

5. The possibility of predicting the future based on an analysis of cosmic principles.

6. The relativity of the material creative order : its finitude, its capacity for spiritual imprisonment and its general ambivalence towards the divine Will while Time lasts.

7. The belief that Time is an inferior projection of eternity and that time and space are dissolvable, leaving a 'new heaven' and (possibly) 'a new earth'. (Note the alchemical parallel).

8. That the destiny of the individual depends on the degree to which he or she lives in consistency with the Divine Plan.

9. That knowledge of the Divine Plan is in itself liberating.

The key apocalyptic texts, for our purposes, are those bearing the name of the prophet Esdras : I & II *Esdras* of the Apocrypha, (also known in the sixteenth and seventeenth centuries as III & IV *Ezra*). Esdras is described in these books as a priest, living in Babylon during the reign of the Persian King Artaxerxes[13]. According to I *Esdras* VIII.9ff, Artaxerxes gave the priest Esdras the right to embellish the Temple in Jerusalem with all manner of gifts to be taken from Syria and Phoenicia for the worship of God, and to support this worship with the proper exercise of the Levitical Law. The whole *corpus* is a eulogy to the establishment of YHWH's Law in the Temple and among the people, accompanied by visions of the consequences for disobeying the Law and the certain judgement of wrongdoers. These visions were vouchsafed courtesy of a visitation from the angel Uriel. I & II *Esdras* have been dated between the time of the Maccabaean Revolts of the mid-second century BC to the first century AD.

There must be something quite archetypal about this literature, for we find it being employed with great fervour and astonished reverence throughout the late fifteenth, sixteenth and seventeenth centuries. Similar psychological conditions applied : frustration with the world, horror at inhuman wickedness, social confusion, religious breakdown, a longing for better times and the security of knowing what was really going on. *Esdras* speaks to both the inner and outer dimensions of human experience. Due to this conflict of interests between political or social turmoil and the urge to turn inwards to the purely spiritual, (anxieties addressed in the Rosicrucian Manifestos with their assertion of imminent revelation and illumination of divine secrets hidden in the life of the earth), mysticism (direct and inward approach to God) and apocalyptic became virtually inseparable. The result was a strange (to us) penetration of the timeless into the temporal, analogous to that odd intermediate psychic territory between the soul and the world of nature explored and experienced in alchemy.

There is a fatigue with the 'wicked world' and its turning away from the knowledge of itself : analogous to the rejection of Rosenkreuz on his return from the East, further expressed in the idea that new knowledge of the world represents a prelude to the End - what the *Fama* calls "the last light":

> Verily we must confess that the world in those days was already big with those great commotions, labouring to be delivered of them; and did bring forth painful, worthy men, who broke with all force through darkness and barbarism, and left us who succeeded to follow to follow them : and assuredly they have been the uppermost point in *trigono igneo* [an astronomical event to be discussed in due course], whose flame now should be more and more bright, and shall undoubtedly give to the world the last light.

The release of the spiritual light (the *mercury* of Paracelsus) is then at once mystical, alchemical, and apocalyptic. The operation of this liberation, on the Hermetic principle of "As Above, so Below" was expected to be paralleled by events in the material sphere : in the stars and in politics[14].

Testimony to the significance of *Esdras* comes at the same time as the Hermetic revelation hits the intellectual life of Europe in force. None other than the extraordinary Pico della Mirandola (1463-1494) was moved to see in *Esdras* the authority for taking the Jewish Qabalah very seriously as authentic and pristine divine wisdom[15]. In 1542, David Joris, a radical Flemish reformer who took refuge in Basle, wrote the influential *T'Woender Boek* and used *Esdras* as part of his vision of a truth revealed only to a select group of believers, coupled with the notion of an inner word received in the heart. This book was very popular among the followers of the radical reformers Valentin Weigel (1533-1588) and Caspar Schwenckfeld (1489-1556). The idea of a secret spiritual fraternity is implicit in this view.

Schwenckfeld and Weigel were in their turn highly influential on the thought of the gnostic Jacob Böhme of Görlitz in Lausitz. *Esdras* was also particularly helpful to sixteenth and seventeenth century Calvinists who battled with the Calvinist idea of predestination, since the Books of *Esdras* stressed the importance of the individual's free will in choosing the path of salvation. But perhaps the strangest instance of the influence of *Esdras* - apart from the Rosicrucian manifestos - lies in the rôle they played in the 'angelic conversations' held between the highly influential English magus John Dee, his 'scryer' or seer Edward Kelley, and a number of what Kelley purported to be angels, from whom Kelley claimed to receive direct messages in the 1580s. Not only did these angels seem to have a thorough and respectful acquaintance with the Books of *Esdras,* but Esdras's own guide, the angel Uriel, appeared to Kelley with instructions recorded in John Dee's quite astonishing spiritual diaries. These strange séances directly affected Dee's career and may have influenced, by the strangest of routes, the course of European history.

John Dee - Apocalyptic Prophet

For John Dee, as for many others in the sixteenth century, *magia*, the art of the *magi*, was a vehicle for spiritual salvation. The split in the Catholic Church with its ensuing violence and hostile invective had left many genuine believers with a feeling of being cut off from the spiritual resources of the old universally practised eucharist. Magic, in its aspect of divine and mystical illumination (made respectable in Neoplatonic writings), was held to be a valid route for divine influences to enter into the life of man to heal his heart. Therefore *magia* was deeply associated with Reformation movements and, necessarily, with apocalyptic prognostications. Men such as Henry Cornelius Agrippa (1486-1535) and the phenomenal Giordano Bruno (1548-1600) believed that a deeper and more powerful reforming movement could be enacted by revitalising the magical basis of religion. This view provides a basis for understanding John Dee's fervent desire to make contact with the angels of the supercelestial sphere. These angels seem to have had more than a passing acquaintance with the Books of *Esdras* and their (ie : Edward Kelley's) interpretation of the books stressed that they applied directly to the late 16th century, and that they promised a magical reunion of the Christian Church as well as a necessary overturning and reforming of the contemporary order. Compare for example the following communication of the angel 'Madimi' with Dee[16] to II *Esdras* and the *Fama Fraternitatis* :

> **Madimi** : And lo, the issue which he giveth thee is wisdom. But lo, the mother of it is not yet delivered. For, if woman know her times and seasons of deliverance : Much more doth he [God], who is the Mother of all things. But thou mayest rejoice that there is a time of deliverance, and that the gift is compared to a woman with childe.
> **II *Esdras* IV.40** : Go thy way to a woman with child, and ask of her when she hath fulfilled her nine months, if her womb may keep the birth any longer within her.
> **Fama Fraternitatis** : ..for Europe is with child and will bring forth a strong child, who shall stand in need of a great godfather's gift.
> **Uriel to Dee** : These are the days wherein the prophet said, No faith should be found on the earth. This faith must be restored again, and men must glorify God in his works. I am the light of God.
> **URIEL** : When you have the book of God before you, then I will open these secrets unto you.

In order to re-establish "the faith", Uriel instructs Dee and Kelley to read II *Esdras* IX.7 and VI.28. The texts from *Esdras* read as follows :

> And everyone that shall be saved, and shall be able to escape by his works, and by faith, whereby ye have believed, Shall be preserved from the said perils, and shall see my salvation in my land, and within my borders : for I have sanctified them for me from the beginning.
> As for faith, it shall flourish, corruption shall be overcome, and the truth, which hath been so long without fruit, shall be declared.

This is, according to Uriel : *That my kingdom may be One.* Another angel, Jubanladace by name, re-iterates the same message with tiresome repetitiveness :

> For I will establish One Faith.. Moreover I shall open the hearts of all men, that he may have free passage through them.
> And there must be One veritie. And Hierusalem shall descend with an horn of glory to the end.

Other angelic prophecies reveal that the Antichrist's arrival was scheduled for 1587; that "the Turk" (the Ottoman Empire) would be destroyed by a ruler in central Europe and, generally, that those who fail to respond to the prophetic call shall be destroyed. Amid all this heaviness, there are lighter moments. The New Age which the angels usher in promises a spiritual joy, then currently being enacted by the radical reformers, such as some Anabaptist sects, persecuted by Catholics, Lutherans and Calvinists alike. The angels put themselves in spiritual communion with the bright and often crazy spirit of the new churches. In Dee's shewstone (which can be seen in the British Museum) Kelley sees and hears a luminous figure declare :

> There is a God, let us be merry. E.K. [Kelley] He danceth still.
> There is a heaven. Let us be merry. E.K. Now he taketh off his clothes again.

Kelley frequently has his angels recommend 'free love' as a fruit of the spirit. It is hard to imagine that such stuff should form the basis of a practical political programme, but that would be severely to underestimate the conviction of authenticity in which Dee held these communications. These revelations would take Dee and Kelley off to central Europe on a mission to save the world.

Frances Yates in her book *The Rosicrucian Enlightenment* (1972) held the view that Dee's activities were instrumental in bringing about the Rosicrucian movement, and that the movement had an essentially English basis. This can no longer be held to be the case. Germany and Bohemia had sufficient magi (if not so universally brilliant as Dee) of their own to initiate their own movement. However there is little doubt that Dee and Kelley's time spent abroad in the 1580s and 1590s - combined with the political configurations of the period (wherein England was seen as a bastion against the Habsburgs) - was a significant influence on the alchemico-magico-apocalyptic reforming philosophy, and Dee certainly contributed to and reinforced the growing expectation of great events soon to be fulfilled in which gnostic influences would play such a significant (if unspoken) rôle. More important than Dee's angelic seances whose prophecies were already widespread in Europe, was the contribution of his book *Monas Hieroglyphica* (1564) which laid out a complex theory of cosmic unity whose aim was to integrate all knowledge in a cosmic spiritual/ mathematical system : an aim implicit in the Rosicrucian endeavour. Dee's *Monas* symbol became a staple symbol in the works of Rosicrucian apologists and even appeared in the 1616 edition of Johann Valentin Andreae's alchemical story, The *Chymische Hochzeit*.

Saving the World

"YOU ARE BECOME PROPHETS, AND ARE SANCTIFIED FOR THE COMING OF THE LORD".

With these words, the angel Uriel launched John Dee and Edward Kelley on what must be one of the strangest adventures of all time. The adventure got off the ground through a strange co-incidence. In June 1583 the Polish Prince Albert Laski was taken by the poet-adventurer Sir Philip Sydney to witness an academic debate held at Oxford University. The principal speaker was none other than 'the Nolan', Giordano Bruno (of Nola), gnostic Dominican with a mission to return the world to the (in his eyes) pure Egyptian "religion of the world" : the worship of the divine immanent principle, the basic magic power to be found in an heliocentric system as part of an infinite universe. The debate went badly for Bruno who was laughed at, ridiculed and unjustly accused of plagiarism from the *de vita triplici* of Marsilio Ficino by the "grammarians and pedants" of Oxford (as he called them).

Sydney suggested Laski might like to meet England's greatest intellectual luminary, John Dee, at the latter's house in Mortlake. Dee obliged Laski with some angelic conversations. Kelley's angels siezed the opportunity to suggest that Laski was the European prince who could fulfill the role of harbinger of a new age. He would defeat the Turk and bring the "One veritie" to the whole wide world. Laski seems to have found the prospect agreable, and so Dee and Kelley packed their bags and returned to the continent with the Polish prince. Laski was probably most moved by Kelley's contention that the angels held the key to alchemical transmutation : gold.

Laski proved not to be quite what the angels really had in mind, and their attention turned towards the Emperor Rudolf II in Prague, whence Dee and Kelley's expansive train moved. On 3 September 1584, Dee finally got his audience with the Emperor. In the full panoply (and doubtless folly) of his new prophetic rôle, Dee announced to Rudolf that "The Angel of the Lord hath appeared to me, and rebuketh you for your sins. If you will hear me, and believe in me, you shall Triumph : if you will not hear me...." Rudolf heard Dee, but found it practically impossible to step into the rôle Dee's angels had in mind for him, which was in effect to take practical spiritual and political advice direct from John Dee. Rudolf *was* interested however in Kelley's vaunted alchemical skills - and so was Queen Elizabeth of England who tried to get Dee - and especially Kelley - back to England to serve their country. But Dee now saw himself as a trans-national figure in the care of God alone. He even celebrated Mass in a Catholic church to demonstrate his eirenicist intentions. He consulted with the Catholic Hannibal Rosseli in Cracow on how to employ the *Corpus Hermeticum* (on which Rosseli was writing a massive commentary) to unite the Christian churches behind the banner of the (Neoplatonic) One. Dee was in an incandescent state for some years. It seemed to him that his message was indicated in the stars, and by the knowledge of the time, he had reason to do so, as we shall see shortly.

In 1586, the year in which Johann Valentin Andreae was born, Dee met Francesco Pucci in Cracow. Pucci was an enthusiast for a mystical and universalist faith which he believed the Catholic Church would or should enact. He also shared Dee's views on the coming Apocalypse and final judgement. These consultations with Catholic savants greatly disturbed the Papal Nuncio in Prague. The Nuncio had Dee and Kelley thoroughly investigated, concluding on orders from the Vatican that the pair should be arrested and put to the stake. Rudolf, compromising as usual, ordered Dee and Kelley out of Prague, whence they became guests of Count Rozmberk on his estates at Trebon in Bohemia. Rozmberk lavished his wealth upon them and encouraged Dee in his mission. We also know that Dee visited Landgrave Wilhelm IV of Hesse-Cassel, where he whipped up the requisite enthusiasm and presented his host with manuscripts on the subject of the secrets of God relating to the Apocalypse. Dee doubtless encouraged other chiliasts, alchemists and dreamers during his journeys about central Europe. All of this took place only twenty-six years before Adam Haslmayr was arrested by the Inquisitor Guarinoni in Innsbruck - well within the living memory of Carl Widemann and Andreae's older friend and guide Tobias Hess. (Hess was sixteen when Dee met the Emperor Rudolf II in Prague in 1584).

Apart from the ministry of angels, what else made Dee so sure that his mission had such extraordinary and apocalyptic significance?

The Fiery Trigons

1584 saw a major astronomical event : a conjunction of three planets in Aires - a fiery trigon or *trigonus igneus*. This was generally held among students of the stars to signify the inauguration of a "Great

Year", a new epoch or *Aion*: a vast cosmic time-unit bringing with it a new set of dispensations - a New Age. Dee received his astrological theory of history chiefly from *De magis coniunctionibus* by Abu Ma'shar (787-836AD), which had been translated into Latin in about 1120. Abu Ma'shar's ideas reflect the teachings of the Harranian pagans or 'Sabians' who took Hermes Trismegistos for their prophet. Their astrology developed within the context of Aristotle's works on the natural world : the *Physica*; *De caelo*; *De generatione et corruptione* and *De meterologia*. Following Abu Ma'shar, it became common to divide the twelve signs of the zodiac into four trigons, corresponding to the four elements. When the superior planets formed a new trigon (as happened in 1584) it was taken to be a sign for such earthly events as the genesis of new empires or new religious movements.

On cue, Dee set about fulfilling the necessary conditions for a New Age, an endeavour further supported by the influential *Astronomisches Schreben* by David Herlizius and, most particularly, by Leowitz's *De coniunctionibus magnis* which Dee had acquired twenty years earlier and had heavily annotated. Leowitz's work had predicted great changes to take place in Bohemia and the Habsburg domains in 1584. Dee believed that the signs for a new movement to establish religious unity - he was heard to say in Prague that he did not care for *religions* - within the context of new scientific understanding of the cosmos were now more than sufficient to encourage him and anyone with whom he came into contact to rise to the task of ushering in the new aeon. He was certainly not alone in this view.

The Breaking of the Seals

One year after Dee's audience with the Emperor Rudolf, Theodor Gluichstein of Bremen published the *Mystica et prophetica libri Geneseos interpretatio* by the Italian heretic Giacomo Brocardo. Brocardo had escaped the fangs of the Venetian Inquisition in 1568 and had taken his vision of the end of the old order through Basle, Heidelberg, England, Holland, Bremen and, in the early 1590s, to Tobias Hess's home-town of Nürnberg. Brocardo's work was to make a great impact on two men whose lives and work are pertinent to our story. They are the Tübingen doctor Tobias Hess (1568-1614) and Simon Studion, author of the apocalyptic work *Naometria* (=the measurement of the Temple), who was born in Urach in Württemberg in 1543.

Brocardo's mystical and prophetic interpretations of the book of *Genesis* generally follow similar lines to those explored by Dee and Kelley. The difference is that in the works of Brocardo and Studion, number-mysticism and complex mathematics are brought to bear on the precise dating of apocalyptic history, in conjunction with other prophecies such as those of I & II *Esdras*. To a large extent Brocardo, like Studion, employs the framework devised by the Calabrian abbot Joachim of Fiore (c.1135-1202). While Joachim's division of history into the three eras of Father (Law), Son (Gospel), all to culminate in the final age of the Holy Spirit (revelation of God's secrets and an era of spiritual liberty), had made a major contribution to apocalyptic expectation in the thirteenth century, his basic ideas were to do much the same for the sixteenth century and beyond. Brocardo saw the date of Luther's birth (1483) as the starting point for the last age. This age would last 120 years (*cf.* the time to elapse given in the *Fama* with respect to the discovery of the tomb of Christian Rosenkreuz).

Hess obtained his copy of Brocardo's work in 1601 and was by this time in communication with Simon Studion, who lived in Stuttgart as a favoured scholar of Duke Frederick of Württemberg and who, incidentally, shared the same tutor at Tübingen as did Johann Valentin Andreae : Martin Crusius. Simon Studion completed his first draft of *Naometria* in 1592, a year after Hess became a doctor of civil and canon law at Tübingen. It will soon become apparent as to how the involvement of Tobias Hess was crucial to the genesis of the *Fama Fraternitatis*, its successor the *Confessio Fraternitatis* and the Rosicrucian movement in general. For Hess in 1601, the destiny of the world was definitely 'hotting up'. According to the *Naometria* he was living at precisely the time when the "first seal" of the Apocalypse would be broken (in heaven) : a time of bloodshed. Two years previously (1599), Tommaso Campanella had been incarcerated in a Naples dungeon. In 1598 he also had seen signs. His interpretation of the signs convinced him that a universal Hermetic-Christian Republic was imminent, and that he should help things along by participating in a rebellion against the Spanish Habsburgs. Like Dee, Kelley and Tobias Hess, Campanella had drawn inspiration from II *Esdras*, in particular chapters XI and XII which speak of a murderous many-headed eagle, a figure uncannily like the double-headed eagle of the Habsburg insignia. II *Esdras* promised revenge and justice :

And therefore appear no more, thou eagle, nor thy horrible wings, nor thy wicked feathers, nor thy malicious heads, nor thy hurtful claws, nor all thy vain body : That all earth may be refreshed, and may return, being delivered from thy violence, and that she may hope for the justice and mercy of him that made her. (II *Esdras* XI. 45-46).

The point is taken up in the *Confessio Fraternitatis* :

> But we must also let you understand that there are yet some Eagle's Feathers in our way, the which do hinder our purpose.

II *Esdras* XI.37 ff. pits a "roaring lion" against the eagle. The lion speaks with a man's voice, and on hearing the speech of the lion, the horrible eagle is annihilated:

> For thou hast afflicted the meek, thou hast hurt the peaceable, thou hast loved liars, and destroyed the dwellings of them that brought forth fruit, and hast cast down the walls of such as did thee no harm.

Likewise in the *Confessio*, false hypocrites and those who seek other things than wisdom from the Fraternity "shall certainly be partakers of all the punishment spoken of in our *Fama*; so their wicked counsels shall light upon themselves, and our treasures shall remain untouched and unstirred, until the Lion doth come, who will ask them for his use, and employ them for the confirmation and establishment of his kingdom."

From the point of view of the authors of the Rosicrucian Manfestos, the Reformation could not be completed so long as the Pope and his political allies remained - and it was the completion of the Reformation in all its fullness that the authors of the manifestos sought. Nevertheless there are different areas of stress within the manifestos themselves - all part of their mystery and fascination - and it is more than likely that these areas of emphasis stem from the difference between the two minds which dominate the manifestos, namely Tobias Hess and the more subtle and ambivalent Johann Valentin Andreae.

Tobias Hess and the Apocalyptic Numbers

John Dee was certainly not the only man alive in his time who had glimpsed the great import of the fiery trigon of **1584**. Dr Carlos Gilly (the foremost authority on the Rosicrucians in the world) has made many discoveries in the last decade pertaining to their origins. Among them was the discovery of a cache of writings by Tobias Hess, commenting on Studion's *Naometria*, as well as a copy in Hess's hand of correspondence between Studion and Duke Frederick of Württemberg. Hess also copied Studion's *judicium* on the writings of Brocardo, in which Studion speaks of a series of seven fiery triangles, beginning with Adam and proceeding regularly through the times of Enoch, Noah, Moses, Babylon, Christ and Caesar Augustus, Charlemagne - all to culminate in 1584, the Great Year. Gilly has also examined correspondence between Hess and Studion in the *Würtembergische Landesbibliothek* wherein Studion defends his work by saying to Hess that should his (unbelievably complex) computations be denied, then the enquirer should recognise that they have been checked by the great mathematician Michael Mästlin, tutor in mathematics to both the astronomer Kepler and to Johann Valentin Andreae.

According to the diary of Martin Crusius (one of Andreae's tutors), Hess spent the years 1597-1605 delving deeply into the work of Studion and indeed anything he could find of value regarding futuristic apocalyptic prophecy. Hess agreed with Studion in 1597 that the Papacy must fall in seven years, according to computation. The key year was **1604**. There must have been something wrong, if not with the mathematics, then with Studion's source of inspiration, for a year after the Papacy was supposed to have fallen (1604), Hess was getting into trouble with the theological authorities in Tübingen for discussing the theory of fiery triangles, while the Pope was still attending to his business in Rome. Nevertheless, something extraordinary *had* occurred in 1604. Apart from Studion's completing *Naometria* in 1800 unpublishable pages, the heavens offered yet another sign for the times. A *trigonus igneus* appeared in March 1604 in the constellations of *Serpentarius* and *Cygnus*, at which point I shall defer to the astrological wisdom of Dr Christopher McIntosh[17]:

At the time when the new stars appeared Jupiter and Saturn were in conjunction in the ninth house. As Jupiter was considered a good planet and Saturn a bad one, there was some speculation as to which was dominant. The general concensus of opinion, however, was that as the ninth house is Jupiter's house, and Jupiter rules Pisces, the sign which was in the ascendent at the time of the observation, Jupiter was therefore the dominant planet. Both planets were also favourably placed in relation to the other planets. When Saturn is well placed it brings forth thoughtful, serious men. The combination therefore, promised the advent of a prophet or prophets who would be wise, just and righteous. It was believed, moreover, that these astrological positions corresponded to the positions at the Creation. According to tradition the Sun first appeared on the fourth day of Creation when Aires was in the ascendent. From this it followed that Saggitarius must have been in the ninth house. Thus, the signs at the appearance of the new stars in 1604 were the same as those for the beginning of the world, proving that **1604** would also see a great new beginning.

For Tobias Hess this event assumed an extraordinary importance - and it must be to him that we must look for an explanation of how it came to be that the tomb of Christian Rosenkreuz, the "compendium of the universe" came to be revealed to the Rose-Cross Brothers in 1604, 120 years after he had been buried and almost exactly 120 years after the birth of Martin Luther, in which time according to Johann Valentin Andreae, the full Truth had been buried beneath sectarianism, academic pedantry, persecution of God's servants and widespread anti-Christian bickering and violence : those very evils which true Christians who most desired a reform of the Church had been expressly against. As Andreae's friend Christoph Besold observed : "Whereas before Luther we were ruled by the Pharisees, now we are ruled by the Scribes." The Rosicrucian Manifestos clearly suggest that the 'old guard' cannot be trusted and that a new attitude, a new openness, an altogether new heart is required : a refreshing spirit of Fraternity and understanding is waiting for the right men to fill its ranks to bring light to the world.

The *Confessio Fraternitatis*, written very probably in early 1610, looks back six years to the wondrous planetary event of 1604, an event which had moved the astronomer Kepler to prophetic poetry[18] :

It was in March when the red orbs appeared
A birth of unparalleled redness
When the matchless ruby stars were brought forth
The wife a matchless golden girl...

Kepler was not sure what the event really meant, but he seems to have expected political catastrophes or a new religious sect. The *Confessio* takes the event as its own.

As we now willingly confess, that many principal men by their writings will be a great furtherance to this Reformation which is to come...yea, the Lord God hath already sent before certain messengers, which should testify his will, to wit, some new stars, which do appear and are seen in the firmament in *Serpentario* and *Cygno*, which signify and give themselves known to everyone, that they are powerful *Signacula* of great weighty matters. ...that great book of nature stands open to all men, yet there are but few that can read and understand the same.

That last line perfectly expresses the ambivalence of the manifestos, a quality of playfulness which can only have come from Andreae, the serious joker. Investigation of the *Book of Nature* is a Paracelsian term which can mean simply sensible scientific experiment and experience - an openness to what nature has to offer as an image of God - or something more mysterious, the interpretation of signs in an astrological or mystical sense. It will become clear that Andreae was definitely in favour of the former but ambivalent or hostile to the latter, while Hess could look both ways at once.

Studion completed his manuscript *Naometria* in the same year as the fiery trigon, and it was perhaps this event as well as Hess's public discussion of the import of the trigon that led to Tobias Hess's being accused of questionable interests by some of the theologians of Tübingen University. Studion himself had bitter enemies at Duke Frederick's court in Stuttgart and they persuaded the Duke to distance himself from Studion. On 2 July 1605, Hess, absolutely unrepentant, wrote an *Apologia* to Duke Frederick. While the academics of Tübingen found Studion embarrassing or even politically dangerous and inflammatory, Hess stood for decency and truth where it could be found, whether it appeared palatable or not. In his *Apologia* Hess maintained that all prophecies will be fulfilled in time, that the enemies of God will be destroyed and that the trigon of 1604 was one of the signs of the last times. He quoted *Matthew* V.18, "until heaven and earth fall apart, nothing will be taken from the law" and, most forcefully, *Habbakuk* II.3 :

For the vision is yet for an appointed time, but at the end it shall speak, and not lie : though it tarry, wait for it; because it will surely come, it will not tarry.

Chapter Eight

Hess and Andreae

Johann Valentin Andreae was born of distinguished Lutheran parents in Herrenberg in 1586. His grandfather, Jacob Andreae had been a staunch and brave pioneer of the Reformation cause. The dreamy and imaginative young Johann was expected to advance the family tradition. The young Andreae seems to have been more interested in theatre, alchemy and mysticism than politics. He had great intuitive powers and an unerring nose for hypocrisy, like many dramatists. In youth he dramatised his own life and early struggles in works published when he was thirty, such as *Turbo* and the *Chymische Hochzeit*, both of which employ alchemical themes - a practice engaged in by the family - while the latter work introduced the character of Christian Rosenkreuz who, doubtless reflecting the family crest of a S.Andrew's cross with four roses, dons a blood-red ribbon bound crossways over his shoulder, and puts four red roses in his hat "that I might the sooner by this token be taken notice of amongst the throng." The boy was clearly a genius, a quality which few either recognise or understand. It means that he was more intelligent than his own explicit thoughts, a condition necessitating irony and a sense of detachment. He found his equilibrium in the embrace of the purest Christianity he could conceive of : that of Christ Himself. It was perhaps this quality which drew him towards friendship with the older man Tobias Hess, the man who was prepared to stand for truth wherever he found it, no matter what sectarian interests it might offend.

Andreae entered Tübingen University in 1601 at the age of fifteen, at which time Hess is reported to have been in a black prophetic mood, deep into his studies of Brocardo and Studion. Had Andreae met Hess at this time the younger man might have found Hess to be rather old-fashioned. Andreae attended to his studies : classical languages, poetry, Renaissance literature, physics, mechanics and chemistry. He realised that in spite of his vast knowledge, he would never know all. This realisation may have brought the *gnosis* out in him : the sense that *orbis non sufficit* : the world is not enough.

His first acquaintance with Hess' name may date from 1603 when Studion sent a letter to Hess, asking for a copyist with good Latin to help prepare the final draft of *Naometria*. Hess may have suggested Andreae's brother Ludwig to execute the task. But it was to be another five years before the two masterminds of the Rosicrucian Manifestos actually met : in 1608, the year in which John Dee died in poverty in Mortlake, ignored and perhaps feared by Britain's King James I. By this time, Hess was beginning to look beyond the end of the world, and had taken a very deep interest in Theology, as well as in the iatrochemical medicine of Paracelsus. It is significant that healing was the basis for Andreae's and Hess's first encounter. It is said in the *Confessio* that the philosophy of the Rose-Cross Brothers "containeth much of Theology and medicine, but little of the wisdom of the law.." Hess had already healed Ludwig Andreae of an *oedemitus* knee, when Hess brought his skills to bear on a serious fever from which Johann Valentin was suffering. Hess brought Paracelsus and Apocalyptic to Andreae, and thus to the *Fama*. It was Andreae's genius tactfully to subsume these elements into an overall mystery-story which prevented the manifestos from coming out as yet another mystico-political pamphlet. The *Fama* is especially well-written, full of the dignity of language which one might expect from an illuminated being. Andreae clearly loved Hess, as can be seen from his *Immortalitas*, written on Hess's death, and published in 1619. "Hess listens to God and no-one else." wrote Andreae of his friend. He was struck by Hess's attempts to live his Christianity, not to get bogged down in theological conflicts over doctrines and dogmas. He took the path of the *Imitatio Christi*, attributed to the medieval mystic Thomas à Kempis which Andreae would have found in his friend Besold's huge library, if he had not read it already.

> Hess, originally an able lawyer and after that an even better doctor, eventually developed into an outstanding theologian, who (please take note) however knew about the older and the more recent scholarly opinions (he devoured their works in large quantities) and he also knew enough about various conflicts and heresies, but he was rather concentrated on the imitation of the life of Christ than on the defence of its teachings, more concentrated on its practise than on its purely scientific approach. (*IMMORTALITAS*. 1619)

We shall need to hear more from this beautiful work in memory of Hess, for nothing else shows as clearly what it was that the two men stood for and what the true intention of the Rosicrucian Manifestos consisted of, for there can be little doubt that the character and life of Hess informed Andreae's conception of Christian Rosenkreuz : the true Christian disciple on his way to the chemical wedding of his soul with God :

The world showed all its enticements and tried to win his noble talent with the promise of great glory. No doubt, there he would have reached important summits, should he have agreed to the laws of this world and said goodbye to his conscience. Melodious conceptions like 'justice' and 'fairness' have always attracted our man who was himself a just man.

..with ardour he tried to grasp the idea of the greatness of God's book compared to the insignificance of the specialist's works. His house underwent a complete change. Bartolus and Baldus were thrown out, Hippocrates and Galen were welcomed. He let them in, being a free man himself. With no obligations and under condition that they were not allowed to affect the higher aspect of his mind, nor would they try to get hold of it. Since the purple clad teachers were too delicate, he added Paracelsus to their number, a man who would not give up so easily and who rightly shows suspicion where nature is not fully involved, but full of patience where hard work and experiments are involved and who, at last, has the courage to concentrate on research after the composition of things.

In the mean time, as a result of his wife's fertility, his house became rather crowded. With such a large number of children - by that time more than twelve - I doubt whether anyone else could easily have managed to run the household along the lines of fair and sacred standards. Anyway, to Hess it turned out to be something like the twelve labours of Hercules, not so much for the faults of that period he had to deal with, and with the problems young people usually bring along, but because some Pandora seemed to have thought up and let loose her proverbial flood of disasters.

Hess was "a friend of God, a servant of Christ, a brother to his fellow-creature, a herald of truth, an executor of goodness, a jewel of literature, a shining star in Tübingen, a treasurer of nature and also a stumbling-block for the world and an enemy of Satan." While the *Immortality of Hess* stands as the greatest obituary and *apologia* a man could possibly wish for - and it was certainly earned - Andreae felt it necessary to address the issue of Hess's reputation, in particular with regard to Hess's interest in Simon Studion and, by implication, his involvement with the genesis of the Rosicrucian movement :

Hess was said to be superstitious, a man who followed his own lines, an eccentric, a phantast and, as a result of the multiplication of lies - a king of Utopia, an interpreter of dreams and a predictor. Whoever belonged to his closer friends and who he called his brother, was said to be a member of a gang of fanatics, of a group of conspirators and a gathering of obscurantists.

In this period of time, when he was a most devoted priest to his own body, all kinds of people turned up - apparently times were ready for it - who introduced the end of the earth and the arrival of the Antichrist, things which are always pushed when the Church is slowing down. Since these people found a rich source in the bible to defend their case, Hess did not feel so much like rejecting them, moreover, while they did not touch the basic principles of faith. And little by little - for curiosity is part of the human kind - he also took to the teachings of holy numbers, in order to find out whether they could reveal anything about similarities between periods of time and between the old and the new Babylonia. In the beginning it was a matter of comparitive innocence (most of the true theologians joined in), but soon Hess came into trouble caused by lack of thought of some young adepts : for they not only expected Hess to give such doubtful drafts of repeating patterns in history, but they wanted him to come up and defend an idea which had never been fully his own. Thus, warned by his friends, he stood up for his point of view that he did not wish to recommend all his ideas to as many people as possible, but at least show the pure and very much to our faith related meaning supporting them, and that he furthermore wished to move away from the irresponsible explanations those supporters attached to his words. This however, was the very moment slander sprang to life. Growing with pride she exclaimed that now she had got hold of Hess - on whom she had vainly tried her teeth when he had studied chemistry - and she called him a naometrist, a chiliast and a day-dreamer. It is amazing to see how her foul talk could smudge so pure a man. And since people are liberal in nothing else so much as in lies, she affected people who were actually not prejudiced at all, but who rather could be called a little bit unattentive towards the noble name he enjoyed in all his innocence.

I am sorry to say that even I was influenced to prefer such a kind of paradox in Hess's mind and some imaginary golden age to the possibility of some playful calculations of the brain.

If Andreae had toyed with Hess's apocalyptic ideas, it could not have been for very long. Andreae tended to lump together those who were obsessed with purely alchemical and magical solutions to the human condition along with those who racked their brains trying to extract complex numerological significance from apocalyptic writings. He called them the "little curiosity brothers" who obscure, rather than illuminate the spiritual life. He found their writings odd, strange, (*insolite*) often arrogant and fundamentally unhelpful. In his book *Turris Babel* (1619), Andreae devotes the fifth dialogue between *Astrologus & Calculator* and *Conjectans* (the interpreter of dreams) to an attack on the *Naometria* and kindred works :

> I would deny nothing to heaven, but I am enraged at you who read lies into the heavens; I respect sacred numbers, but I suspect that they have nothing to do with these tortured interpretations.

In the *Immortalitas* he says that when Tobias Hess "was admonished in a friendly way, he moderated the defence of his opinion" and "finally withdrew himself from these exceedingly rash speculations."

Andreae was deeply suspicious of what he saw as misguided attempts to suugest that if one wanted to know God, then one should needs have access to occult, alchemical or specialist mystical knowledge. The exclusivity of much alchemical literature, seen as a *single* or reserved path to the truth appalled him. The mysterious Fraternity of value for Andreae was simply the Fraternity of Christ, best expressed in love for one's neighbour and an open hearted and open-minded response to new knowledge. So while in a sense the spiritually regenerated imitator of Christ has indeed become a member of a Brotherhood - which has (note the metaphor) become *invisible* to the (blind) eyes of the world and exists as it were, underground, Andreae cleverly (perhaps too-cleverly) attracts attention to it by playing dramatically with the mythology of secret gnostic adepts. Speaking of Brocardo, Studion and, by implication, astrologers like Paul Nagel and alchemists like Heinrich Khunrath, Andreae complained of their inability to talk to ordinary people in their own language, preferring an idiom Andreae calls : "Persian, Chaldean, Brahmanic, Druidic, of Fez or of Damcar." The ambivalence of the *Fama* in attempting to get responsible science and scientists into positive and non-sectarian shape by using the imagery of mystical and magical secrecy, while at the same time clearly approving of men of learning such as Paracelsus, practically ensured that 'in the wrong hands' the *Fama* would attract attention very much at odds with what Andreae originally had in mind.

Happily for us, Andreae's precise views on 'natural magic', or what we would call simply 'science' are laid out in a very amusing dialogue between a 'Christianus' and a 'Curiosus', in a playlet called *Institutio Magica pro Curiosis* (The institution of magic for the curious), which appeared in Andreae's brilliant polemical work *Menippus* in 1617.

Taking place in the book-filled study of Christianus, the dialogue is a masterpiece of terse, intellectual comedy. Curiosus drops in for a chat, to find out how much magical power the famous Christianus really has. Curiosus is portrayed as a man who is desperate to find an occult explanation for everything; a man looking for the easy way out, and a fool obsessed with illusory powers. Here are some relevant extracts. The stage-directions are mine :

CU : It is said, Christianus, that you have knowledge of all things, both serious and diverting...And - this is the most important point - that you have achieved all this within the space of two or three years.

CH : And of course, as well as that, I'm able to produce gold and nourish the eternal flame!

CU : All agree on one point, that you are a magician.

CH : 'Magician' is an ambitious name, don't you think? Perhaps you mean necromancer?

CU : I am not quite sure of the distinction but I mean the person who through intimacy with and servitude to the spirits achieves great and wonderful things.

CH : I would rather prefer another definition of 'necromancy'. But please tell me, do you really believe I am able to do the things you just mentioned? [Curiosus squints, nods his head & then wonders. Christianus decides to play with Curiosus on his own level. He looks significantly at the curtains. Curiosus gets the point, rises and closes them, crossing himself as he does so.] Well then, Curiosus, as it is now of prime importance to become a magician - or a *wise man*, we must incessantly invoke God's help.

CU : [rubbing his hands] Excellent.

CH : So [handing paper and pen to Curiosus], please write here, on the first line of your piece of paper : 'Invocation of God'.

CU : That's done.

CH : Now please, examine *yourself*, whether you have been born with an earthy, a watery, an airy or a fiery character.

CU : [looks up] This is all new to me.

CH : You force me to consider opening up for you, a thing as yet known to nobody, not even to my brethren.

CU : [earnestly] Please do.

CH : But would I dare to entrust you with my secrets, lest they reach the common people?

CU : Here, I give you my right hand in promise.

CH : Please Curiosus [looks deeply into Curiosus' eyes], please consider and consider again where you lead me : for necromancy is a very serious business.

CU : Please trust me, and if I fail you, so may the supreme God have me-

CH : Please do not swear - I cannot stand it! I will believe you without any oaths. But tell me, are you really longing for this magic of mine?
CU : Very much indeed, if only [he coughs] it can be exercised with a *clear conscience*.
CH : Why, as surely as if you were studying the Bible itself. [Christianus gestures for Curiosus to close his eyes, very tightly. He tip-toes to the curtains and opens them. He touches Curiosus' shoulder, who opens his eyes to see his mentor pointing at the Bible, opened at *Genesis* I.1., over which he immediately places a Mercator map of the known world and then the works of the *Polymathia*.]
CU : [both astonished & disappointed] So...your magic is nothing more than this?
CH : By the Holy Trinity...there is no other magic but the persistent study of the different sciences.
CU : But if I follow your advice, I might as well throw my studies overboard and start work with a - with a craftsman or a sailor.
CH : What you say there is not bad, but it's what you're thinking when you're saying it.
CU : Would you make a farmer or a mining expert out of me?
CH : No, Curiosus, all I want to do is to make a philosopher out of you so that you may become a citizen of the world - and not the alien wanderer.
CU : - And that special Art whereby you can learn all sorts of things in no time at all?
CH : Have I not told you that this Art is called hard work and perseverence? ...The foremost stars of learning and the princes of the arts were always highly versed in many branches of science - this is testified by their books, densely filled with every kind of knowledge.
CU : Perhaps they too were *magicians*!
CH : O Curiosus - you always sing the same old song - everything that is inelegant, unlearned and vulgar is God's intention. But if it be spiritual, rare and admirable, then it is taken as the devil's work. But it was God who gave man a mind so aristocratic that when we *refine* our mind and abstain from worldly matters, then we can work wonders.
CU : [a sudden afterthought] Do you have anything to say on medicine?
CH : By all means. As there has taken place such a great accession of new land, that the world is now known to be twice as big as before - and as all this has been meticulously described, do you have any doubts that medicine too will make some progress? Is it such an absurd idea to try to reconcile, at least in part, Galenus and Paracelsus, as both ways round it appears that the one's remedies are not always happily applied and the other's not always unhappily - and as we cannot be sure whether Galenus, had he lived today, would not have borrowed a few things from chemistry? We know that this was done by, amongst others, Josephus Querceteanus, a thing greatly enhancing his reputation, but

even more beneficial to his patients! In the meantime the other members of the medical profession are perpetually poised in battle array - as if they were to fight for their altars or their hearths - with such bitterness that many a patient has already succumbed to his pains amidst such sighing and suffering, as from neither side no helping hand was offered.

I take the same line as to mathematicians. From them I only demand one thing, that they should show me the celestial phenomena regardless of whether the earth moves within them and the sun is fixed, or the sun moves and the earth is at rest, or the earth moves in one place and turns around its own axis - and so on and so on. All these things are beyond proof to us. For not because we think one way or another will the sun move rather than be fixed. Let it suffice for us to measure time exactly and to get a clue to the *harmony* God has equipped all things with.

CU : Goodbye Christianus, carry on ridiculing man's folly!

CH : That I will do. But for now, Curiosus, goodbye.

This dialogue squarely places Johann Valentin Andreae in the centre of the European scientific *avant garde* of his day, albeit as a very well informed theologian and ideological activist. It also makes much more sense of the story of Christian Rosenkreuz as outlined in the *Fama*. We can now see that the journey of Father C.R.C. is a pure allegory for the transition of knowledge from the East to the West *via* Spain[19]. That transition of course included a great deal of knowledge of gnostic provenance. The underground (when not sky-high) nature of the Rose Cross Brotherhood, for 120 years, can also be seen as the burying of Renaissance and medieval Christianised science and cosmosophy during the ravages of the Reformation. Andreae is picking up the torch of the Renaissance and, as we have seen, calling out for a second spiritual and scientific reformation to encompass all men of goodwill in the true Christian spirit of love and brotherhood.

In order to get an idea of how advanced Andreae was, one only has to recall the famous lines of Isaac Newton on the limitations of science. Newton - who took an interest in the Rosicrucian movement while being aware that its precise origin was an "imposture" - was not born until 23 years after the publication of Andreae's *Menippus*. (Newton was born in 1642). They make a stunning comparison with Andreae's words printed above, that mathematics can at best only offer a *clue* to the harmony of the cosmos :

To explain all nature is too difficult a task for any one man or even for any one age. 'Tis much better to do a little with certainty, and leave the rest for others that come after you, than to explain all things. ...I do not know what I may appear to the world; but to myself I seem to have been only like a boy playing on the sea-shore, and diverting myself in now and then finding a smoother pebble or a prettier shell than ordinary, while the great ocean of truth lay all undiscovered before me.

Newton was the kind of man with whom Andreae hoped his *Fama* would put him in contact. Andreae - alas - was ahead of his time.

Andreae and Radical Reform

According to the archives of the senate of the university of Tübingen, there occurred in 1620 the trial of the Tübingen librarian Eberhard Wild, accused by the Theological Faculty of having sold books by the radical reformers Caspar Schwenckfeld, Valentin Weigel and Sebastian Franck, and of being friendly to the Austrian gentleman Michael Zeller, a 'notorious' Schwenckfeldian. Wild had edited the *Imago*[20] and *Dextera porrecta*[21] of Andreae. The trial further revealed that the condemned books had been printed by Andreae's 'secret friend' Abraham Hölzl, even though no printer or author was mentioned on the title pages. Andreae, as a Lutheran deacon in the parish of Calw (near Stuttgart) was thus put in a delicate position. Hölzl had printed a catechism by Andreae and was known to be a visitor to Andreae's house. It was further suspected that Andreae and Hölzl exchanged heretical and occult books. After examination however, the theologians could establish nothing particularly reprehensible in Andreae's conduct. What *was* so terribly wrong with these radical reformers that Andreae should have had to defend himself from being associated with their works?

115

Caspar Schwenckfeld (1489-1561)

> I cannot be one in faith with either the Pope or Luther,
> because they condemn me and my faith, that is, they
> hate my Christ in me. To have the real Christ according
> to the spirit is very important. Christ does not condemn
> Himself. He does not persecute Himself.
> (Caspar Schwenckfeld*)

Schwenckfeld was a prince of Leignitz in Ossig, Lower Silesia. He was an aristocratic evangelist and a knight of the Teutonic Order, the exponent of an eirenic and evangelical spiritual Christianity with gnostic resonances. Schwenckfeld was a spiritual hero. In 1518 Schwenckfeld converted to Lutheranism, but with reservations. He believed that the Spirit should be free of all institutions. He followed the "royal road", tending neither to the right nor to the left - a road trodden by a few : "To my mind, I am one with all churches in that I pray for them, in that I despise none, because I know that Christ the Lord has his own everywhere, be they ever so few."

In 1524 Schwenckfeld wrote *An Admonition to all the brethren in Silesia* urging the adoption of the inward eucharist. Taking as his cue *John* VI.35 : *I am the bread of life : he that cometh to me shall never hunger, and he that believeth on me shall never thirst,* Schwenckfeld posited a mystical flesh upon which only those who perceived Christ spiritually might feed. Christ was "killed in the flesh and made alive in the Spirit" declared Schwenckfeld. He recommended his followers cease taking the external eucharist of bread and urged instead an inner, meditative feeding on Christ's true nature. He later regarded the correct institution of the Lord's Supper as impossible to reconstruct, its true nature lying in the "sealed book of the Apocalypse". It may well be a Schwenckfeldian eucharist that Andreae has Christian Rosenkreuz celebrate in the first paragraph of his *Chymical Wedding* :

> On an evening before Easter day, I sat at a table, and having (as my custom was) in my humble prayer sufficiently conversed with my Creator, and considered many great mysteries (whereof the Father of Lights his Majesty had shewn me not a few) and being now ready to prepare in my heart, together with my dear Paschal lamb, a small, unleavened, undefiled cake...

The spiritual inner eucharist was part of a process of deification : a distinctively gnostic understanding of human potential. This process

---

* Quotations from Schwenckfeld (pp. 116 - 118) appear in Williams, George, *The Radical Reformation* (Westminster, US, 1962, pp. 106 - 112, 257f., 466ff.).

of deification - becoming divine (a process which was thought even to affect the nature of the flesh) - was predicated on a special understanding of Christ's and of human-nature :

> The bodily food is transferred into our nature, but the spiritual food changes us into itself, that is, the divine nature, so that we become partakers of it. (Schwenckfeld)

Schwenckfeld developed his views through engaging his beliefs with those of the radical reformer Melchior Hoffmann, a man who had thoroughly imbued the 'celestial flesh heresy' of the Bogomils and Cathars. For Hoffmann, Jesus Christ is the "heavenly manna which shall give us eternal life" - that is, Christ's body, which in the words of the eucharistic institution, "I give unto you", must have been of a wholly spiritual nature. The second Adam (Christ) has a wholly heavenly origin, and is symbolised as *heavenly manna*, or *heavenly dew*, tangible only insofar as say water becomes ice through the blowing of the cold north wind. For Hoffmann, the 'wind' or 'breath' of the Holy Spirit made Christ's body tangible. (This conception has a highly alchemical ring to it). The teaching of the Catholic Church on the other hand was, and is, that Christ was emphatically the "Word made flesh", in order thoroughly to redeem humanity in its full terrestrial identity; He was both God and man. Schwenckfeld held to this latter view, but with a difference. Schwenckfeld believed that human nature was, to an extent, already spiritualised. His flesh, when *progressively spiritualised*, is not as other flesh. (Attentive readers will note the parallel here with the "whole and unconsumed" corpse of Christian Rosenkreuz, discovered, according to the *Confessio Fraternitatis*, in 1604). Schwenckfeld describes human nature as "uncreaturely", scarcely distinguishable from the divine nature in Christ. In this sense Schwenckfeld understood humankind to be the sons of God (*Luke* XX. 34-36).

In principle, according to Schwenckfeld, God can bring pure visible flesh from a virgin. Through the persistent feeding on the inward flesh/bread of Christ, man can become progressively deified through the *spiritual processes* of transfiguration, resurrection, and ascension. This view is echoed in the gnostic alchemy prevalent at the time, and from whose imagery Andreae and others borrowed freely to describe the transformation of leaden, blackened man into spiritual gold : the theme of Andreae's *Chymical Wedding*. Schwenckfeld's view of man is very close to William Blake's "Divine Humanity" and is ultimately derived from the Heavenly Man (*Anthropos*) of the gnostic Hermetica.

Schwenckfeld wrote that "Justification [before God] derives from the knowledge [*Erkenntnis*] of Christ through faith." Participation in the bread of heaven (which according to John's Gospel feeds the *kosmos*) made Schwenckfeld a free man : a member of the true church behind the visible church - the spiritual fraternity, and the central concept implicit in Andreae's Fraternity of the Rose-Cross, which meets in a building called the *House of the Holy Spirit*. Schwenckfeld was 'freed-up' to act as Adam did before the Fall. He became the "new regenerated man" who was able, because he was spiritually free, to keep the commandments of God, since he was truly in love with God.

In 1526, Schwenckfeld was rebutted by Martin Luther on the eucharistic issue, and his teachings were condemned as heretical. Two years later, the Catholic Ferdinand of Bohemia and Hungary annulled the evangelical reforms which had taken place in Silesia, and Schwenckfeld went into exile to Strasbourg in 1527. While in Strasbourg, he disputed with Anabaptists - the most anarchistic and physically courageous of the radicals - but who Schwenckfeld thought lacked the true knowledge of Christ. He considered the Anabaptists to be too preoccupied with the end of the world and the 'second coming', and begged them rather to consider how things are in the presence of God. Schwenckfeld was not an apocalyptic millenarian.

> Nor can we wait here on earth for a golden age. We hope to attain to the perfect knowledge of Christ yonder in the Fatherland. Here we know only in part.

The Anabaptists might well have sought an end to time. In 1522 the Holy Roman Emperor, the Habsburg Charles V, had introduced the Inquisition into the Netherlands, and it is claimed that during his reign 30,000 of these revolutionaries met grisly deaths in the seventeen provinces under his control. The Anabaptists, abandoned by Luther along with the peasants, were to be tortured, drowned, burned, and roasted over slow fires. For Andreae, the Anabaptists were the *boni*, the good people, whose word was ignored and whose martyrdom was exemplary. In Andreae's eyes, it was better to be a Waldensian[22] or an idiot whose life and preaching harmonised than to show off many learned books of orthodoxy, while neglecting Christian practice and the love of one's fellows. Andreae did not need to be in agreement with their entire outlook (which in the case of the Anabaptists was egalitarian and socially revolutionary - and not infrequently quite hysterical) to feel scandalised by the treatment meted out to radical reformers. Andreae also regarded the burning of witches as a stain on mankind.

Sebastian Franck (1499-1542)

While in Strasbourg, Schwenckfeld became close to the radical reformer Sebastian Franck, who was also in temporary sojourn in that 'free' city. Franck, an itinerant printer and effective radical, had been hounded out of more cities, free or otherwise, than he could properly recall.

A key belief of Franck's was that of the *celestial assumption of the apostolic church*. According to this picture the primitive Christian Church had in distant times become corrupt, and the true church had become a spiritual body. The visible church was, according to Franck, a mere husk that the Devil had perverted. The spiritual church would remain scattered and hidden among the heathen and the nominal christians until the second advent, when Christ would gather his own and bring them home. This vision of an invisible fraternity would impact itself in the conception of the invisible Rosicrucian Brotherhood, as well as providing a source for much later neo-gnostic and neo-Rosicrucian beliefs regarding a hidden sanctuary of adepts or invisible cabal of 'Secret Chiefs'. Indeed, when you add this image to that of Wolfram von Eschenbach's Gral castle (Munsalvaesche) in *Parzifal*, you have the fundamental itinerary of a good deal of contemporary neo-gnostic and theosophist mythology[23].

It is noteworthy that Franck translated Agrippa's *de vanitate scientiarum*, (very much in tune with Franck's notable 'learned are perverted' theme as we shall see). Agrippa was of course steeped in Neoplatonic-occult lore. Franck was also acquainted with Paracelsus when both these giants resided in Basle, and in Franck's book *Die Gulden arcke*[24] he says of Hermes that "he hath all that in him which a Christian must needs know." In the same book, (written in 1538), Franck gives an extensive paraphrase from the *Poimandres* of *Corpus Hermeticum I*, a translation of which provided Holland with her first printed acquaintance with the *Corpus Hermeticum*. Sebastian Franck stood for the *Ecclesia Spiritualis*, the spiritual church which, as with the Cathars, required neither wood nor stone but subsisted in the hearts of the faithful. Franck wrote that :

The unitary spirit alone baptizes with fire and Spirit all the faithful, and all who are obedient to the inner Word in whatever part of the world they may be. For God is no respecter of persons but instead is the same to the Greeks as to the Barbarian and the Turk, to the lord as to the servant, so long as they retain the Light which has shone upon them and the joy in their heart.

In 1531, Sebastian Franck was accused of being a revolutionary and kicked out of Strasbourg. Schwenckfeld received the same treatment two years later.

Anyone who doubts the influence of the radical reformation on Andreae need only consult his brilliant *Menippus* (1617), described by Wilhelm Kühlmann as "a satire which cannot be more highly regarded as the summing-up of the conflicts of an entire epoch." The theme of the 86th Discourse, *Paradoxa*, is taken completely from the *Paradoxa* of Sebastian Franck : *quo doctorium, eo perversiorem* or more bluntly, *the learned are perverted*. Andreae was heartily sickened at the arrogant conceit of academics who thought they knew everything, did nothing, and stood by while good men and women went to the stake for the very thing with which they ought to have been most concerned : the truth. Andreae says he would rather have been a witness of the truth than a doctor; those thought by the world to be impious (such as the radical reformers) are the truly holy; the truth is always revolutionary. Theology is an experience, not a science; belief is not an art. The will and the thoughts are free and no judgement can restrict them. In short, the learned are perverted. In fact, the very same theme had been used by Andreae nine years earlier in the *Fama* : "the pride and covetousness of the learned is so great, it will not suffer them to agree together".

The 23rd Dialogue of the *Menippus* tells of how pious people have to starve because they give themselves freely and without ceremony. The 24th Dialogue says that too many books prevent the ordinary man from finding God and gaining understanding, while the teachers and priests call anyone an Anabaptist and a heretic who is simply going his own holy way. The 25th talks of the downfall of the universities, calling them schools where empty meaning, vanity, wastefulness, manure, intolerance of dissenters, hypocrisy, flattery, idle talk and lying dominate, and where talkers armed with "scholastic guns" are aimed against Christ and his foolish disciples, while the whole travesty rules over the poor people[25].

By the time Andreae was born, in 1586, the political effectiveness of the radical spirituals had been suppressed. In 1535, the wild

Anabaptist 'kingdom' of Münster fell with the death of every inhabitant, while spiritual prophets tried to recruit disappointed Anabaptists into sects of 'invisible churches'. Five years later, Franck and Schwenckfeld were condemned by Lutherans and Calvinists at Smalkald. The 'inner word' of the radicals was denied. The Holy Spirit, said the Judges - speaking on its behalf - works exclusively through the exterior Word, written and preached. As George Williams expressed the consequences in his brilliant book, *The Radical Reformation* (1962) :

> The ruthless suppression of the radical Reformation by the Catholic and Protestant princes alike led to the permanent disfigurement of the social and constitutional structure of central Europe, culminating in the treaties of Münster and Osnabrück with their sanction of the complete disintegration of the great medieval ideal of a universal Christian society. ...they [the radical reformers] were covenanters of the ongoing Israel of faith, died confident in their election to live obediently at the suffering centre of redemptive history, in imitation of Him who taketh away the sins of the world.

Piety and Mysticism

There was another link which bound the genesis of the Rosicrucian Manifestos to the radical reformers. That link subsists in the development of German Pietism from out of the streams of radical reform, mysticism and theosophy (direct investigation of the life of God in the soul, expressed in terms of philosophical and alchemical dynamics).

A key author in this development was Valentin Weigel, who was born in Dresden in 1533 and who died in 1588 - the year of the Spanish Armada. Weigel published only one book in his lifetime, *On the Life of Christ* (1578), but after his death his works gained considerable underground currency. Some even crossed the Channel to England.

121

Astrology Theologized was published in London in 1649 under the gnostic rubric *Sapiens dominabitur Astris*. Pirate copies emerged from all kinds of places, including, Carlos Gilly surmises, Augustus von Anhalt's secret printing-press at Plötzkau, (Augustus being, according to Gilly, the first known recipient of the *Fama Fraternitatis*). Weigel was certainly influenced by Caspar Schwenckfeld while his *Life of Christ* displays much erudition influenced by Paracelsus. The microcosm-macrocosm theory, so central to the thought-world of the 'Rosicrucian' is quite explicit in Weigel's work on the superiority of the light of grace to the natural cosmic dominants expressed in the images of the stars in *Astrology Theologized* :

> Everything which is without is as that which is within, but the internal always excels the external in essence, virtue and operation, so we bear God within us, and God bears us in Himself. God hath us with Himself, and is nearer to us, than we are to ourselves. We have God everywhere with us, whether we know it, or know it not.

Weigel, a Protestant minister, came to consider his own professional calling vain, and the ordained ministry in general as the work of the Antichrist. He was against the Lutheran Formula of Concord (1577) with its emphasis on formal dogma and the straight-jacketing of the inner spiritual movement. His view of the cosmos was that of the Neoplatonic Theurgist : the Three Worlds, (as detailed in Agrippa's *Three Books of Occult Philosophy*, 1533) : the material world, (a world of darkness in itself), the invisible celestial (angelic) world, and the supercelestial domain of God. God for Weigel is the *summum bonum*, reception of Whom is blessedness. When a person accepts salvation, he or she becomes a god. He followed Schwenckfeld's view on the supercelestial nature of Christ's flesh and the general Schwenckfeldian scheme of progressive deification.

Weigel's theosophic vision represents a Neoplatonic, gnostic reworking of orthodox Christian theology. He saw the magical power inherent in the theology but unexpressed by the orthodox Lutherans. Due to the synthetic and harmonising nature of Weigel's thought, he found approval among Andreae's circle and among all those who believed that true Christian spirituality was, in a very special sense, *magical*. Weigel's works had a practical, helpful and above all spiritual character. He was a great influence on Jacob Böhme (1575-1624) whose profound theosophic system was compared by his follower Abraham von Frankenburg to the Valentinian Gnostics in the manuscript *Theophrastia Valentiniana* (1627), as well as upon Andreae's friend and spiritual mentor Joannes Arndt of Anhalt (1555-1621). Arndt reworked Weigel's writings, and in so doing became the father of German Pietism, a movement which persists in influence to this day. Arndt wrote that "Christ has many servants but few followers."

In 1618, while Böhme was busy writing his spiritual masterpieces in Görlitz, Johann Valentin Andreae founded his Christian Society, the *Societas Christianae*, whose twenty-six members included Tobias Adami, Christoph Besold and Joannes Arndt. (Andreae included the name of the late Tobias Hess on the list as well). Arndt was particuarly close to Andreae's friend Christoph Besold, the last link in our chain of association. Besold called Arndt "the most meritricious man in Christ's Church" and shared with him and with Andreae an extraordinarily deep and well-informed knowledge of medieval mysticism.

Christoph Besold (1577-1649)

Born at Esslingen in 1577, Besold was nine years older than Andreae, gaining a chair in Jurisprudence at Tübingen in 1610, three years after Andreae had been sent down from the university for writing a lude poem about a tutor's wife. Andreae learnt a great deal from the older man's encyclopaedic knowledge. Besold knew nine languages, including Hebrew and Arabic, was familiar with the Qabalah and occult sciences, was brilliant at Theology, at home with the Patristics, the scholastics and, above all, the Platonist mystics and cosmologists from the thirteenth century to his own : Ramon Lull (c.1232-1316); Cusanus (who used the Hermetic *Asclepius*, 1401-1464); Pico della Mirandola (1463-1494); Giordano Bruno (1548-1600); Eckhart (c.1260-1328); Heinrich Suso (c.1295-1366); Ruysbroek (1293-1381); Joannes Tauler (c.1300-1361) and the author of the *Imitatio Christi* (called Thomas à Kempis) : all vital links in the chain of the intellectual presentation of a spiritual *gnosis*, and who together represent a veritable catalogue of some of that movement's greatest literary moments. Andreae had unrestricted access to Besold's library (now housed at the *Universitatsbibliothek* in Salzburg).

Besold was also politically aware. He was passionate about Campanella's utopian *Civitas solis* (*The City of the Sun*, which became a model for Andreae's *Reipublicae Christianopolitinae* or *Christianopolis* of 1619, dedicated to Joannes Arndt), and was an enthusiast for the

Italian anti-Habsburg liberal satirist Trajano Boccalini whose *Ragguagli di Parnaso* (*News from Parnassus* 1612-1613 - an extract from which was published with the 1614 *Fama*) was probably translated by Besold.

Besold's philosophical outlook, as revealed in his *Signa temporum* (*Signs of the Times*, 1614) and *Axiomata Philosophico-Theologica* (1616) was exeedingly profound and made a great impact on Johann Valentin Andreae, to whom it was dedicated. Like Andreae, Besold was fully aware that the hoped-for spiritual reformation had been hi-jacked by the ruling classes and soured by the theologians and ecclesiastical authorities. He set about trying to establish a basis for the true and authentic spiritual Christianity. In spite of the huge scope of this endeavour, and his vast knowledge, Besold himself was sincerely humble, favouring the doctrine of 'learned ignorance' detailed by Cusanus in the latter's famous work of this name. Besold realised that no theory or external knowledge-system could ever constitute absolute and everlasting knowledge. Following the mystics, Besold saw that God Himself can mostly only usefully be described in terms of what He is NOT. Ultimately, the highest wisdom is to know NOTHING[26].

Besold preferred act to theory and disputation. He saw the Church as an embattled ship calling on Christ to save it. The world to Besold was a sect : separated from God. The good man passes through the world as a voyager : "he must not be in the world as if it were his native land; he passes by as a traveller" said Besold in an utterance highly reminiscent of views expressed in the Nag Hammadi Library such as the imperative to "Become passers-by" so as to remind Gnostics of the relative character of this world. According to Besold, the pretended sages of the world in their blindness, regard people who behave as Christians as mad, and insofar as they claim to be Christians themselves do the name a dishonour. Besold shares with Hess, Andreae and Comenius the theme of the folly of the world - to be in right relation to it must mean appearing foolish to the worldly.

Besold regarded erudition as an obstacle to true devotion. Besold cites the melancholy voice of *Ecclesiastes* : *With much knowledge cometh great sorrow*. Even the most assiduous researches reveal the full profundity of neither nature nor the human-being in spite of vaunted claims to the contrary. The false sage is like a caged bird : always turning around on himself. Pious philosophy on the other hand does not make for multiple theories, but it does make us better. The demon of the savants (the *learned-perverted*) is curiosity, offering much work for poisoned fruit. This theme will have a great influence on Andreae, and arm him with a useful category to describe many of the absurd responses to the *Fama*.

For Besold, curiosity obstructs the revelation of God in man. The "curious" are like Martha who obstructs calm and confidence with her incessant worries about domestic necessities. Rather, Besold advises, man should strive for the "most simple simplicity"*. Humility is the true foundation of all Christian life. It is the trunk of the Cross, the other arms being according to Besold, obedience, poverty, and chastity. The Cross is the only intimate knowledge of the Word of God. The 'real thing' is interior; the Reformation had failed to reform the heart. Those who were closest to genuine spiritual regeneration were attacked from all sides. While before the reform of Luther the Church had been dominated by Pharisees, now it had been taken over by the scribes. Whereas religion is firstly communicated through acts of love, the religion of the letter kills. Christianity, according to Besold, is not a system or theory but a practice through which we advance by Grace. Luther's 'justification by faith alone' is insufficient if not followed up and accompanied by good works, acts of love, remembering that it is not the earthy 'I' (ego) that does these good things but God within, without Whom we are helpless, though we may consider ourselves powerful and impervious to circumstance. The Godless are obsessed with insurance; death will cure us of the illusion. We are not saved by our own efforts, externally generated, but by the sole merits of Christ dead and raised within us. We must die and be resurrected with Him : an inner alchemy. Without Christ-the-Stone we are lead, truly dead. (As the "living Jesus" of the Nag Hammadi Library says : "The dead are not alive and the living will not die").

Penitence is "the best of all medicines". We must lose confidence in ourselves, and in the world. Once the flesh is mortified, that is governed by the Spirit, the Spirit of God lives in us. Wisdom destroys man to renovate him; she humiliates him to exalt him. She darkens him to make in him a new light. This is accomplished by the alchemy of regeneration. The more frequently the metal 'dies', the more it is transmuted into noble metal, the more it abandons its old 'body'. The better the metal, the more it must die, to reveal the gold. If you are especially gifted, expect to suffer. The more often he dies, the more death illuminates him by the resurrection of Christ in himself. The imitation of Christ is the real alchemy, culminating in the real New Man.

---

* Quoted by Roland Edighoffer in his analysis of Christoph Besold in his excellent and invaluable study of the Rosicrucian phenomenon, *Rose-Croix et Société Ideale* (2 vols. Paris, 1982).

125

Besold uses the image of the Christian knight and of 'the sleeping fiancé', brought in time to the rose-garden. Few are called there, and few are chosen. The chosen are the elect : nothing to be proud of. The elect are not a sect, which is always a human invention and therefore ultimately sterile. Besold quotes Augustine : "I was searching for you outside of myself, and did not find the God in my heart." God is at the centre of the soul.

Regarding the path of the mystics and the seeing-of-visions, Besold says that visions are dangerous for those not thoroughly schooled in humility, (as occult and mainstream history makes abundantly clear). The divine garden is always there, but no-one can force entry. The door is always ajar, but not everyone can enter. We make our own barriers. Besold regrets the blindness of man who cannot see the signs sent to awaken him. Paraphrasing the gospel (*Matthew* XIV. 22-27), Besold writes how Christ returned at the fourth watch of the night to the boat of the disciples (meaning the time of Luther), but was unrecognised and taken for a ghost. The Church-boat is still rocking with the winds of doctrinal conflict and will continue to do so until the moment comes when Christ will re-enter the boat and the ocean will become calm.

But the ocean will not be calm. The already wild surface is about to receive a colossal splash whose waves will billow for a generation.

Christoph Besold

"I was searching for you outside of myself,
and did not find the God in my heart"

126

Chapter Nine

The Greatest Publicity Stunt of all Time

A ROSE, as fair as ever saw the North,
Grew in a little garden all alone;
A sweeter flower did Nature ne'er put forth,
Nor fairer garden yet was never known :
The maidens danced about it morn and noon,
And learned bards of it their ditties made;
The nimble fairies by the pale-faced moon,
Water'd the root and kissed her pretty shade.
But well-a-day! - the gardener careless grew;
The maids and fairies both were kept away,
And in a drought the caterpillars threw
Themselves upon the bud and every spray.
God shield the stock! If heaven send no supplies,
The fairest blossom of the garden dies.[27]

The Rose

1613 : a year before the publication of the *Fama*. While two responses
to the manuscript version emerge - one from 'I.B' in Prague, the other
from Joannes Combach in Marburg - the Czech genius and Rose-Cross
enthusiast Johann Amos Comensky (*Comenius*) enters the city of
Heidelberg. He is just in time to see the Elector of the Palatine Frederick
V returning to that city in a triumphal parade with the King of
England, Scotland and Ireland's daughter, the learned and beautiful
Princess Elizabeth as his bride.

There were great hopes for the Elector Frederick. He was identified
with the symbolic animal of the Palatinate : the lion - and was not the
lion the beast who defeated the many-headed eagle in the second,
apocalyptic Book of *Esdras*? That fearsome Habsburg eagle was now
flapping its feathers in Bohemia, where the new Emperor Matthias
was overseeing a growing reversal of Rudolf II's laws of Toleration :
laws which had been established to protect the Bohemian Protestants.
The Bohemian Protestants looked to Frederick as their future king.
Now he was wed to the daughter of the most powerful Protestant
monarch in the world, surely their cause was not only just but

politically powerful. Those who had seen and remembered Simon Studion's *Naometria* (completed in 1604) may have recalled the conclusion to that gigantic work : a six-part choral canon which had called for King James of Britain, Frederick of Württemberg, and the Lily of France (in the person of the tolerant King Henri IV of Navarre, now dead) to rally behind the banner of the *Rose*. In spite of signs of a growing political crisis in central Europe, great men in England, Scotland and Germany saw the union of Frederick and Elizabeth as one full of extraordinary promise : a great expansion of neo-Elizabethan culture, a new beginning for the whole world : a time of toleration, wisdom, knowledge and art : an age of *gold*.

During the previous year (1612) the Paracelsian doctor and alchemist Michael Maier of Rostock (1568-1622), formerly physician to the Emperor Rudolf II, had been in England. Soon he was to work for both Moritz von Hessen and for Augustus von Anhalt. He would also become, along with England's very own Paracelsian Hermetist Dr. Robert Fludd, the most determined supporter of the Rosicrucian cause. While in Britain, (where he met James I's physician Sir Wiliam Paddy and very probably the aforementioned Fludd), Maier sent a curious Christmas card to James I. The card, on parchment three feet by two, consisted of a huge rose divided into eight petals : a rose formed of various pious and optimistic Latin phrases whose dominant message offered "Greetings to James, for a long time King of Great Britain. By your true protection may the rose be joyful."

The *Fama's* strong bias towards medicine may well have attracted Maier to the Fraternity - had he seen it at this stage. (Maier was in Prague at the time of I.B's early response from that city). We certainly cannot be sure as to what significance the word "rose"[28] had for him in this context, any more than that "rose" of Simon Studion behind which enlightened princes were invited to gather round in 1604 (the year of Christian Rosenkreuz's exhumation, according to the *Confessio Fraternitatis*). Holding back the supposition that the Rose referred to the Fraternity of the Rose-Cross, let us first consider more pertinent avenues, principally in the realm of alchemy, that art so dear to the hearts of Fludd, Maier and Maier's patrons.

The rose had undoubted symbolic, alchemical associations with, for example, the alchemical *Pleroma* and with Christ; with the womb of the Virgin (wherein the Christ-*Lapis*=Stone is born) and above all with the *lapis philosophorum*, the philosopher's Stone itself[29]. Furthermore, there is the red-and-white rose, the "golden flower" of alchemy and birthplace of the *filius philosophorum* - the regenerated human-being -

which appears in the English alchemical *Ripley Scrowle* of 1588[30]. The "rose-garden of the philosophers" is one of the favourite images of alchemy, with a many-layered matrix of appropriate meanings. The Rose might have indicated an eloquent and simple password for those seeking the Stone - at whatever level (for the Stone is polyvalent) : *including* the Stone of political and religious unity.

In the *Rosarium philosophorum* (1550), well-known to Maier and to most alchemists of the time, the *lapis* says : "Protect me and I will protect you. Give me my due that I may help you." This could make sense as a meaningful symbol for political and spiritual co-operation. Meanwhile, close inspection of the unique Christmas card which Maier sent to James I reveals at the Rose's centre a point in a circle. Not only does this bring to mind the heavenly rose at the heart of Dante's *Paradiso* (=Garden)[31] but it also symbolises the fountain at the centre of the Rose-garden : the unifying spiritual heart from which all Good flows : the analogue for the spiritual stone - the lost stone of unity, lost when the Reformation split Europe into religious pieces. (The symbolism of the point in the circle also pertains to the ideal of the Third Degree Master Mason in early 18th century Freemasonry). It would then I think seem reasonable to take the Rose as representing a gathering-point or shorthand for the deepest political and spiritual endeavours of the time. A simple question such as : "Are you for or against the Rose?" would immediately elicit knowledge of the correspondent's political and spiritual proclivity.

Sure enough, history suggests something of this nature was indeed being assiduously sought by powerful and not-so-powerful people in Germany and Great Britain[32]. Ludwig and Christian of Anhalt (the politically active elder brothers of Augustus) were already planning a new union of Protestant Princes to centre around Frederick and his English wife Elizabeth, whose parentage seemed to suggest British support for their schemes. Comenius, who had come from Bohemia (where Protestants put hope in Frederick's legitimate candidacy for the Bohemian crown) to Heidelberg for his studies, must have gazed in wonder at the great celebrations in Heidelberg, as the bells rang out across the Neckar to welcome the English Rose, Elizabeth[33].

Meanwhile, word was getting about (in highly select circles) of a secret Fraternity of the Rose-Cross. The Rose *and* the Cross - could Johann Valentin Andreae ever have dreamed that his family coat-of-arms - the S.Andrew's cross with four roses : might suddenly gain such powerful

129

meaning to those steeped in symbolism, in a world where politics was frequently expressed in symbolic references? We know that Augustus von Anhalt had seen a copy of the *Fama* and wanted to know more. Did he speak about it with his brother Ludwig (based a few miles away at Köthen), friend of Frederick of the Palatinate, a man with whom he shared 'literary interests'?

The Furore Begins

The publication of the *Fama Fraternitatis* represents not only the "greatest publicity-stunt of all time", sparking off a movement which persists to this day, but it also provided Europe with its first multinational conspiracy story. Indeed, every occult conspiracy story since owes its basic shape to the excitement generated by the prospect of a secret, underground body of initiates pledged to change the world by invisible means, privy to all knowledge, advanced science and vast wealth. Whether or not readers thought such a prospect dangerous or as something wonderful to be welcomed with open arms depended very much on whether that person was in fundamental sympathy with the aims of the Brotherhood. Since the *Confessio Fraternitatis* (published as a follow-up in 1615) made it clear that the Brotherhood stood against the Papacy, response to the Brotherhood was likely to be split according to religious affiliation. Furthermore, it did not take long before the plea for universally shared knowledge and the announcement of enlightenment began to appear as an attempt to subvert the established order of government, education and religion. It *was* - but not in the way its enemies thought.

From 1614 until the mid-1620s when the Thirty Years War began to take the steam out of the furore, Europe was split between those in favour of the Rosicrucian movement, and who wished to join its ranks, and those who were against it. Wiser commentators stayed on the fence, a few aware of the method behind the apparent madness of the Rosicrucian self-publicity : to stir up debate on fundamental issues regarding the nature and orientation of religion and science. One thing was for sure, whoever had published the *Fama* had taken any control the Tübingen circle might have had over its dissemination right out of their hands. As a published work the *Fama* began to look very different indeed from a select manuscript submitted for private consideration and intimate response. This no longer looked like an enquiry into the minds of men of learning; this was a broad, politico-religious manifesto. The authors may well have been shaken by the reaction - although in the first instance one does suspect a mite of ribald laughter at the sight of people looking for an invisible fraternity while remaining completely blind to that fraternity which could be realised all about them. The Philosopher's Stone was, according to the alchemists, everywhere to be found but *nowhere seen*. Andreae and others pondered upon the words of John's Gospel (I.10-11) : *He was in the world, and the world was made by him, and the world knew him not. He came unto his own, and his own received him not.* The world, Besold said, is a sect.

The Stone Falls

Initial response to the *Fama* came in the form of a bewildering number of books and pamphlets which flew back and forth across northern and central Europe. Many wished to join; some defended the movement, some even said they were members of the Brotherhood - or knew somebody who was. Others virulently opposed the Brotherhood, accusing it of heresy and worse crimes. Some writers wrote defending the Brotherhood one day while repudiating it the next. The Brotherhood was sought everywhere, but found nowhere. Surely, some surmised, the Brotherhood must be *invisible*! The *Fama* had fallen like a catalyst into the religious and intellectual bosom of Europe, winnowing out a vast array of *pros* and *contras*.

In Tübingen: Wilhelm Schickhard, Wilhelm Bidenbach, Thomas Lanz, Abraham Hölzl, Samuel Hafenreffer - all *pro*. Caspar Bücher, Theodor Thummius[34], Lucas Osiander[35] - *against*. In Darmstadt: Theophilus Schweighardt (real name, Daniel Mögling[36]) and Heinrich Nollius[37] - both *for* the Brotherhood. In Frankfurt : Johann Bringer and Lucas Jennis - both printers and both *pro*. In Marburg: Rudolph Goclenius, Georg Zimmerman, Raphael Eglin[38], Johann Hartmann, Joannes Combach and Philipp Homagius[39] - all in favour. In Ulm: opposition from Zimbertus Wehe, Johann Hebenstreit and Conrad Dieterich. In favour: Johann Faulhaber, a brilliant mathematician[40]. In Augsburg, carrying a torch for the Brotherhood were Carl Widemann, David Ehinger and from 1617 Adam Haslmayr, lately returned from sea.

In Coburg lived one of the most active and virulently anti-Rosicrucian writers: Andreas Libavius[41]. Libavius was a famous 'chymist' who, while approving Paracelsus' introduction of chemistry into medicine, absolutely despised the magical interest in Paracelsus and stood as a staunch defender of traditional Galenic and Aristotelian medicine. In fact Libavius was against the whole gamut of Renaissance occult philosophy : John Dee, Magia, Cabala, Hermes Trismegistus, Agrippa, Trithemius - anyone of a gnostic tinge. He was also deeply suspicious of the politics of the manifestos, linking their hopes to extravagant plans for a 'Paracelsist Lion'. Following the defeat of Frederick V at the Battle of the White Mountain in 1620 (after the fateful monarch had acceded to the Bohemian Protestants' wish that he take the throne of Bohemia) the 'Rosicrucians' were even more strongly attacked as political renegades, utopian subversives and spiritual terrorists in a series of vicious pro-Habsburg pamphlets.

Another regular contributor to the anti-Rosicrucian pamphlet war was Friedrich Grick, a private tutor from Altdorf near Nuremberg who also wrote under the pseudonyms *Irenaeus Agnostus* (Irenaeus being of course the chief patristic anti-Gnostic theologian), *Menapius* and other fanciful names. Grick seems to have been obsessed by the Rosicrucians and one suspects that his perpetual forays into print, approving of this and disapproving of that, evinced some conflict in his own mind; he really could not let the matter drop. Like so many others at the time, he was hooked. He may also have been enduring an identity-crisis. In *Tintinabulum Sophorum* (Nuremberg, 1619) he talks of "our" *Fama* and "our" brotherhood. Indeed, he blames the Brotherhood for trickery and then tells his readers that Christian love is the gold of their alchemy. He seems rather confused and admits as much himself in a reply to one Justus Cornelius who had written to him - he was now setting himself up as an expert on the subject - (not difficult to do when the 'real' Rosicrucians refused to stand up) :

> The first author of the *Fama and Confessio R.C.* is a great man and wishes particularly to remain a while longer concealed. He desired, however, only to learn the opinions of people and of these he experienced many kinds. ...I originally took [him] for a mad or capricious innovator; for this reason I set myself against him and wrote the *Fortalitum Scientiae* but when my first writing saw the light I learned that I had written a tragedy with jesting words and, at least with the curious, had provoked judgement and condemnation.

Grick devoted his future works to rebutting those who used the Rosicrucian works for their own ends; he was embarrassed.

Meanwhile, Leipzig gave a good showing of pro-Rosicrucian works: Kerner, Schwanbach; Paul Nagel[42] (Augustus von Anhalt's astrologer) and Paul Felgenhauer[43]. Erfurt's Johann Weber was *against*. Herrn

Isaias Stiefel and Meth from Langensalzach were *pro*. Dresden's Matthias Höe was in favour, while Johann Francus of Bautzen had a foot in both camps.

The case of the gnostic Jacob Böhme of Görlitz, Upper Lusatia, is an interesting one. Even today some Rosicrucian enthusiasts count Böhme the German Theosopher as one of the Brotherhood since he had absorbed so much of the mysticism and Paracelsian terminology for which the manifestos appeared to demonstrate such approval, and clearly Böhme was an illuminated man. Böhme read the manifestos and thought them interesting but mad. His devoted follower Balthasar Walter, on the other hand, admired both the Rosicrucians and the messianic-type mystagogue Steifel. Böhme wrote against Steifel (the latter had used Böhmist theosophy), in response to which the astrologer Nagel and his friends moved to suppress Böhme's work, since they admired Stiefel so much. Nagel claimed he knew a nobleman who was a Rosicrucian (he might have been thinking of his patron Augustus von Anhalt) and himself went to great lengths to find the Brotherhood but, as for everyone else, the search proved vain. The mist thickened into fog, the fog into darkness. The less hard fact was forthcoming, the deeper and more fantastic the speculations became. One man appeared, Philip Ziegler by name, who claimed to be the *King* of the Rosicrucians, declaring that John Dee was one of their Fraternity. Confusion reigned. Recriminations flew thick and fast. Madness was in the air, and Andreae sighed.

Joachim Morsius, a very gifted scholar who had studied at Rostock and Cambridge, wrote to the Brotherhood (care of the printer), received no reply and then wrote a work defending their secrecy (*Theosophi Eximii*, Frankfurt 1619). He was friendly with Balthasar Walter (a Paracelsian alchemist) who informed Morsius that his spiritual master Böhme knew all about the true Rosicrucian doctrines. Böhme's reply to Morsius' enquiry into the Rosicrucian Reformation merely informed him of the need for the true reformation in Christ. Morsius then went to Stockholm to talk to the Swedish pansophist Johann Buraeus who was himself fascinated by the Fraternity of the Rose-Cross, but never seems to have found the satisfaction he craved. Morsius even met Andreae in Calw in 1629. Andreae did not, it seems, disillusion him in his quest. Morsius comes over as something of a romantic figure, belonging perhaps to a later time when poets throughout the continent would again pack satchels and head off in search of the Absolute.

The list goes on : Daniel Sennert of Wittenberg, Galenist and

Aristotelian: *against*. Alexander Rost of Rostock, prolific anti-Rosicrucian: *against*. Joannes Arndt and Melchior Breler[44] in Lüneburg: in favour. Wenceslas Budowez, Comenius (initially), 'I.B.' - all in Prague - all in favour. Ratke in Köthen : *pro*. Christoph Bismark and Joachim Krusicke of Halle : *pro*. In Schleswig Holstein: Nicolas Tetting, Banier, the poetess Anne Hojers: all in favour. David Fabricius, also in Holstein: *against*. In Hamburg: Georg Froben: *pro*; Nicholaus Hunnius and Muller: *anti*. In Oppenheim in the Palatinate the publisher Theodor De Bry (publisher of Robert Fludd's *Utriusque Cosmi Historia* (1617) and other massive Hermetic works): *pro*. In Danzig, Corvinus: *against*, while Hermann Rathmann and Martin Ruarius were in favour.

The frequent vagueness of the manifestos concerning details of the Brotherhood's beliefs enabled champions and opponents to paint the non-existent Order in whatever colours they fancied. For Julius Sperber, based in Danzig and a convinced apocalyptist attending on the New Age as fervently as Simeon in the Temple waited upon Jesus, Christian Rosenkreuz was the inheritor of the ancient secret doctrine stemming from Adam and which then passed through Noah, the Patriarchs, Zoroaster, the Chaldeans, the Egyptians, the Persians, the Jewish Qabalah, and then in a secret wisdom tradition begun by Jesus and reserved to the few Christians who could 'take it' - (this man seems to have had a very penetrating insight into the gnostic tradition) - it was passed on to Cornelius Agrippa, Johann Reuchlin (the great Christian Qabalist), Marsilio Ficino, Pico della Mirandola and Aegidius Guttmann (1490-1584), spiritual alchemist, esotericist and author of *Offenbärung gottlicher Majestät* (Revelation of the Divine Majesty). In Sperber's *Echo der von Gott höcherleuchteten Fraternitet* (Echo of the God-illuminated Fraternity. Danzig, 1615), Sperber saw the Rosicrucian Fraternity as having a claim on this inherited pristine *gnosis*. Sperber held an official position in Anhalt lands for Ludwig, Augustus' brother, at Köthen. I have seen some of Sperber's handwritten manuscripts held in Köthen castle in the former DDR: commentaries on the *Apocalypse* and on the work of Simon Studion - and I would say that the visions of the farthest-out psychedelicist would have a hard time 'out-freaking' the mind of this extraordinary person. Andreae found this sort of speculation too far-out-of-this-world for his taste, and no doubt began feeling something like regret. But the Rosicrucian *furor* had a momentum of its own.

In Strasbourg: Johann Friedrich Jungius (who got another pro-Rosicrucian, the printer Zetzner, to print Andreae's *Chymische Hochzeit* in 1616 - "someone brought the text" he said) was *pro*, along with Figulus and Walch. Isac Harbrecht[45] was against. In Lübeck, Joachim Morsius and Count Michael Maier were *pro*; Rochel and Dame : *against*.

Michael Maier, the man who had sent the strange Christmas greeting to James I in 1612, becomes the single figure most identified as a classic 'Rosicrucian'. He writes in his many works on the subject - always in staunch defence of the Brotherhood - with what appears to be great insider-knowledge. He strives to be acceptable to the Brotherhood but never claims to be on the inside. The inside of the Brotherhood has become for him, as for his correspondent Robert Fludd (1574-1637) in England, an altogether exalted fraternity : a spiritual body, not existing on this plane at all.

It is never clear whether this spiritual body actually represents a body of unearthly initiates guiding humankind with occasional gifts of knowledge and insight or whether Maier has got Andreae's trick, that is, that the 'Brother' is a truly Christian person with a spiritual approach to all things, subsisting on angelic guidance and a member of the invisible fraternity of Christ's body : the Church which transcends space and time. It seems to me that Maier held both views at once : that the essence of the Fraternity was spiritual but there was yet some kind of organisation somewhere - or that there *ought* to be. It is noteworthy in this context that in 1619 Augustus of Anhalt, for whom Maier was working, along with Moritz von Hessen proposed a *Societas Hermetica* for the explicit study of Hermetic science while Augustus' brother Ludwig founded the *Fruchtbringende Gesellschaft* (Fruit-bringing society) : a select order dedicated to the cultural renewal of Germany in the same year (Andreae was a member). Maier may also have known of Andreae's ideological centrality to the original movement. Maier's *Themis Aurea* (Frankfurt, 1618) not only gives the rules of the Fraternity (extrapolations from the *Fama & Confessio*) but also offers clues as to where it could be found :

> We cannot set down the places where they meet, nor the time. I have sometimes observed Olympick Houses not far from a river, and known a city which we think is called S.Spiritus - I mean Helicon or Parnassus, in which Pegasus opened a spring of overflowing water wherein Diana washed herself, to whom Venus was handmaid and Saturn gentleman usher. This will sufficiently instruct an intelligent reader, but more confound the ignorant.

Here Maier clearly sees himself as one of the intelligent as distinct from the (already) confounded ignorant. Maier was brilliant at linking up Greek and Egyptian mythology into a complex alchemical system, regarding the ancient myths as allegories for alchemical processes. A dedicated reader might well check up with his beautifully produced collection of alchemical emblems[46] where he or she would find in Emblem XII a delightful engraving, almost certainly by Matthieu Merian (De Bry's son-in-law), of a figure with a scythe (Saturn) flying above a mountain whilst vomiting out a large indigestible rock or (rejected) stone. Below the mountain is a little chapel with a cross on it, built into the side of an escarpment (into Nature?) whose steps lead down to a stream which flows about the mountain (Helicon). Behind the mountain is a river with a graceful city built on the opposite banks. Venus is present in the lush vegetation which surrounds the scene. The theme of the Emblem is written in Latin and German and tranlates as follows : "The Stone which Saturn ate for his son Jove, vomited, is then put on Mount Helicon for the remembrance of mankind." Without pursuing the eloquent symbolism to the ends, we can say that Saturn (as Cronos : Time and Death), famous in the Greek myth for swallowing his children and vomiting them out again, is here placed in the positive rôle (following Plutarch's *On the Ei at Delphi*) of Saturn as a *redemptive* figure, that is to say that the *swallowing*, according to the Neoplatonic scheme, represents *the return of the Many to the One*. Partaking of the Chemical Stone re-unites the cosmos to its source. This is the fundamental theme of the emblem. Plutarch wrote that :

> When the god is changed and distributed into winds, water, earth, stars, plants, and animals, they describe this experience and transformation allegorically by the terms "dismemberment" and "rending". They apply to him the names Dionysius, Zagreus, Nyctelius, Isodaites, and they construct allegorical myths in which the transformations that have been described are represented as death and destruction followed by restoration to life and rebirth.

Plutarch (AD 46-120) was a priest at the centre of the Greek Mysteries at Delphi, and Delphi lies between the great mountains of Parnassus in the west and Helicon in the east[47]. The German humanist Conrad Celtes took the idea of Pegasus the winged horse producing a fountain on Helicon (when brushing the mountain with his hooves) as the theme for a woodcut made in 1507 after learning of the 'pagan trinities' of Neoplatonic interpretation in Italy. Pegasus clearly stands as an image for the *Holy Spirit*.

Furthermore, Andreae was also more than familiar with the Christian interpretation of classical mythology. It had become both customary and somewhat prosaic in sixteenth century Germany simply to equate Greek gods and goddesses with respectable Christian figures *viz* : Jupiter=God the Father; Apollo=Christ; Minerva=Mary; Hermes=S.John the Baptist; Pegasus=the dove of the Holy Spirit. Andreae's *Chymical Wedding* is peppered with such associations. Note for example the copper kettle upon the tripodic sepulchre in the vault of Venus on Day Five of the Chemical Wedding. In the kettle is a tree which drops its *fruit* into the kettle and then into three smaller golden kettles from which the lustrous liquid overflows. Christian Rosenkreuz is informed that when the tree is all melted, its fruit will produce a King. This triadic arrangement is almost certainly a reference to the three Neoplatonic Graces who in their outgoing, receiving and return, embody the dynamic Venus. Whoso partakes of the melted tree which has flowed through the three golden kettles (the Graces) will be "a King", that is : the philosophical Child whose mother is Venus, that is: *Love*. Where there is active Love, *there* is the Fraternity : the children of Love.

Andreae's theatrical romance *TURBO*, published (like the *Chymische Hochzeit*) in 1616, declares its mythical source on the title page (on which is an engraving of a tree weighed down heavily with fruit). The book derives this time not from Lazarus Zetzner but from *HELICONE juxta parnassum* : Helicon near Parnassus (Parnassus being the mountain of the poets) - and that is of course the same artistic source as the *Fama Fraternitatis*. It would seem that Maier was at least to a degree 'in on the gag'. It should also be stated that acquaintance with this kind of rich initiatic symbolism, whose aim can best be described as *gnosis*, does in fact produce an invisible fraternity among those who have glimpsed the mysteries. In this sense a secret Fraternity *does* exist - and anyone can enter in who *sees* and siezes the point. This was certainly the point-of-view of Andreae and Besold. The question, as always in Hermetic matters, is one of perception.

The Devil in Paris

In 1621 - a late date in the history of the Rosicrucian furore - one of the rare Catholic commentators, Philip Geiger, weighed in with his Counter-Reformation inspired *Warnung für der Rosenkreutzer* (Warning against the Rosicrucians) after Frederick and Elizabeth (the 'Winter King and Queen of Bohemia') had been defeated and exiled to the

Hague while their beautiful capital of Heidelberg was being sacked by the Catholic army of the Duke of Bavaria. It was being widely touted by Catholic opponents that Frederick had used witchcraft in (what they saw as) his machinations against the Catholicity of the Holy Roman Empire. The Rosicrucians became objects of a witch-scare as part of a massive pro-Habsburg propaganda campaign. In France the conspiracy-angle really took off. According to Gabriel Naudé's *Instruction a la France sur la verité de l'histoire des Frères de la Rose-Croix* (Paris. 1623), placards appeared in the capital announcing that the Invisible Brothers were about to put in an appearance :

> We, being deputies of the principle College of the Brothers of the Rose Cross, are making a visible and invisible stay in this city through the Grace of the Most High, towards whom turn the hearts of the Just. We show and teach without books or marks how to speak all languages of the countries where we wish to be, and to draw men from error and death.

Naudé's view was that 'their' mission was altogether more sinister. Another work published in that year of 1623 was more specific : *Horrible Pacts made between the Devil and the Pretended Invisible Ones*. The publication of this nonsense was clearly intended, and seems to have succeeded, in creating a witch scare. This was no joke. The burning of witches was a regular occurrence during this period, and the justice available for such cases was invariably a mass of prejudice. According to the latter work - a kind of prototype for 300 years of Satan-scares - 36 Invisibles were dispersed about the world in groups of six. The meeting to decide to send their 'reps' to Paris had occurred, it says, in Lyons the previous June, and was followed by a Grand Sabbath at which a demon appeared in great lustre. His appearance then made the adepts imitate the accusations made against the Templars i.e : that they prostrated themselves before the evil-one and swore to abjure Christianity in all its aspects. For so selling their souls they obtained the power to travel with full pockets to whereso'er they wished and were granted the eloquence to attract dupes for the Devil. In a perversion of the *Fama's* rules, it says that they could not be recognised because they were attired as ordinary men.

Another book from the same year, *La doctrine curieuse des beaux ésprits de ce temps* (Paris, 1623) by the French Jesuit François Garasse, informs its readers that the Rosicrucians are a secret German sect run by their secretary, one Michael Maier. Their learning comes from the east - therefore it is heathenish - and in spite of appearances they are wicked, subversive sorcerers of universal danger who should be put to ignominious death on the gallows or wheel if captured. All this happened as Catholic armies poured into northern Germany : a progress of rapine and destruction characterised by a multiplication of witch-trials. It was all so much easier to murder your neighbour if you could pin on him or her an appropriate label : witch, sorcerer, heretic...*Rosicrucian*.

Naudé in his *Instruction* to victim-France does not go as far as Garasse. He says that the placards were put up to cause a bit of excitement by "some people". Furthermore, his position against the Rosicrucians is compromised since he favours much of the philosophy with which they are associated. He gives a fascinating list of the kind of authors approved by the Brotherhood. They include John Dee, Trithemius,[48] Francesco Giorgi,[49] the Hermetic *Pymander* (translated by François de Candale), Pontus de Tyard's Musical Theories (occult and Neoplatonic, and very influential), Giordano Bruno (and his book *On the shadows of ideas*. Paris, 1582), Ramon Lull (Alchemy), and a commentary on Magic by Paracelsus. Naudé cannot really say that these books are in themselves bad - 'tis the use they are put to - and that use is pernicious. The Rosicrucians must be charlatans, telling fables and distorting the truth. Interestingly he lumps their fancies in with Thomas More's *Utopia* and with Rabelais' *Abbey of Thelema* : a mythic establishment which will not gain concrete form for just under 300 years - when Aleister Crowley will found an 'Abbey' of this name in Sicily, abandoned in a flurry of press-led Satan-scares not entirely unrelated (from the psychological perspective) to the witch-scares of the 1620s.

Naudé must have felt conscious of having somewhat confused the issue by throwing in some favourite authors into the pot of paranoia brewing in Europe, for in 1625 he published an *Apology for Great men suspected of Magic*. In this work he maintains that innocent people are being attacked because the proper distinctions between types of magic are not observed. There are, he says, four kinds of magic : divine magic, Theurgy (freeing the soul from the body), Goetia (witchcraft), and natural magic, which is good science. Only *Goetia* is wicked. He suggests that people often become suspect for the wrong reasons : mathematical diagrams, because of their incomprehensible nature to the uneducated, frequently draw suspicion. This is not right, says Naudé. He wishes people could see John Dee's book on Friar Roger Bacon, then they would know that Bacon did not conjure demons. Try witches by all means, says Naudé - if, that is, you are sure that they are not religious magi or men of learning. The good magi according to Naudé are Zoroaster, Orpheus, Pythagoras, Socrates, Plotinus, Porphyry, Iamblichus, Ramon Lull, Paracelsus, Henry Cornelius Agrippa, Pico della Mirandola, and John Dee. It must have taken a certain amount of courage to publish the second book during the collective hysteria of the 1620s.

A kind of picture-magazine called *The Miseries and the evils of the War* was published in 1633 in Paris. It is a bit like the old *LIFE* magazine only instead of photographs there are a series of engravings made by a man called Israel for his friend Jacques Callot. The pictures come from the distant war. We see women being chased out of houses at the ends of halberds, the raising of armies, multiple violation of women, merciless hand-to-hand combat, men being suspended over fires and slow-roasted while their comrades cut throats and steal; regiments blasted by cannon-fire, the burning of churches, the looting of whole towns; whole armies watching burnings at the stake; men and women publicly broken on wheels erected in market-places while priests with crucifixes beg for recantation; row upon row of veterans with one leg, or walking with sticks to support wooden stumps while others pull themselves about on little sleds, limbless; beggars and starving peasants; men tearing the hearts out of victims and showing off severed heads to their fellow Christians; men hung from trees, young girls left in the mud as mothers and fathers weep; small bands of renegades and mercenaries out for anything they can find; public torture : men trussed up like turkeys and hung by the wrists from great gibbets built in town-squares, a great tree with over thirty captured enemies suspended from its branches, hung until their torsos fall from their necks; mass executions by firing-squad. This was the Thirty Years War - as real and cold and weird as any passage from the Apocalypse. And the verdict of the picture captions : "see how the guilty rebels pay for their treason!"

The Assassination of Truth

How did the authors of the Rosicrucian Manifestos react to this decade and more of mystery and madness - following the publication of the *Fama* in 1614? We shall never know what Tobias Hess thought of the *furor* because he died in Tübingen in the same year as Wessel published the *Fama*, much missed by his close friends Andreae, Joannes Stoffel, Wilhelm Bidembach and the lawyer Thomas Lanz, who wrote of Hess on 27 November of that year :

My Hippocrates has died, my Machaon, HESS, whose abilities made him a God to the sick. Sorrow protests here : "either he should not have been born, or he should not have passed away so soon." But reason said : "Hess was a peer to Job, unless he has born more crosses than he". But since this worn out world treads down on virtue and rewards those without merit instead of the meritorious, God has called this man of merit and now he is a citizen of Mount Olympus and he is full of joy, he, HESS, who before has been so unhappy.

For Christoph Besold the *furor* merely confirmed what he had always suspected about the stupidity and waywardness of humankind : curiosity satisfies, the truth can 'go by the board'. In 1634 he would convert to Catholicism : "A long-time wanderer got snatched away by the wind" is how Andreae described the occurrence in his Autobiography. Andreae reckoned Besold's knowledge was too vast for his move to Rome to carry much conviction. Andreae regarded the move as spiritual death. What seems most likely is that Besold's tired mind was simply sick to death of controversy. The on-going atrocities of the war must have made him see again that fighting over religious affiliation was utterly pointless. It seems his spiritual homeland was, in a sense (like the frustrated Victorian romantics who followed Cardinal Newman to Rome) in the (so-called) undivided Church of the Middle Ages. When his encyclopaedic *Orbis Novis Thesaurus* was published after the war he was content to use Libavius' entry to sum up the Rosicrucians : "Chiliasts, Prophets, reformers, Paracelsians, Paradise and Rose-garden dreamers..." In Besold's copy of the *Fama* (now in the university library of Salzburg) he wrote : "*Autorum suspicor J.V.A.*" There was no suspicion about it; he knew perfectly well of Andreae's contribution - but with the insanity of the war raging, it was wise to be discrete.

Besold's view of the world seems to be well embodied in the extract from Boccalini's *News from Parnassus* which was printed with the *Fama* in 1614. It is highly likely that Besold was the translator. The inclusion of the text ought to have alerted readers to the true nature of the manifesto : a *ludibrium* (as Andreae called it) - a dramatic joke with a serious intent. The "Reformation of the whole wide world" is presented in the Boccalini extract as universally desirable but practically impossible. In it we have the picture of Apollo holding court on Parnassus (remember *Helicon juxta Parnassus* as the source of Andreae's *Turbo* in 1616) where Pico della Mirandola is complaining that the noise of the reformers is preventing him from thinking! The news of the world heard on Parnassus is so bad - people are committing suicide rather than endure it any longer - that Apollo calls as many wise people as possible to debate how to reform the world. The big guns arrive : Socrates, Solon - all have their say. One suggests that the problem is that people lie, therefore it would be a good idea to put a window in their chests so you could see what their heart was thinking. Another objects that this would make social intercourse a matter of frustration. Another suggests that the problem is greed and money - therefore why not get rid of gold altogether and let everybody have the same? This is in turn rejected as producing social sterility, sameness, tedium and a loss of value. And so the arguments rage. Nobody can agree on the ideal solution to the ills of the world. Eventually, Apollo sighs at the terminal wisdom of the world and suggests announcing to the expectant crowds at the foot of the mountain - who are anxiously attending the court's deliberation - that the prices of vegetables are to be lowered. The result : widespread rejoicing![50] It should not be difficult to imagine how a man who saw the humour of this would regard the Rosicrucian *furor*.

And Andreae, what of him? In April 1614 he married the niece of Bishop Erasmus Grüninger (Besold became godfather to his three children, along with Abraham Hölzl and Wilhelm Wense[51]) and settled into a tireless Christian ministry in Vaihingen, not far from Tübingen. What with the death of Hess and these new assumptions of responsibility, Andreae's imaginative mind was doubtless steadied to some extent. However, that mind had already been moving towards a more serious approach to the problems of Germany before the *Fama* was published. He was under the eye of his father-in-law. Furthermore, Andreae was attacked by members of the university as a dreamer with dangerous views, as a friend of the Paracelsian Hess, as a social revolutionary, suspected heretic, secret magician. At some stage he would have to justify himself and make it clear to all what it was that he stood for. His first task was to clear his table of unpublished writings so that he could devote himself to his main work of presenting unambiguously his own conception of the ideal fraternity.

Andreae was twenty-eight years old when he began the editing and re-writing process, and his work had attained a new maturity. It would be easy for him to disown his older work to some extent as the peregrinations of a young mind. With regard to the *Fama*, that task would be even easier since the *furor* demonstrated the need not only for himself, but for German religious culture in general to 'grow up'. In his Autobiography[52] Andreae wrote that he had devoted the early months of 1610 to a number of writings which were later brought to the light of day by the agency of other people. It is difficult to find any candidates for these works other than the *Fama Fraternitatis* and a reworking of the *Chymical Wedding of Christian Rosenkreuz*. Perhaps it was Andreae or one of his associates who brought the *Chymical Wedding* to Jungius, Lazarus Zetzner's reader in Strasbourg. After the publication of the *Confessio Fraternitatis* in 1615 - the second 'manifesto' almost certainly conceived and directed by Tobias Hess (but not intended for publication) - it might have struck Andreae that it would be interesting for someone to consider his youthful work written (he notes in his Autobiography) in 1605. The *Chymische Hochzeit* would have to appear to all but the dullest dolt as a work of fiction, he doubtless thought. Thus people might get the idea that the *Fama* should also be regarded as a specialist type of literature. It could be that Andreae was trying to save the day before the Rosicrucian business got completely out of hand. Alas the *Chymical Wedding* was taken as yet another hieratic pronouncement from the mysterious Brotherhood.

The *Chymical Wedding* was published in 1616 along with two other works which should have had the effect of neutralising the absurd notion that the weird Brotherhood of Christian Rosenkreuz actually existed, as well as guiding enthusiasts of the *Fama* into the direction in which Andreae wished them to go. One gets the feeling that for the first two or three years after the publication of the *Fama* Andreae was more or less pleased to keep the pot boiling so long as his works might influence the outcome of the *furor*. Andreae's initial pleasure in the sport is revealed in a speech put in the mouth of *Alethea* (=Truth) in his *Christian Mythologies*, published in January 1618 :

> When it came about, not a long time since, that some on the literary stage were arranging a play scene of certain ingenious parties, I stood aside as one who looks on, having regard to the fashion of the age which seizes with avidity on new-fangled notions. As spectator, it was not without a certain quality of zest that I beheld the battle of the books and marked subsequently an entire change of actors.

Andreae after 1617 would change his tune, and, as we shall see, it is not difficult to see why. Nevertheless, 1616 marked a good beginning for Andreae's life as a published writer. We can see him facing up to his own youthful escapist drives in *Turbo*.[53] *Turbo* is a beautiful work on a Faust-like theme but with the emphasis on the search for wisdom rather than power. The play tells of how Turbo (a play on the alchemical work the *Turba philosophorum*) studies, then goes to France where he has a disappointing love-affair. He puts all his hopes into alchemy. The treatment of alchemy is somewhat ambiguous, since it is a scenario for charlatanism, especially where the "accursed gold-making" is concerned : a practice ridiculed in the *Fama*. Andreae is emphasising the spiritual alchemy which leads to the regenerated human-being. Alchemists are mocked in *Turbo* as devotees of 'Beger', an anagram of that famous Arabic alchemist known to the west as Geber. We are also introduced to Andreae's *alter-ego* Peregrinus, who reappears in two works, one published in 1618 and the other in 1619.[54] In these succeeding works we find the signs of the new Andreae. After years of wandering among the errors of the world - the "land of errors"- Peregrinus arrives in Elysium. His steadfastness in the face of the world's manifold illusions (cf : Bunyan's later Vanity Fair in *The Pilgrim's Progress*) earns him a new life given by God, the "highest doctor". Peregrinus changes and becomes a new man. In fact he becomes a Christian. The new attitude is clear in the dialogue between 'Christianus' (a kind of retired Peregrinus) and 'Curiosus' written for *Menippus* a year before *Civis Christianus* in 1617, and which was quoted at length earlier. Now I hope we are beginning to get a glimpse of where Andreae 'was coming from' and why he was to become so impatient with the Rosicrucian Furore.

Later in the year (1619) Peregrinus will appear yet again, washed up on the shore of a mysterious island while his heart is being cleaned. The island contains the object of Andreae's utopian masterpiece : the city of Christianopolis[55], Andreae's ideal civic society, full of science, medicine, art, idealism, harmony, cosmic consciousness, practical charity - all running under benign angelic care. This latter work must have been in England's Sir Francis Bacon's mind when he published *his* ideal island civilisation in his *New Atlantis* (1627), another Utopian, Rosicrucian-inspired classic, and itself an inspirer of enlightened scientific advance throughout the years of the Civil War in Britain and the Thirty Years War in Germany.

Andreae's first batch of printed writings also included the *Theca*[56]. This book offers clear evidence that Andreae and Hess participated in the production of the *Confessio Fraternitatis*[57]. The *Theca* retains those passages of the *Confessio* with reference to the superiority of the Bible and associated pious observations. The words of the *Confessio* regarding the highest philosophy which "containeth much of Theology and medicine, but little of the wisdom of the law" reappear in the *Theca*. The Naometrian and chiliastic material is rejected outright, considered by Andreae to be products of the *curiosi*. The references to the R.C. Brothers are replaced by references to "the good", the "humble" : those chosen by God as 'His own' who can interpret his signature in His Creation and in His Word. Was this work put out to defend Hess's reputation after the calumny thrown at him in his lifetime by academic 'colleagues' at Tübingen? The book says that it owes its authorship to Hess "in part from published works" chosen and "in part suggested by the consideration of pious thoughts." However in 1642 a communication from Andreae to Augustus of Braunschweig contradicts this, saying that it was his own work.

There is still an enigma surrounding the *Theca* but happily it is of no great importance to us - suffice to say that it shows the literary involvement of Andreae and Hess in the genesis of the Rosicrucian movement, an involvement also supported by Joannes Arndt's close friend Melchior Breler who was physician to Augustus of Braunschweig (Andreae's friend and patron) and who wrote that the *Fama* was assuredly written by "three eminent men" in order to discover the Philosopher's Stone.

In 1617 Andreae had a shot at hitting two birds with one (philosopher's) stone. Firstly, the incessant communications begging entry into the Fraternity of the Rose-Cross and secondly, Andreae's first explicit printed attempt to define the essence of Christian spirituality. His method was gentle. He invites his readers to join the *Fraternitas Christi* : the Fraternity of Christ. Entry is free. No magical skills are necessary but it might require some very hard work[58]. How many would wish to be a candidate for membership in a spiritual Brotherhood whose only aim was sacred love? There was no furore.

In this beautiful little book Andreae contrasts the world, inspired and governed by Satan, with the little number of real Christians. Although they are few, they are yet secure on the perfidious ocean in the little *barca* of Christ, whose mast is the cross. (Journeying across the oceans to the mystical homeland is another favourite image of Andreae - as is that of discovering wonders in secret vaults). Christianity in its deepest and purest form (invisible to the world) is the great fraternity worth responding to because Christ's love wanted it to be so. Those who enter become "friends of God", a designation used, incidentally, by the medieval Cathars for those who joined them. Andreae links the life of this Fraternity to the exploration of nature. Looking at the magnificent harmony which men of learning have discerned in the cosmos, what more beautiful task exists, asks Johann Valentin, than to discover the wisdom of the creator in all its creatures?

Such study requires effort, disciplined, arduous, prolonged *work*. Renunciation is required, not lust for power. The true scientist, if he is to be true, needs be a man of God Whose Mind is discernible in all things. In the same year Andreae will personify this attitude in the figure of Christianus. Magic is neither more nor less than the diligent study of all the sciences. The method of magic : hard work and perseverence. *Christianus* is contrasted to *Curiosus*, the person who believes that magic is a short-cut to the truth. According to Andreae the search for the Truth requires self-mastery and Christian discipleship : disciple, as in *discipline*. The greater part of mankind are characterised as the *curiosi*, forever distracted by the latest new thing, unconsciously gripped by the Satan of the world; trapped among the vanities of the world, they live in chains they cannot feel. The supreme reason is not to listen to human reason but to believe in God who is omnipresent, omniscient, just and merciful and to manifest faith in reality. Only the heart inhabited by God is really aware of the authentic philosophy, the aim of whose study is to regenerate man who, on becoming regenerate, is made son, brother and heir to the wealthiest fraternity imaginable : true cosmic citizenship.

What a contrasting sight greeted Andreae's eyes in October 1617! The potential citizens of the cosmos had other things on their minds. Pamphlets flew from one end of Europe to the other. Theologians bickered, tempers flared, knives were drawn. It was the centenary year of the Reformation - 100 glorious years of 'freedom'!

Meanwhile, news was arriving from Bohemia. Ferdinand, persecutor of the Styrian Protestants had been advanced to the thrones of Hungary and Bohemia and planned to succeed his elderly cousin Matthias as Holy Roman Emperor. Ferdinand did not give a *mark* for promises made to the Bohemian Protestants. He was a Counter-Reformer and believed that the sword was more powerful than the pen. Back in Tübingen, self-congratulation was the order of the day. Lutheran orthodoxy was there to stay. *What a joy to be in the Truth! What a pleasure to have taken the Right Side!* This is how Andreae saw through what he sincerely considered to be a vast hypocritical illusion. He put pen to paper and wrote one of the most brilliant and precise works of practical satire ever written : *Menippus*[59].

The title-page gave its source as *Cosmopolis* : City of the Cosmos. The book was dedicated to the "sensible and simple" people of the Antipodes, implying that his own hemisphere was ridiculous. Andreae took on the whole German situation. He declared that the true Christian athletes for evangelical purity, Luther and his friends -

men who aimed in the first instance to spiritualise and revive the Church had been betrayed by a fantasy, a joke. (The reference to Luther and the popular reformers was a necessary courtesy which, once made, slips out of the main picture. Andreae was no simple Protestant).

The author of *Menippus* did not pull his punches. As far as he was concerned, to serve Christianity was to serve the Truth : to tell it like it is. Andreae set about pouring some light into the dim cave in which the fools lived, congratulating one another, backbiting each other, jealous of one other, impatient with one another, judging one another, destroying one another. Johann Valentin Andreae believed the pen was mightier than the sword.

Dr Carlos Gilly (to whom we should all be indebted for having discovered and undertood the value of so much 'new' Rosicrucian material) has described *Menippus* as a work coming from the "radical left-wing of the Reformation", and I believe him to be absolutely right. The 61st discourse, for example, calls in no uncertain terms for full religious tolerance. A person's belief should not be linked to the state he was born in. All religions contain good people. Andreae followed the Spanish radical Giacomo Aconcio in declaring all theological disputes to be unimportant. Heretics do not exist. They are created in the minds of theologians, who seem to have nothing better to do. It is always pious people who are branded as being "impious" or heretical. University professors should listen to the "exemplary martyrdom" of the Anabaptists who are rejected by those who consider themselves educated. Christ will recognise His own, even in the flames.

Andreae denies the right of Christians to make religious judgements. It is clear that there are Christians who surpass even the barbarians in cruelty and torture, frequently applied over matters where no definitive judgement exists, frequently applied in dark places with torture instruments, threats and fire. Those who shout loudest against the Machiavellian character of the aristocracy are themselves the most Machiavellian. Machiavellianism has always existed. All Machiavelli was doing was plainly stating the perennial wheelings and dealings of the ruling classes. If Andreae had wished 'to make friends and influence people' he would not have written *Menippus*. It brought him more hatred and envy than any other work. He was on his way to becoming an intellectual exile. Copies of *Menippus* were confiscated in Tübingen. Andreae had upset the *status quo*.

An extremely dangerous attack came in vocal and printed form from Tübingen's professor of oratory, Caspar Bücher. Bücher described *Menippus* as an "alchemical abortion" : the author biting the hand that had fed him, putting him in the rank of low-level ranters, haters of learning such as Karlstadt : a notorious anti-intellectual and Anapbaptist radical. In disguised form, Bücher hinted that all the world knew who this 'Menippus' was. (The book had been published anonymously). Everyone knew that he belonged to the circle of Tobias Hess and that they planned a quixotic 'reformation of the whole world'. Was Andreae thinking of Bücher and his slander against his late friend Hess when he wrote the following in *The Immortality of Hess*?

> Now, where are you, who force your paper peerage down everyone's throat, while he [Hess] covered his noble birth, you, who pretend to have friends in the highest circles, where he just stayed away from them; you, who beg the great ones to tip you, while he disdained huge salaries, you, who gather the crumbs of the rich, while he did not wish to brush shoulders with the upper-classes. No-one else but our Hess would have been able to resist the temptations of court life, the ambushes of money and the tickles of homages, for he was inaccessible to the invitations of the wealthy, but free and open-handedly reacted to requests of anybody else.

The storm around *Menippus* led to a swift second edition, but Andreae hesitated to follow it up with his next work, *Christian Mythologies*.[60] He had already lost friends over *Menippus* and there was his family to think about, and his future as a writer. Andreae thought it out and with the encouragement of genuine friends set to publishing his new collection. Andreae says he must speak out; not to do so would be a criminal sin. If Truth hides herself, even the stones would cry out : "We are not going, by the horror of our predecessor's faults, to sin by default where they sinned by excess", wrote Andreae. This time he would nail his colours to the mast and put his name to the work. The theme of the book is nothing less than the *Truth*.

The title-page shows the gates to a temple. On either side of the gates are simple pictures showing all the creative deeds of man, precisely portrayed so that every visitor can learn a basic framework for knowledge without having to wade through an entire library: Theology; Mathematics; Grammar; Politics; History; Mechanics and Agriculture. At the base is a head with three faces. Looking to the left towards the word 'Truth' is the face of a youth. In the centre : middle-age; and looking to the right, where is written the 'Good' is an aged face. The three ages each bear an inscribed imperative : for youth, *discuss it*; for middle-age, *pursue it*; for old age : *be wise*.

Andreae followed Theodore Zwinger, whom he much admired, in using simple pictures as educational aids (rare at the time), an educational ideal more fully expressed in Andreae's *Christianopolis* which both Zwinger and Andreae's younger contemporary and correspondent Comenius both believed in. The aim was to make the entrance to the Temple of Science as straightforward a matter as possible, without pomposity and obscurantism, so prevalent and damaging a feature of the university life which he parodies so successfully. *Christian Mythologies'* collection of allegories and fables 'takes on' alchemists, astrological calendar-makers, the Rosicrucian Furore, the class-system, Scepticism, the Universities, Error and the exile of Truth. Andreae also gives an answer to Bücher's savage personal attack on him.

> There are two kinds of *literati* I especially fear; the too-talkatives and crafty exponents of dialectic and rhetoric. Because they try to convince me of what they want and want to blame me for anything they like.

Andreae says that such people are always trying to make people believe that they live in the most learned and God-fearing time of all times, and that anyone who criticises this is guilty of treason against the Fatherland[61].

> If anyone dares saying that one should not let the unworthy become teachers and doctors, then he is immediately interpreted as trying to undermine the upper-classes. If a man says that the young should learn languages, then he gets the answer that you should emigrate to the Garamants of Libya. Should one criticise that the doctor and tutor title could only be had by paying large sums of money, the answer comes back that society cannot consist of tailors and cobblers alone. If one maintained the view that to address people with very long titles is barbaric, then you would be for all times proclaimed as an adherent of Karlstadt. And if one further objected that the poor people are treated like animals, this would mean refusal to accept your superiors. If a man should preach reciprocal love, he would immediately be called a Rosicrucian. If you would ask for more freedom, the people would fear that all the barriers were coming down. And more : if you don't like to swear, then you're an Anabaptist. If you dislike boozing and feasting, then you're a Papist; if you fight against prostitution, then you will be taken for a fanatic and a dreamer; if you try not to lie, then you must be a disciple of Schwenckfeld; and if lastly you dislike pictures and pomp, then you are certainly taken to be a Calvinist.

Andreae hits the nail on the head, time and time again. Regarding the Rosicrucian Furore, Andreae comes up with an extraordinary and painful inversion of the myth of the discovery of the tomb of Christian Rosenkreuz, linking it directly to his attack on corruption.

Andreae envisions a scene where a number of his contemporaries, following certain indices, discover a secret vault. In an almost sick parody of the *Fama* the explorers break down a wall, whereafter torches in hand they enter the darkness. Bearing their fiery torches aloft they discover a modest sarcophagus with an inscription upon it : *mea tempora* - 'my times'. The men anxiously remove the lid. Inside the sarcophagus lies a cadaver, horribly mutilated, soiled and decaying, the flesh consumed. After great effort they succeed in uncovering a beautiful bronze plaque by the cadaver's rotting head :

I, THE TRUTH
DAUGHTER OF GOD
ASSASSINATED
BY THE DUPLICITY OF SATAN
BY THE CORRUPTION OF THE WORLD
BY THE FEEBLENESS OF THE FLESH
BY THE DESPOTISM OF TYRANNY
BY THE INDOLENCE OF THE PRIESTS
BY THE MALIGNITY OF POLITICS
BY THE SUPERFICIALITY OF HISTORIANS
BY THE FOLLY OF THE WISE
BY THE STUPIDITY OF THE PEOPLE

I REST HERE
WITHIN THE MUD OF THE LIE
IN ONE HUNDRED YEARS
THE SUN WILL SEE ME AGAIN
GREETINGS O POSTERITY!

This is the tomb of Truth. In a startling image, Andreae has succeeded in condensing his entire outlook and the real substance of the *Fama* as well. As the 'myth' continues, once this crushing epitaph is published all who read it react with a mixture of sadness and joy. The past is vilified for not understanding the error. The response of one observer (Bücher?) is to exalt the present, while another erects a magnificent funerary monument to dignify the rediscovered Truth, adding the following words to those on the plaque :

If we had lived
in the times of our fathers
We would have been their accomplices
in the assassination of the Truth

This is Andreae with the gloves off. It is a sign of the perversity of the world that while his Rosenkreuz fantasy is remembered, this devastatingly truthful work lies rotting in obscure libraries. The Truth *is* assassinated...

As ought to be crystal clear by now, the essential proposition of the *Christian Mythologies* is the resurrection and the return of the Truth. Truth is not to be found in the world but in the *sacra universitas*, the holy city. The door to this bastion is inscribed with the following : *The Word of God*. Andreae is still working for the spiritual reformation. Rejected by the masses, dishonoured by the philosophers and pseudo-savants, unwanted at court and repudiated by the Church, Truth had no choice but to exile herself. In Andreae's dialogue between *Philalethes* (Lover of Truth) and *Alethea* (Truth), the former seeks refuge in *Eleutheropolis* (from the Greek *eleutheros*=liberty) the City of Liberty, but this country of Liberty is only a Utopia[62]. Besides, Truth is faithful and still hopes that the darkness extending over Germany is only an eclipse, and that at some time the Light - not the 'last light of the apocalypse' - will shine again in all its startling glory. Social inequalities will cease as will all things that stem from the gulf between belief and practice.

With regard to the Rosicrucian Fraternity - *what, **that** again!* one can almost hear Andreae saying - the imaginary fraternity which promised so much in its conception, the whole business has gone beyond a joke:

> Most indubitably I - Alethea [Truth] - hold nothing in common with this Brotherhood... seeing that at this present the theatre is filled with altercations, with a great clash of opinion, that the fight is carried on by vague hints and malicious conjectures, I have withdrawn myself utterly, that I may not be involved unwisely in so dubious and slippery a concern.

Andreae's succeeding works represent not only an elucidation of what he stood for but also, it seems to me, a kind of expiation for his share of the responsibility in setting off such a cavalcade of bizarreries, for encouraging the "little curiosity brothers", those who preferred, as he put it, "some artifical or strange way" to the simple, beautiful truth. And yet even in the madness was method, for it is without doubt true that the search for the fictitious Brotherhood has led - and *still* leads people to a real experience of the spiritual life - and if the Rosicrucian idea was truly inspired, then are we to deny that it was anything less than the spirit of love which inspired him?

Perhaps most touching in the *Christian Mythologies* are Johann Valentin Andreae's heartfelt words reserved for the two men who, he says, have influenced him the most : Tobias Hess and Christoph Besold. Indeed, the last of the three books is dedicated to Besold :

> I owe a little to a lot of people. To very few, I owe a lot. To you, excellent man, I owe everything. Because whatever you initiated in and for me for so many years, now others who were jealous and envious of you, now shout out with trumpets, as if it were their own.

Andreae calls Time

In 1619 Andreae turned his attention for the last time to his most remembered creation, the Fraternity of the Rose-Cross. The *furor* was getting in the way of the truth; the *Fama* had ceased to be an enlightening phenomenon. While initially it had made people stop and think - and Andreae was content to watch its progress with a chuckle, now it was a "fantasy": "the heart and scandal of occultism in our time". "Would that the remaining chimes and little bells by which this fable was noised abroad be melted down; I mean that I wish their prolific writings would all go up in smoke!"[63] It should be noted that he refers to *their* prolific writings : the dozens of comments on the *Fama*, the speculations, the claims, the hysteria. *He* knew what the *Fama* was all about, and he was content to know some few others now did as well. He did not stand in the way of Joachim Morsius when the latter visited him in Calw in 1629. Ambivalence was central to Andreae's genius.

In *Turris Babel*[64] Andreae finally 'called time' on the furore. He reckoned that those who claimed to be Rosicrucians could well be Christian (the implicit but *unseen* fraternity of humankind) but that the manifold writings referring to his non-existent Brotherhood tended to attract the *curiosi* who want fancy spectacles without having tried to use their own eyes first. Andreae set his sights clearly, once and for all :

> I shall cultivate the religion of Christ; I shall respect the government of Christ; I shall devote myself to Christian knowledge; I shall embrace the Christian way of life; I shall delight myself with the roses of

Christianity and shall bear its cross; I shall uphold Christianity's order, and shall submit to its discipline; I shall live as a Christian and I shall die as a Christian. And then it will truly happen - to use their words - that IESVS MIHI OMNIA.

Johann Valentin Andreae and History

The following statement appears in Dame Frances Yates' last book, *The Occult Philosophy in the Elizabethan Age*[65] :

> Many suggestions as to the origin of the name [Rosicrucian] have been made, but in moving along the historical line which we are following, the suggestion which seems most likely is that the [Francesco] Giorgi type of Christian Cabala acquired this name when it became associated with Elizabethanism, with the Tudor Rose, with [John] Dee's scientific British imperialism, with a messianic movement for uniting Europeans against the Catholic-Habsburg powers.

The Yates view of a British origin for the Rosicrucian movement, tied in directly to movements around the election of Frederick V of the Palatinate with Christian Rosenkreuz a Germanicised version of Spenser's 'Red Cross knight' from the *Faerie Queen* will simply not hold water. It is almost completely misleading. A full analysis of the life and associations of Johann Valentin Andreae removes the need for such a broad-sweep approach.

Andreae has been too often regarded as a kind of weird, strange or fringe figure, at one with the kind of literature sparked off by the publication of the *Fama*. Andreae was a most serious 'player' in the period, intellectually exiled not for strange occult opinions but because he had the courage to describe things as they were. Was then the man who wrote the *Fama* a 'Rosicrucian'? In terms of what that word has come to denote, we had better say that he was not. It would be more correct to think of him as a 'left-wing' radical reformer of exceptional wisdom, knowledge, inspired cynicism and practical spiritual experience; he was certainly not a hot-head or automatic rebel. His writings on the social system of Germany in his day are remarkably prescient and advanced. Christian Socialists of the nineteenth century such as F.D. Maurice could claim him as a (superior) predecessor without doing violence to Andreae's real place in history (which of course utterly transcends politico-religious socialism). Furthermore, his scientific views were extremely advanced and aware. In the battle

(1623-1633) between the Rosicrucianist and Paracelsian Dr Robert Fludd and the 'mechanistic philosophy' of the Jesuit Marin Mersenne (friend and promoter of René Descartes) stimulated by the Rosicrucian Manifestos, it is obvious to this author that Andreae would have sought a harmony between the world as experienced by the senses and the world as conceived in the spirit.

The appalling split between spirit and matter, of which Descartes has been seen as the harbinger, could easily have been avoided if truth had not been buried in sectarian squabbling. (Scientists and philosophers can be sectarians too - a mentality Andreae tried so hard to abolish). It has taken well over 300 years to establish the open-mindedness which could have been, and should have been established as a principle of learning in the seventeenth century. This split between the respective realities of mind and matter lies behind the intuitive suspicion of the *modern* which has driven people of feeling and intuition into near-despair as the orthodoxy of single-minded, blind and pathetically confident materialism has been thrust ever more desperately upon the world : a vain sense of security which is still held to be the 'distinctive contribution' of the West to world culture[66].

Was Andreae an occultist? This question is anachronistic for the early seventeenth century. The idea of 'occultism' as a separate subject or fringe discipline is a relatively late development. What we would call 'scientific' and occult mentalities interwove in this period. One needs only to recall the now generally recognised fact that Sir Isaac Newton spent more time on alchemy than he did on gravitational science to realise that *Nature* for the men of learning had become an infinitely fascinating vista where all manner of unknown energies operated. Newton was happy simply to illuminate one area of the cosmic picture which indicated an harmonious, mathematically intelligible structure. Andreae would have been delighted to read Newton's *Principia*. Undoubtedly the greatest praise for mathematics as a discipline in the Renaissance and its aftermath came from highly gnosticised magi such as Pico della Mirandola and John Dee. The gripe of men like Andreae was not against the *idea* of Magic, (Andreae was a keen and advanced mathematician) but of its perversion in cheap, marketable form as in for example, popular astrology, and claims for all-embracing knowledge systems built on a portion of insight (such as Khunrath's *Amphitheatrum Sapientiae Aeternae*. 1598).

'Magic' for Andreae embraced all aspects of knowledge, since it is above all a *natural* system of thought, resting on the awareness that nature is magical : seen through the right eyes it bears a spiritual quality ("*Was Solomon in all his glory arrayed as one of these?*"). For Andreae, Magic does not mean Myth. It does not mean woolly-thinking and above all it does not mean escapism. While the image of the stage-'magician' has unfortunately dominated the usage of the word magic in the West (when it is not seen as a 'black art'), it is clear that the cosmos can be seen as one vast magician's topper, continually bringing forth the unknown and the marvellous. If we limit our emotional and spiritual response to the universe as scientists, it is merely to concentrate on the measuring of new phenomena. Scientists without awe and wonder do not make the *best* scientists. It is not surprising that our culture is experiencing a reaction to the myopic dogmatism of *scientism*, that is, science as a belief system. It is, I think, remarkable and regrettable how many second-rate theologians and philosophers have hung onto the hem of dogmatic scientism's garment in the hope of godless miracles.

Was Andreae a Gnostic? Dr. Carlos Gilly put it this way to me in 1989 :

> The Rosicrucian Movement was undoubtedly a gnostic movement. However, if any of the authors of the Rosicrucian Manifestos had been asked if he considered himself a Gnostic, he'd have answered that he did not. At that time, the image that people had of Gnostics was practically handed to them by the writings of the opposing side : the one-sided writings of the Fathers of the Church who had fought Gnostics from the first centuries of Christianity. However, within the Rosicrucian Manifestos can be found many elements of traditional Gnosis so that the Manifestos can be seen as a kind of ring in the chain which goes from Valentinian Gnosis, the Gnosis of the 2nd and 3rd centuries after Christ; passing through the Cathars, passing through the alchemists of the Middle Ages, passing through the mysticism of the Middle Ages; the Neoplatonic and Renaissance movement - and, above all, passing through Paracelsus.

Furthermore the gnostic character of the Rosicrucian thought-world was recognised at the time both by their enemies and particularly by the admirers of Jacob Böhme (such as Abraham von Frankenburg and Gottfried Arnold) with whose writings the Rosicrucian works were frequently associated and often read side by side with. There are many elements of Andreae's thought - not counting his early and fecund immersion in the world of alchemy - which are clearly of Hermetic provenance : the discipline of the senses; the refining of the mind in order to receive divine guidance; the suspicion of the material/ego -

(divorced from spirit) world as in the grip of Satan; the idea that life is a journey upon a perilous ocean towards a spiritual homeland; the idea of man locked in a prison[67] ; the emphasis on spirit and love over formal beliefs and works; the recognition of the transmundane light existing in all religions; his overwhelming sense of the Dignity of Man and the sorrow at seeing such a potentially divine creature behaving as a monster and, above all, his dramatic sense of the cosmic dimensions of human problems and the realisation that Christ's Kingdom - which for Andreae is a kind of joyful, anarchic, truly free-willed and spiritually-minded collective - is *not of this world*.

Nevertheless, Andreae's sense of the spiritual does not make him cower away from the fundamental facts of life. He would have us be "citizens of the world and not the foreign wanderer." This belief represents his fundamental faith in the mystery and magic of life - and the necessity to fully experience life so as to appreciate, when it comes, the divine *harmony* which, though Andreae believed it to be frequently invisible to us, nonetheless informs the 'system' as a whole.

Some Sufis have held the view that Christianity is an esoteric form of Judaism in its widest sense, and that the effort to make it into a formalised Church has obscured the heart of the matter. Andreae might have gone along with the substance of this view but only so long as we do not mean by the word 'esoteric' a side-line or specialist concept of the religion. The truth within Christianity was for Andreae as for other 'radicals' hidden to the eyes of the worldly : only in this sense might the truth be thought to be esoteric. He certainly saw the truth as exiled from the Church of his day, but his radicalism subsisted only in being faithful to the spirit of truth which has forever been to the mind of man something elusive, non-possessible, ambivalent and paradoxical - always confounding the "wisdom of the world". At first sight it always looks difficult. The obliqueness of the truth is merely a sign that the eyes of material perception are unfocused and out of kilter with reality. That *The Truth will make you free* was the Christian message Andreae most wished to be understood and acted upon.

Chapter Ten

Others have Laboured

And the king commanded, and they brought
great stones, costly stones, and hewed stones,
to lay the foundation of the house. And Solomon's
builders and Hiram's builders did hew them,
and the stone-squarers: so they prepared timber
and stones to build the house.
(I. *Kings*. V. 17-18.)

What are those golden builders doing? asked William Blake in his epic poem *Jerusalem*.[68]   A certain mystique once surrounded the art of building. Builders exhibited mighty powers; their successes were exemplary, their failures symbolic. Piercing spires strained for the supreme architect: the Creator Himself, architect of the infinite. And if, as John Dee maintained, the root of architecture lies principally in the imagination, then we may also consider the Hermetic principle whereby the cosmos is seen as the divine imagination projected, becoming visible to those in whom that divine imagination has been awoken. Thus enlivened, the architect or master mason becomes a spiritually significant figure. Dee the magus paraphrased the great Augustan architect Vitruvius' *Architectura* in his *Mathematical Preface* of 1570:

> An Architect (sayeth he) [Vitruvius in his *Architectura*] ought to understand Languages, to be skillfull of Painting, well instructed in Geometrie, not ignorant of Perspective, furnished with Arithmeticke, have knowledge of many histories, and diligently have heard Philosophers, have skill of Musike, not ignorant of Physike, know the aunsweres of Lawyers, and have Astronomie, and the courses Caelestiall, in good knowledge.

For the Hermetist, architecture is potentially magical. Therein lies its dignity, a dignity linked, moreover, to what the building contains. What of a building designed to contain that which cannot *be* contained? I refer of course to the Temple of Jerusalem which biblical tradition asserts was first built under the auspices of Solomon the Wise (c.961-922 BC).

And king Solomon sent and fetched Hiram out of Tyre: he was a
widow's son of the tribe of Naphtali, and his father was a man of Tyre,
a worker in brass : and he was filled with wisdom, and understanding,
and cunning to work all works in brass and he came to king Solomon,
and wrought all his work.   (I *Kings* VII. 13ff.)

A close reading of the New Testament and extant Dead Sea Scrolls
suggests that at the critical crux of 1ˢᵗ century Jewish religion lay the
question of the proper administration, meaning, and essential nature
of the Temple.

Documents from Qumran base much of their opposition to the
ruling priestly party in Jerusalem on the conception of a strict, purified
and ideal Temple. The first Christian martyr, Stephen, was stoned to
death for announcing its imminent destruction. Jesus himself[69]
entered Jerusalem to attack the Temple's commercial wing with
righteous indignation, thus securing his eventual arrest and
crucifixion. The 'abomination of desolation', whose appearance
would signify the final apocalypse (*Daniel* XI.31; *Mark* XIII.14) was
expected to appear in the Temple. The return of the Jews from exile
in Babylon in the fifth century BC was predicated on an imminent
reconstruction of the Temple. Figuring prominently in the gospels
and *Acts*, the Temple is where Jesus is presented to Simeon; it is where
the boy Jesus astonishes the chief rabbis. John the Baptist's father
Zacharias is a priest of the Temple. Jesus teaches his disciples in the
Temple. The Apostles pray in the Temple. Paul comes and goes to
the Temple in performance of the Nazarite vow. The Temple is
frequently the Big Question. But there is more to the matter than
mere ubiquity.

Therefore thus saith the Lord GOD, Behold, I lay in Zion for a
foundation a stone, a tried stone, a precious corner stone, a sure
foundation: he that believeth shall not make haste. Judgement also
will I lay to the line, and righteousness to the plummet and the hail
shall sweep away the refuge of lies, and the waters shall overflow the
hiding place. (*Isaiah* XXVIII.16)

The stone which the builders refused is become the head stone of the
corner. This is the LORD's doing; it is marvellous in our eyes. This is
the day which the LORD hath made; (*Psalm* 118. 22-24a).

Jesus of Nazareth based much of his radical doctrine on a precise re-
interpretation of the nature of the Temple.

And he beheld them [in the Temple], and said, What is this then that is written, The stone which the builders rejected, the same is become the head of the corner? Whosoever shall fall upon that stone shall be broken; but on whomsoever it shall fall, he shall be winnowed. (*Luke* XX. 17ff.)

Hit by the Stone

The stone that falls from heaven has left a traceable pedigree within Jewish apocalyptic and prophetic literature. It appears in the prophecies ascribed to Daniel (*Daniel* II. 34-35. c.160 BC) as a fatal projectile sent by God against the great image symbolising the empire of Nebuchadrezzar. The false image with 'feet of clay' is smashed on impact. Transformed into a mountain which covers the whole earth, the mountain reminds us that it is God who "rules the heavens". The polyvalent stone is supernatural.

In the quotation from *Luke* above, the falling stone of heavenly origin "winnows" the one on whom it falls; it divides the grain from the chaff. (Grain has a long-standing alchemical association with gold - Christian Rosenkreuz is described in the *Fama* as a grain hid in Christ for example). This process of winnowing occurs when the wheat is tossed into the air for the wind to do the work of division. The Hebrew word for 'wind' or breath is *ruach,* the word for spirit. The winnowing by the stone may be seen as a spiritual process, equivalent to the action of the philosopher's stone in alchemy. Perhaps Jesus knew of alchemy. It can certainly be argued that he understood the spiritual principles underlying it.

The coming of the stone is a salvific operation; it would be consistent for the believer to say that the best thing is to be *hit by the stone,* and remade into a new being. This is spiritual alchemy. In the alchemical context, the stone releases the divine spirit. Jesus identifies *himself* with the cornerstone of the Temple, the "precious" stone referred to by Isaiah.

And the chief priests and all the council sought for witness against Jesus to put him to death; and found none. For many bare false witness against him, saying, We heard him say, I will destroy this temple that is made with hands, and within three days I will build another made without hands[70]. (*Mark* XIV. 55-58).

The *Gospel of John* is more explicit. Following Jesus' rout of the Temple commerce, his enemies ask Jesus for an explanation:

> Jesus answered and said unto them, Destroy this temple, and in three days I will raise it up. Then said the Jews, Forty and six years was this temple in building, and wilt thou rear it up in three days? But he spake of the temple of his body. (*John* II.19ff).

Should we follow the symbolism literally, the Jesus of the *Gospel of John* is responsible for his own raising: "*I* will raise it up". Jesus appears to have the art of building at its highest degree. He can raise stones. He can raise himself. He can raise himself in another; he is an initiator:

> And he [Andrew] brought him [Simon] to Jesus. And when Jesus beheld him, he said, Thou art Simon the son of Jona: thou shalt be called Cephas, which is by interpretation, a stone. (*John*.I.42).

The new Temple envisioned by Yeshua ben Josef is made up of those who "worship God in spirit and in truth". These living stones, rejected by prevailing powers, are set in place by the appearance of the keystone within themselves, those who have been, as it were, 'hit' by the Stone and become divine: golden builders.

> The Jews answered him, saying, For a good work we stone thee not; but for blasphemy; and because that thou, being a man, makest thyself God. Jesus answered them, Is it not written in your law, I said, Ye are gods? (*John*. X.34).

The highest state for man, according to the Johannine *Logos*, is absorption in God whence the Logos derives, when "I and my Father are one." (*John* X.30). The *Logos* acts as the hidden stone, buried in the soul - and if fallen man is to be 'rebuilt', the stone must be recovered. The saviour's 'body' is made of the regenerated stones: the Temple. His followers become the new temple-in-the-making: a spiritual body.

The parallel of language here between alchemy and architecture is extraordinarily striking. However, much of that surprise comes from our being accustomed to imagine stone as an inert material; this was not the case among the ancients. Stones themselves could contain a secret power. Certain features of landscape might be indwelled by spirits. S. Paul in I *Corinthians* X refers to a rabbinic legend whereby the rock from which Moses drew water for the Children of Israel in the wilderness actually followed the Israelites around in their wanderings. Paul then goes on to say that "that spiritual rock which followed them: that rock was Christ." - a quite extraordinary idea until we consider that stones were associated in the ancient world with healing.

Josephus referred to how the Essenes had knowledge of healing stones. Thus was architecture deeply bound up with the idea of health: spiritual and consequently physical transformation. We are to 'put our own house in order'. This should help us to understand the origins of such alchemical terms as the 'philosopher's stone' and the 'elixir of life'. They denote the power to transform lower being into a higher state, to regenerate that floppy idiot called man into a living stone, a "house of fire" embodying God. According to gnostic tradition, the great stone - like the *Gral* of von Eschenbach and the *krater* containing divine *nous* of *Corpus Hermeticum* IV - comes from above:

> And he said to them [his opponents], Ye are from beneath; I am from above : ye are of this world; I am not of this world. *(John* VIII.23.)

The *Logos* is the 'lost word' of Free Masonry.

The Stones in Action

The value of the preceding metaphysics will become apparent as we examine two giants of the 17th. Century: two builders, two men who were 'hit by the Stone', and who in seeking the Stone became 'living stones', dedicated to the rebirth, renewal, and reconstruction of the temple of knowledge, nature and of the divine society. In the process, they contributed to the spiritual genesis of two significant institutions which have, at their best, attempted to aid the liberation of humankind from the bondage of material constraint: freemasonry and the Royal Society. I refer to Johann Amos Comensky (or Comenius, 1592-1671), and Elias Ashmole (1617-1692).

161

Comenius (1592-1671)

Between the Westerkerk and Damrak in the city of Amsterdam, visitors still come to the house where Comenius lived in the 1660s. This house was only one of many havens in a long life lived on the move.

In the year in which the *Fama Fraternitatis* was published in Cassel (1614), Comenius returned from the Palatinate to his beloved Bohemia. There he wrote a vast pansophic encyclopaedia, an integration of all knowledge written on the micro-macrocosmic principle, envisioning all natural things as part of an unbroken whole, the which whole included the human mind and the spiritual activity of God. He was encouraged in this work by Johann Valentin Andreae, for Comenius dedicated his efforts not to the private world of academe but to the cause of public enlightenment. The new age would be built on the principle of opening the 'book of nature' and the house of wisdom to all. In learning lay the key to liberation, the freedom of mind over matter. Learning was not to be the servant of the state or of industry or capital. Capital, industry and the state were to be the servants of learning - a principle we may consider of no little value today.

This passionate and good man was further encouraged in his efforts by the configuration of two events. Firstly, the public diffusion of the Rosicrucian manifestos, and secondly, the political movement supported by many of his Church (the Bohemian Brethren) to install Frederick of the Palatinate and his wife the Princess Elizabeth as King and Queen of Bohemia. These events seemed to promise a new age of religious toleration, release from Catholic Habsburg domination and the rebirth of science.

To the delight of Comenius and many others suffering religious persecution, Frederick accepted the throne of Bohemia in September 1619, journeying south for the coronation in Prague Cathedral, an event witnessed by the joyous Comenius himself. Optimists expected James I to support his daughter (Elizabeth) should the Habsburgs intervene, but James did nothing. The Duke of Bavaria's Catholic army invaded. Only the outnumbered army of Christian of Anhalt (Augustus' brother) came to Frederick's aid. After the Battle of the White Mountain (8 November 1620), the "Winter King and Queen of Bavaria" were toppled, the Prague Palace was sacked, and the Thirty Years War began.

Comenius would lose his house, his library, his wife and one of his children in the ensuing conflagration. Shattered, he escaped to the protection of Count Zerotin at Brandeis. In 1622 he poured forth his despair into a masterpiece of Czech literature, *The Labyrinth of the World and the Paradise of the Heart*. To all those who have dreamed a great dream, attempted to manifest it in the public domain only to receive the rebuttal of the world's perennial wickedness, stupidity and blindness, this volume speaks.

The 'Labyrinth' of the world is in a sense Campanella's *City of the Sun* and Andreae's *Christianopolis* turned into a nightmare. The ordered streets of science lead nowhere; all knowledge is unsound. The Pilgrim is lost in the world. Then he hears the sound of a trumpet: the trumpet of *Fame*. It is the announcement of the Fraternity of the Rose-Cross, the sound of universal reformation. Pilgrim is tempted to take an interest. Many books appear with promising titles of pansophic enlightenment but are found empty. Pilgrim is confused. The Brotherhood "said that they had the stone, and could by means of it entirely heal all illnesses and confer long life." He dreams of Paradise, a paradise reborn through access to divine wisdom, but still the Brotherhood is silent. Pilgrim can wait no more; he resumes his journey, falling into greater despair at the sight of war:

Oh, most miserable, wretched, unhappy mankind! this then, is your last glory? this the conclusion of your many splendid deeds, this the term of your learning and much wisdom over which you glory so greatly?

A voice penetrates the darkness: "Return! Return whence thou camest to the house of the heart, and then close the doors behind thee!" Comenius is forced by the pressure of events and by profound torment into a cathartic inner experience, a descent into the depths of himself. In the process he encounters a new light, and unexpected aid:

Yet I saw that they [the Godly] were well sheltered; for I saw that their whole community was encompassed by a wall of fire. When I came nearer I saw that this wall moved, for it was nothing else but a procession of thousands and thousands of angels who walked around them; no foe, therefore, could approach them. Each of them also had an angel who had been given to him by God and ordained to be his guardian. I saw also...another advantage of this holy, invisible companionship - to wit, that the angels were not only as guards, but also as teachers to the chosen. They often give them secret knowledge of divers things, and teach them the deep secret mysteries of God. For as they ever behold the countenance of the omniscient God, nothing that a Godly man can wish to know can be a secret to them, and with God's permission they reveal that which they know...

The period of repairing his mind seems to have taken several years. Eventually he revived and found, at the end of it all, that far from his ideals having been extinguished, they had matured and even intensified. Comenius never again seems to have lost the sense of divine guidance, and he was certainly cared for to the end of his seventy-nine years.

A new Court at the Hague

In 1626, four years after writing the *Labyrinth of the World and the Paradise of the Heart*, Comenius visited the court-in-exile of Frederick and Elizabeth, still regarded by their many supporters on the continent and in England as the rightful King and Queen of Bohemia. This impoverished court was a catalyst for the rebirth of science. On this occasion, Comenius presented Frederick with an illuminated manuscript of *Lux in Tenebris* (Light in the Darkness), a work containing the strange prophecies of Bohemian clergyman Christopher Kotter[71]. In Comenius' preface, he says that Kotter had warned Frederick not to use force against the Habsburgs in 1620. Kotter also prophesied the eventual return of Frederick to Bohemia in triumph and though this might have cheered up the dejected king, it was vain.

After her husband's death in 1632, Elizabeth's court continued to be a magnet both for those who believed that the Reformation had been betrayed, and for those who saw it entering a new phase of educational and philosophical enlightenment.

Comenius enjoyed other connections to Frederick and Elizabeth. Of his Heidelberg tutors, Abraham Scultetus had accompanied Frederick to Prague in 1619 as his chaplain, while Johannes Henricus Altingus remained Frederick's close friend until the latter's death. These connections deepened further after meeting the reformers Samuel Hartlib and John Dury in Poland, both of whom, like himself, were encouraged by Queen Elizabeth and her son, Charles Louis.

Comenius first met Hartlib when he went to Poland in 1628 to form a community of exiled Bohemian Brethren. Both Comenius and

Hartlib wrote educational works extolling the liberation of knowledge. Hartlib the Pole had also met the Scot John Dury at Elbing in Poland and decided that England was the best place to get the new reforms under way, encouraged by the writings of Rosicrucian-readers Dr Robert Fludd and Sir Francis Bacon.

Dury and Hartlib had good contacts. Sir William Boswell, Queen Elizabeth's diplomatic supporter, was not only Britain's ambassador to the Hague but was also Sir Francis Bacon's executor (Bacon had died in 1626). Was it co-incidence that Hartlib set out for England within a year of the publication of Bacon's fable of a perfected spiritual and scientific society, the *New Atlantis* (1627)? The story told in Bacon's *New Atlantis* is not only strongly reminiscent both of Andreae's *Christianopolis* (1619) - including a journey by sea to reach it and the appearance of a cross and cherubim's wings on an official scroll (the Fraternity of the Rose-Cross was "under Jehovah's wings") - but it also presents us with the image of a new temple of science:

> Ye shall understand, my dear friends, that amongst the excellent acts of that king [of the island], one above all hath the pre-eminence. It was the erection and institution of an order, or society, which we call Saloman's House; the noblest foundation, as we think, that ever was upon the earth, and the lantern of this kingdom. It is dedicated to the study of the works and creatures of God.

'Saloman' is explained as a corruption of 'Solomon'. The House (so similar in concept to the vault of Christian Rosenkreuz: "a compendium of the universe") is a kind of distant temple, housing not so much God Himself as the knowledge of His creation in all its aspects, physical and spiritual. New Atlantis sends out agents (again like the Fraternity of Christian Rosenkreuz) to gather new discoveries:

> we have twelve that sail into foreign countries under the names of other nations (for our own we conceal), who bring us the books and abstracts, and patterns of experiments of all other parts. These we call Merchants of Light.

I suspect that Samuel Hartlib, when he left his Christian mystical and philanthropic society in Poland for England in 1628, saw himself as a figure not at all unlike a "Merchant of Light". After founding a school for Protestant refugees in Chichester, Hartlib went to London in 1630, establishing himself as a leading reformer in England, keeping in close touch with both Comenius and the Hague[72].

In 1640 he addressed *A Description of the Famous Kingdome of Macaria* to the newly instated 'Long' Parliament. Hartlib compared his ideal tolerant state to the Macaria of Pico della Mirandola-enthusiast S.Thomas More's *Utopia*, and to Bacon's *New Atlantis*. Hartlib, in telling words, hoped that Parliament would "lay the corner Stone of the world's happinesse before the final recesse thereof..."

A general clamour for reform was fuelled by a profound excitement that a new Elizabethan age or *Great Instauration* (to use Bacon's words) might be returning to shower her blessings on a thirsty nation. The poet and later revolutionary Parliamentarian John Milton (1608-1674), friend of Hartlib, was moved to song:

> Yea Truth, and Justice then
> Will down return to men,
> Th'enamelld Arras of the Rain-bow wearing,
> And Mercy set between,
>
> Thron'd in Celestiall sheen,
> With radiant feet the tissued clouds down stearing,
> And Heav'n as at som festivall,
> Will open wide the Gates of her high Palace Hall.
> (*Hymn on the Morning of Christ's Nativity*)

Would King Charles I, brother of Elizabeth, Queen of Bohemia, get off the fence of political expediency and declare for Britain's rôle of defending and expanding the Reformation, bringing all Britons together of whatever religious persuasion in peace and prosperity? Would he welcome the Merchants of Light? For a heady moment it seemed so.

Hartlib wrote to Comenius and begged him to come to England. As Frances Yates put it in *The Rosicrucian Enlightenment* (1972): "he [Comenius] believed that he had a mandate from Parliament to build Bacon's New Atlantis in England." In 1641 John Williams, bishop of Lincoln, welcomed Comenius to England with a great banquet and informed Parliament that in considering much-needed reform the names of Comenius, Samuel Hartlib and John Dury should be considered exemplary[73].

Inspired, Comenius wrote *Via Lucis* (the Way of Light) in London. *Via Lucis* presents the world as a comedy in which the divine wisdom plays with men of many lands. The play is not yet over, for the highest light - like the dénouement of a play - is reserved for the end. In order to bring this *Light* forth, Comenius advocated the establishment of a College or sacred society devoted to the common welfare of man. The idea had clearly lingered in Comenius' brain since the time of the Rosicrucian manifestos over two decades since. According to Comenius, a new science needs a universal spiritual and educational reformation to go with it:

> When all instances and rules have been collected, we may hope that an Art of Arts, a Science of Sciences, a Wisdom of Wisdom, a Light of Light shall finally be established.

Comenius hoped that his educational primers, his "universal books", would become available to all. The word of enlightened learning must be spread over the earth: "For though it is true that the world has not entirely lacked intercourse, yet such methods of intercourse as it has enjoyed have lacked universality." The principle of universality is an important one, suggesting both the pristine wisdom of the ancients and the possibility of finding a common basis in *knowledge* that will transcend religious divisions, social divisions and national divisions; *fraternity* is the keynote. Comenius believes the "agents of general happiness and welfare" should be many. These agents must be guided by some kind of order (reminiscent of the Rules for the Fraternity of the Rose-Cross), "so that each of them may know what he has to do, and for whom and when and with what assistance, and may set about his business in a manner which will make for the public benefit."

Nevertheless, King Charles had little interest in national reform, while parliament was in any case divided on what reforms were necessary. There was, however, one area of broad unanimity, that Charles should relinquish absolute authority over the collection of taxes, that is, that there should be no separate law to that established by parliament.

It is clear that the eirenic approach of such men as Hartlib and Comenius forebore partisanship in the burgeoning conflict. Comenius left for Sweden to undertake that country's educational reform while Dury left for the Hague in 1641. Samuel Hartlib stayed in England.

On 20 May of that same year, Hartlib's friend Robert Moray, quarter-master to the Royal army of Scotland, entered the Scottish Old S.Mary's Chapel Lodge (No.1) of Masonry at a place near or in

Newcastle. This was one of the earliest masonic initiations on record. Moray, learned enthusiast both of the Rosicrucians and of alchemy, was the first president of the Royal Society.

The Royal Society

The precise origins of the Royal Society are still debated. There is in its earliest history (that of Thomas Sprat, published in 1667) a certain cut-and-dried yet nonetheless vague quality as to its genesis, suggesting there may have been much more to the matter than met the eye. Some of this vagueness is due to the fact that the institution (originally called the 'Royal Society of London, for Improving of Natural Knowledge') was born at a time when the Restoration of Charles II seemed insecure. Furthermore, many linked science with diabolic magic or utopian, revolutionary reform.

There is general agreement that the Society was conceived in the 1640s, arising from discussions which took place during the Civil War and its aftermath. These activities, regardless of the political views of its earliest proponents, were then linked firmly to the Restoration of Queen Elizabeth of Bohemia's nephew Charles II. Thanks to Sir Robert Moray, who had laboured tirelessly for the exiled Charles between 1654 and 1657 in France, Holland and Scotland, it became the *Royal* Society.

According to Royal Society member John Wallis, writing in 1678 and 1697, the Society grew out of meetings held in London in 1645 in private homes and at Gresham College. The meetings included founder members Dr John Wilkins (later bishop of Chester), but then chaplain to the Prince Elector Palatine in London, and Theodore Haak, a German from the Palatinate. These men were, like Comenius and Hartlib, patronised by Elizabeth of Bohemia. According to Wallis, it was Haak "who, I think, gave the first occasion, and first suggested these meetings and many others."

Further evidence comes from the letters (1646-1647) of alchemist and experimental scientist Robert Boyle. Boyle, a correspondent of Hartlib, mentions an 'Invisible College', a phrase with which we should be familiar, recalling how Descartes was held in suspicion in Paris in the 1620s for being a member of the "Invisibles", that is, the Fraternity of the Rose-Cross[74]. In one letter, Boyle asks his tutor to send him some books, a favour "which will make you extremely welcome to our Invisible College", while in a letter for February 1647 Boyle writes excitedly about his having made the acquaintance of a quite remarkable group of people:

> The best on't is that the *cornerstones* [my emphasis] of the Invisible or (as they term themselves) the Philosophical College, do now and then honour me with their company... men of so capaceous and searching spirits, that school-philosophy is but the lowest region of their knowledge... as they disdain not to be directed to the meanest, so he can but plead reason for his opinion; persons that endeavour to put narrow-mindedness out of countenance, by the practice of so extensive a charity that it reaches unto everything called man, and nothing less than an universal good-will can content it. And indeed they are so apprehensive of the want of good employment, that they take the whole body of mankind to their care.

This almost sounds as if Boyle has entered the bosom of Andreae's Christian Fraternity or *Societas Christiana* - or even the Rose-Cross Fraternity itself! Somebody or bodies were presumably living out the ideals which Andreae, Comenius, Hartlib, Dury and Elizabeth of Bohemia held so dear: courage, spiritual idealism, open-mindedness, loving care and systematic science. To be fair this does not sound quite like the Royal Society, but it does sound like the kind of atmosphere in which such an undertaking could develop. It begins to look as though Comenius and Hartlib had played their part as "Merchants of Light" very well.

According to Thomas Sprat's official history, the Royal Society grew out of meetings held in John Wilkins' rooms at Wadham College, Oxford between 1648 and 1659. Regular visitors included the polymath Christopher Wren, William Petty[75] and the famous diarist John Evelyn. Evelyn described the rooms as having been filled with "many artificial, mathematical and magical curiosities."

Wilkins, who as we have seen was chaplain to Elizabeth's son Charles Louis was also the author of a book called *Mathematical Magick* (1648) based on the work of both John Dee (*Mathematical Preface*, 1570) and on a section on mechanics from Robert Fludd's *Utriusque Cosmi Historia* (Oppenheim, 1619). Wilkins cites the magician-scholar and Hermetic enthusiast Henry Cornelius Agrippa (1486-1535) as his authority for employing the term "mathematical magick" for that branch of science dealing with mechanical invention. This was a fairly bold statement to appear in an era of regular witch-trials - for both

Agrippa and Dee had been accused of diabolical pacts. Wilkins also demonstrates a loose knowledge of the Rosicrucian material. In describing an underground lamp (an example of mathematical magick), he compares it to the lamp "seen in the sepulchre of Francis [*sic,* clearly taking *Fra.,* ie: *frater* to mean 'Francis'] Rosicrosse, as is more largely expressed in the Confession of that Fraternity." (still unpublished in English at that time).

The Return of the Fama

Perhaps it was due to Wilkins' inaccurate rendering of the substance of the Rosicrucian manifestos that led Thomas Vaughan to publish (for the first time in English) a printed version of both the *Fama* and *Confessio* in 1652. Indeed it appears that the 1650s, with their uncertainty regarding the future of the nation after the execution of Charles I in 1649, saw both a revival of interest in the Rosicrucians[76], as well as a ferocious attack on the Renaissance spiritual tradition which fed into that interest. Thomas Vaughan, twin-brother of the poet Henry Vaughan, author of the beautiful poem *Peace,* is an example of a second-generation 'Rosicrucian' - English-style - a man who made no apology for his magical interests:

> That I should profess magic... and justify the professors of it withal is impiety to many but religion with me ...Magic is nothing but the wisdom of the Creator revealed and planted in the creature. It is a name - as Agrippa saith - not distasteful to the very Gospel itself. Magicians were the first attendants our Saviour met withal in this world, and the only philosophers who acknowledged Him in the flesh before that He Himself discovered.
> (Quoted by Francis King in his *Magic, the Western Tradition,* (BCA, 1975).

Thomas Vaughan was connected with the first English version of Agrippa's *Three Books of Occult Philosophy* (Moule, 1651)[77], writing an Enconium on the magus of Nettesheim under the same pseudonym by which he published the *Fama* the following year, Eugenius Philalethes, 'Lover of Truth'. This name also appeared in Andreae's *Christian Mythologies* (1619). Vaughan's ideological position lies firmly in the extra-curricular school:

Now a new East beyond the stars I see
Where breaks the Day of thy Divinitie :
Heav'n states a Commerce here with Man, had He
But gratefull Hands to take, and Eyes to see.
Hence you fond School-men, that high truths deride,
And with no Arguments but Noyse, and Pride;
You that damn all but you your selves invent,
And yet find nothing by Experiment;
Your Fate is written by an unseen Hand,
But his Three Books with the Three worlds shall stand.

Vaughan would plainly like to have seen a reform of science, but is doubtful whether even the Baconian approach would yield the kind of spiritual awareness he found in Agrippa. The magician was suspicious of the imminent move towards a scientific method that would exclude the wonders of spiritual magic. For him these wonders constituted the heights of human perception. Within the context of the hopes of such as Hartlib and Comenius - that in seeking the truth through the works of God manifest in nature one may return to the Light – Vaughan's is an almost refreshingly sceptical view. One senses that Vaughan is waging a (not quite) private war for the place of Magic in the reform programme, and he does it explicitly since it might appear that few others would dare to. This was a very dangerous area, especially for those in the universities (such as Robert Boyle and Christopher Wren) who were attempting to establish reformed science as an academically legitimate activity.

The faltering ecclesiastical domination of the universities (during the Protectorate) and the particularly Aristotelian bent of Oxford meant that Magic in its fullness was regarded by some as a suspect deviation from what was considered to be a sound classical, theological and humanistic education, or, simply, diabolical witchcraft. The nature of this conflict would have a definite effect on the exoteric character of any established scientific society.

Witch Hunt

Vaughan's publication of the *Fama* and *Confessio* may have emboldened the puritan divine John Webster to write an extraordinary plea for the teaching of Hermetic and Paracelsian philosophy, along with Jacob Böhme, in British universities. These subjects were "in some measure acknowledged" by the Rosy Cross Fraternity, he writes, while mathematics as described by John Dee (from whose *Mathematical Preface* he quotes) is also recommended[78]. Webster was obviously very well versed in the field of contemporary Hermetic studies, including Bacon and Fludd in his programme, believing them to be in agreement. (Bacon did not accept the micro-macrocosmic philosophy.) The book received a stinging reply from Seth Ward, an habitué of Wilkins' philosophical discussions in Oxford[79].

Ward had no time for the Hermetic tradition in its Rosicrucian form and ridiculed Dee and Fludd. Frances Yates' *Rosicrucian Enlightenment* (p.187) takes the view that this work indicates some kind of change of tack in the core group which was to become the Royal Society, veering away from the *magic* which Wilkins had been happy enough in 1648 to attach to the word mathematics. I doubt this. Ward's work is clearly titled to be a vindication of the academic establishment; Webster's book was an attack on the universities' core curriculum. Furthermore, there may have been some smarting from Vaughan's tirade against "fond school-men". The last thing Oxford needed was a witch-trial drummed up because some felt threatened by science.

The men who were to make up the eventual 114 founder members of the Royal Society were men of very different outlooks, as one might expect. Furthermore, the Royal Society was not at its inception a purely academic institution or university society. It included men from different backgrounds who doubtless held contrary opinions on many matters. Nevertheless one *can* see why spiritual magic might not be placed at the centre of the Royal Society's interests. The subject was contentious, by its nature a private pursuit, from which knowledge of natural science *might* come but, as with the *Fama's* conception of gold deriving from spiritual alchemy as a *parergon*, such knowledge would be a by-product of the spiritual *opus*.

The aim of the Royal Society was to present in good conscience a universality of natural knowledge, that on which *all* men could agree. Spiritual experience, whether magical or otherwise, goes beyond reason. The men of the Society would obviously differ in their ability to grasp the rational but they were not setting up reason as a god, only as a yardstick.

The real conflict twixt reason and spirituality, (the so-called 'Enlightenment'), while still to come, may still in small part be attributed to the Royal Society's meetings eschewing contentious questions of religion and the spirit. Such a division went against the pansophy favoured by members of the old guard such as Comenius, falling perhaps into too cosy a harmony with that Cartesian dualism which sundered the worlds of mind and matter. We can now see, for example, Newton's mathematical vision as a *parergon* of his mystical insight, demonstrated in his extensive devotion to alchemy.

The case of Vaughan's 1652 publication of the *Fame and Confession of the Fraternitie of the Rosie Cross* is a case in point where the varied private and public interests of the first Royal Society fellows are concerned. According to F.N Price's preface to a facsimile reprint of this publication[80], Thomas Vaughan was to some degree patronised by Robert Moray (c.1600-1675), a devoted seeker after the Philosopher's Stone. Then as now, devotees of the alchemical art were usually well aware of each other's existence. Connection between them might also explain how it came to be that the version of the *Fama* employed by Vaughan was identical to that formerly in the possession of the Scots Hermetist and fervent alchemist Sir David Lindsay, Earl of Balcarres (1585-1641)[81]. In about 1647 Moray married Sophia, Lindsay's daughter, and it may have been through this connection that Moray obtained a copy of the *Fama* suitable for Thomas Vaughan's purposes.

The 1650s saw a flurry of Hermetic works published in English and there is circumstantial evidence of co-ordination. In the same year Vaughan published the *Fame and Confession*, Elias Ashmole published his great collection of English alchemical manuscripts, the *Theatrum Chemicum Britannicum* as part of *his* search for the Philosopher's Stone. (Ashmole called himself *Mercuriophilus Anglicus*, the English lover of mercury.)

Ashmole was also a Free Mason, joined fraternally to Robert Moray and a founder-member of the Royal Society. The *Theatrum Chemicum* also contained a positive vindication of Count Michael Maier, an account of the esteem in which English alchemy was held by Maier, and a report of the tradition that Maier had been treated in a manner not befitting his station when he was in England. Ashmole clearly saw Maier as a very significant envoy. Was Bacon also thinking of such as Maier when he wrote of the "Merchants of Light" who travel unnoticed in the world? Not many people would have known of this or cared much about it - other than men like Robert Fludd, a man who showed himself on many occasions to be willing to stand out from the crowd and come to the defence of those attacked for Rosicrucian, mystical or Paracelsian interests.

Between 1621 and 1633 Fludd published work after work defending Rosicrucian, micro-macrocosmic and Paracelsian philosophy against the criticisms of the astronomer Kepler, Libavius, Patrick Scot and, most especially, the Jesuit proto-mechanistic philosopher and protector of René Descartes, Marin Mersenne. This debate held the attention of all the thinking part of Europe. Mersenne regarded Fludd's ideas as the height of philosophical and theological impiety and summarised some of them thus, in his *Lettres*, (II.p.441):

> Compounded from God and this ethereal Spirit is the *Anima Mundi*. [soul of the world, or, sometimes, Logos]. The purest part of this Soul is the Angelic nature and the Empyrean heaven, which is understood to be mixed into all things. The Demons are part of the same essence, but joined to evil material. All souls, whether of men or of brutes, are none other than particles of this same Soul. This Soul is also the Angel Michael or *Misattron*. What is more, the same Soul is the true Messiah, Saviour, Christ, *corner-stone* and *universal rock*, on which the Church and all salvation are founded.

Fludd's interest in the symbolism of the rock or stone is also evident in his pseudonymously published *Summum Bonum* (1629), another (late) defence of the Rosicrucians. Fludd says that the *House of the Holy Spirit* referred to in the *Fama*, (which will always remain invisible to the unworthy) is in fact a spiritual dwelling resting upon the rock that is Christ. He quotes S.Paul in support of his contention:

> Your habitation was not made by the lords of men, but we have a spiritual building in the heavens, which is the House of Wisdom on the Mount of Reason, built upon the spiritual rock.

This view is directly paralleled in Thomas Vaughan's own *Lumen de Lumine* (*Light from Light,* 1651) where Vaughan writes as if he is himself a Rosicrucian brother. Vaughan clearly feels a spiritual identification with its dwelling-place, writing of a mountain "situated in the midst of the earth or centre of the world that is both small and great. It is soft, also above measure hard and strong. It is far off and near at hand, but by providence of God invisible. In it are hidden the most ample treasures, which the world is not able to value." Vaughan has been, it seems, 'hit by the Stone'. His works, which successfully introduced the general public to Rosicrucianism, produced a significant wave of supportive material which continued to appear for about a decade adding a (perhaps useful?) mystique to the efforts to establish an ordered scientific community.

For example, in 1656 an anonymous translation of Michael Maier's *Themis Aurea* (1618) appeared, giving the rules of the Rosicrucian Fraternity. Probably published by Nathaniel and Thomas Hodges, men with strong astrological interests, it was significantly dedicated to Elias Ashmole, "the onely Philosopher in the present age" - clear evidence of an attempt to get the socially rising Ashmole on the side of the independents. Indeed in the 1650s we see the spiritual alchemists fighting back, attempting to win the thinking part of England over and Robert Moray, behind the scenes, in encouraging Vaughan, is plainly sympathetic - and there can be little doubt that that sympathy would also extend to Comenius' pansophic enterprise as well. However, the main catalyst for all these efforts was the *Fama* itself - surely "the greatest publicity stunt of all time."

The struggle was well worth the effort for what was at stake involved nothing less than the question of what would constitute the theoretical and practical basis of reformed learning in England. That struggle was in my opinion chiefly a struggle between British ideological freelancers and the English academic establishment caused, in the 1650s, by the Church of England's having temporarily lost its grip on ideological power. There was an endemic crisis of authority which was not resolved until the Restoration of the monarchy in 1660 (and then only partially).

Haunted by Dee's Spirits

Robert Moray, in his efforts to help the exiled King Charles, did the scientific movement an inestimable service in at last achieving a clear authority and stamp of approval for the development of learning and investigation of science in this country. Before this could take place however, the enemies of the Hermetic interpretation of reality were to cast a missile straight to the centre of the debate.

In 1659 Meric Casaubon published extracts from John Dee's Spiritual Diaries, (*A True and Faithful Relation of what passed for many years between Dr John Dee and some Spirits.*). The presentation was anything but sympathetic. Casaubon wished to leave his readers in no doubt that the great mathematician was a conjuror of devils, a Faustian figure who had given up his sanity to serve the servitors of darkness. On the frontispiece Dee is associated with what the editor considers to be other dangerous 'illuminati' - a telling expression tainting the entire Renaissance magical tradition by association. In his editorial stocks Casaubon places Paracelsus, Mahomet, Trithemius, Appolonius of Tyana, Edward Kelley, and of course John Dee himself. Throughout the editing and footnotes Casaubon especially stresses a supposed kinship between devilry and "Enthusiasm", dangerous to public order and spiritual health. These men, he holds, are nothing short of subversive, and their learning is a cloak for Satanism.

In 1659, with Tumbledown Dick (Richard Cromwell) struggling to maintain control, 'enthusiasm' could only mean one thing: religious anarchy of the type which had appeared most alarmingly (to some) in the Civil War period: the Levellers, Anabaptists, holders of Conventicles, Ranters, Prophets, Quakers. Casaubon is saying, 'tolerate this, and you'll know what to expect: demonic possession, witchcraft, apocalyptic subversion'. But who is being attacked? Casaubon's motives may be mixed - and it is still a mystery how he got hold of the diaries in the first place - had they been doing the rounds? It is well known that Elias Ashmole for one was a keen collector of anything to do with Dee[82]. Is Casaubon's book a covert attack on Ashmole? Ashmole's activities and magian reputation were well known. How many knew of his Free Masonry and his connection with several of the founders-to-be of the Royal Society? The government had tried to ban the book - Dee had been a government agent for Elizabeth I - but it had already reached the public. Its publication further damaged Dee's reputation, except among the discerning few, and put the whiff of conspiracy forever around the concept of the *illuminati*.

Frances Yates believed that this publication may have sealed the determination of the Royal Society to confine its meetings to purely scientific problems, to avoid mention of religion or social utopias and to adopt that sobriety which in its dryness is the unmistakable mark of much of British academe. I am not convinced. The beginnings of the Royal Society were in fact a somewhat ramshackle affair. Like all new things it took time to find its feet, and most work as was done was done by individual fellows in private. Furthermore the discussions and interests of the scientists of this period were frequently regarded as absurd by the popular Press, impious by the Church, and of little interest to the classically and theologically dominated universities. It seems to this author that the attack of

176

Casaubon was, again, an attack on the overall *direction* of learning. It was genuinely feared by some that Dr Dee's brand of private interests might subvert the public welfare or even give the magi not only the magical, but the political power to effect changes in the natural (read divine) order of things. Hermetists tend to consider the highest knowledge to be the privilege of *initiation*. The sober meetings of the first Royal Society would have allayed such fears; people enjoyed mechanical gadgets.

It is remarkable that the question of spiritual orientation was put before the Royal Society as early as 1668 by one of the very men without whom the Society may never have existed. That now very old man Comenius appears once more on the horizon, grey, wizened, sharp as a knife. Like the Ancient Mariner he was there, and he was watching. Very well informed, he knew exactly what was going on. He had seen all the tricks long, long before, when the *Fama* was young, and he was too. In 1668, he published *The Way of Light* in Amsterdam and wrote a dedicatory epistle to the "illuminati" of the Royal Society:

> Illustrious Sirs,
> It is not unfitting that a book entitled The Way of Light should be sent to you, illustrious men whose labours in bringing the Light of Natural Philosophy from the deeper wells of Truth is coming to be proclaimed and published throughout Europe. It is the more appropriate since the work was conceived in that country where the territory offered to us for the search for Light and Truth has passed into your keeping, according to that word of Christ, (applicable in its proper sense to this occasion): *Others have laboured and you have joined them in their labours.*

Comenius continues:

> Throughout the world the news will be trumpeted that you are engaged in labours the purpose of which is to secure that human knowledge, and the empire of the human *mind over matter*, shall not forever continue to be a feeble and uncertain thing.

And then came the warning. Should knowledge for its own sake be pursued, or for power over nature only without thought as to the *ends* of that knowledge (the *Way of Light*) then that house of knowledge would surely turn out to be "a Babylon turned upside down, building not towards Heaven, but towards Earth."

Alas!

Notes for Part Two

[1] In March 1610 Galileo published his epoch-marking *Sidereus Nuncius* (The Starry Messenger) in which he described seeing "stars in myriads, which have never been seen before, and which surpass the old, previously known, stars in number more than ten times."

[2] Possibly a comment on the inadequacies and conceit of pre-Renaissance scholastic learning in the universities.

[3] The "inhabitants of the elements" were described in detail by Paracelsus in his book *On nymphs, sylphs, pygmies and salamanders* published by Johann Huser in 1591. Paracelsus says that there are two sorts of flesh: that issuing from Adam, the first earthy man, and secondly, a 'subtle' flesh, filled with extraordinary possibilities, such as being able to travel through walls. Adamic flesh has soul and has been redeemed by Christ. Non-Adamic creatures do not have soul but in other respects resemble man : in mores, language and reason. Undines and nymphs live in water, sylphs in the air, pygmies in the earth and salamanders in fire. God makes them appear to human eyes, lets them live so as to show man the marvels of His natural *opus*. If they marry with man, they gain a soul and have descendents. Nevertheless, dallying with these creatures can be fraught with danger for humans, since they dispose of knowledge which is not theirs. They know the future as well as the past and present, joining to human reason the science and intelligence of spirits. Christian meets them again on the fifth day of the *Chymical Wedding*. They conduct the seven symbolic boats to the Olympus tower to witness the nuptial regeneration.

Belief in the elemental inhabitants implies knowledge of the *virtues* or *divine signatures* inherent in things, and speaks of a time before the poetic and truly imaginative consciousness was sundered from academic science. As late as 1791, the brilliant botanist and natural scientist, Dr Erasmus Darwin of Lichfield (instigator of theories of evolution completed by his grandson Charles Darwin), used the images of the elemental creatures to announce his important *Botanic Garden*, (illustrated by William Blake among others), calling them 'Rosicrucian'. To study the 'elements' in plants, animals and minerals in order to discover their mysterious inner life was *magia naturalis* and is the origin of modern botany and genetics. According to Paracelsus' contemporary Heinrich Cornelius Agrippa (1486-1535), *magia naturalis* permits the magus to determine mysterious relations in the very bosom of nature, the action of 'that which is above and that which is below' : the 'vital fluid' or 'mercury' which penetrates, crosses and animates all the universe. The same "magic panvitalism" is at the basis of Paracelsus' theories, enabling him to see magic as the art of reading the hidden realities of the "Book of the Universe". The fact that God tolerates this activity was taken as a sign that we are capable of making use of it. Furthermore, *magia naturalis* might yet reveal man's truest nature. Nature veils consciousness. The *Fama* announces the unveiling.

[4] Some time in the 1590s, Johann Valentin's close friend Tobias Hess, while investigating the vogue for apocalyptic prognostications, obtained the book

Mystica et prophetica libri Geneseos interpretatio, published by Theodor Gluichstein (Bremen 1585) and written by the heretic Giacomo Brocardo. Brocardo saw the date of Luther's birth (1483) as the starting-point for the last age. This age would last 120 years. The significance of the number 120 was taken from *Genesis* VI.3 : "And the LORD said, My spirit shall not always strive with man, for that he also is flesh : yet his days shall be an hundred and twenty years." This is almost certainly the origin of the account in the *Fama* whereby the body of Christian Rosenkreuz is interred for precisely 120 years, and the tomb is opened to find the prophecy fulfilled.

5   Paracelsus was not born until 1493 - nine years after R.C. is supposed to have been interred - another good reason for seeing the account as an allegory.

6   Men like John Dee's avaricious scryer Edward Kelley, who fell from a wall in Prague while trying to escape imprisonment in 1595. Kelley had promised to produce alchemical gold to the Hermetic enthusiast and Habsburg Emperor Rudolf II.

7   The reference to Paracelsus demonstrates just how closely intertwined were the major thought-streams of the period. It was an easy matter to cross from apocalyptic, to alchemy, to radical spiritual reformation, to mysticism, magic and back again to apocalyptic. Little wonder that Andreae, for one, craved a cleansing and general tidying-up of the European knowledge-base. Men had lost sight of the wood for the trees.

8   Not only would the fact that the *Fama* issued from Lutheran territory (Tübingen) have alerted Catholic authority. In the city of Freiburg in the Austrian Habsburg lands of Breisgau, a man could be arrested for practising the iatrochemical medicine of Paracelsus. Fifty years previously, Thomas Erastus had demanded the death penalty for followers of Paracelsus' 'heresy'. See Article by Carlos Gilly: *'Theophrastia Sancta' - Paracelsianism as a religion, in conflict with the established churches.* (BPH, Amsterdam, 1999)

9   Haslmayr sent letters and essays to Widemann from Genoa. He even wrote a commentary on John Dee's *Monas Hieroglyphica* (1564) : *Monarchia stellae signata,* but accidentally dropped the manuscript into the sea at Messina in 1613.

10   Augustus' immersion in the field of alchemical transmutation is recalled in the guide book sold to visitors to the castle of Plötzkau since unification.

11   In 1625, Joachim Morsius, the itinerant scholar from Lübeck, published the legendary catalogue of magical manuscripts *Nuncius Olympicus*. The work mentions 228 very rare mss. From references to a "pious man" who had been in the galleys for four and a half years, it is to be presumed that these were the manuscripts of Adam Haslmayr brought by Figulus to Eglin in Marburg in 1612.

12   Dr. Christopher McIntosh (author of *The Rosicrucians*. Weiser. 1998).

13   Artaxerxes introduced a reformed calendar in 441 BC, employing the names of the deities which had accrued to Zarathushtra's dualist religion, including the god Mithra, a task executed by the mysterious caste of the Magi.

14   One can also see in all of this the beginnings of science as a 'new religion': find the inner knowledge secreted in nature and so cause progress to perfection. Interpretations of Darwin have led to assumptions that progress

and ultimate perfection are inevitable within a 'natural selection' process : an implicate intelligence is at work at the 'sub-atomic' level beyond current understanding. The psychology of apocalyptic is still with us, whether 'objective' science 'likes it' or not. Just look at the 'eco-crisis' : science appears to suggest a moral imperative little different to that of the first few chapters of *Genesis* : to get back to 'Eden', we should perceive our 'oneness' with the Garden of Nature, completely forgetting that it is our very experience of 'conscious objectivity' which has banished us from such a simple 'home-coming' in the first place! Spiritual men and women have known better than to put their faith simply in the natural world.

[15]   Pico refers to II *Esdras* XIV. 44-46 : "In forty days they [five men whom Esdras is instructed to take apart from society] wrote two hundred and four books. And it came to pass, when the forty days were fulfilled, that the Highest spake, saying, The first that thou hast written publish openly, that the worthy and the unworthy may read it : But keep the seventy last, that thou mayest deliver them only to such as be wise among the people : For in them is the spring of understanding, the fountain of wisdom, and the stream of knowledge." Pico takes these seventy secret books to be the basis for the hidden *gnosis* of the Jews, the Qabalah, which he has employed to prove the essential concordance of all philosophies, and to prove that Jesus Christ Himself employed this magical secret wisdom in order to transform the world.

[16]   *A True & Faithful Relation of what passed for many years between Dr John Dee and some Spirits.* (Ed : Meric Casaubon. 1657). Casaubon took his material from Dee's diaries, chiefly from those of 1583-4.

[17]   *The Rosicrucians.* (Weiser 1998.)

[18]   *De stella nova in pede Serpentarii : De stella incognita Cygni.* 1606.

[19]   Damcar and Fez had similar reputations to Harran and Baghdad for medieval Arabic learning. Andreae could have got his background information from his friend Wilhelm Schickhardt the Tübingen orientalist, while Damcar, wrongly in some English versions of the *Fama* changed to 'Damascus' appeared on the 1569 Mercator map of Arabia, as 'Damar' easily read as 'Damcar' – see end of Bibliography.

[20]   *Christianae Societatis imago.* Tübingen, Eberhard Wild. 1620. (The model of a Christian society).

[21]   *Christiani amoris dextera porrecta.* Tübingen, Eberhard Wild. 1620. (The right hand of Christian love offered).

[22]   A Waldensian was a follower of Peter Valdès, who around the year 1173 believed in sharing property and living communistically, like the first apostles.

[23]   It is curious how so many of the radical spiritual views of men such as Schwenckfeld and Franck would resurface as magical or occult ideas, where they can still be found today. It is a matter of debate whether such archetypes derived from magical circles in the first place - certainly there are gnostic precedents for beliefs associated with the radical reformers.

[24]   *The Golden Ark.* Willem Gaillairt. Emden. 1560.

[25]   Franck's observation on the perversion of learning was to extend right through to Gottfried Arnold's *History of Heretics and Churches* (Frankfurt. 1700), which was not only the first published book to explicitly link the thought of

the first Valentinian Gnostics to that of Jacob Böhme, the Rosicrucians and the Paracelsians, (while referring to Giordano Bruno, Meister Eckhart, Thomas à Kempis and Johann Tauler on the way), but also based the entire theme of the book on the problem of the learned-perverted. On page two, Arnold asked the question, (a kind of summary observation of the previous two centuries' religious conflicts) : "Are not those who accuse and who are intolerant of dissent, not themselves either hypocrites and learned, or Godless and perverted?"

[26] cf. the climactic message of the (apparently unfinished) *Chemical Wedding*, written by a young Andreae : "The highest wisdom is to know nothing. Brother Christian Rosenkreuz. Knight of the Golden Stone. A.D. 1459." (Of course, if the highest wisdom is to *know* Nothing, then we may infer that to know Nothing is to *know All*).

[27] William Browne of Tavistock (1588-1643). *The Rose*. This poem is quite possibly an allegory for the condition of Elizabeth of Bohemia ("The Rose"), daughter of James I, threatened in Prague by the Catholic armies of the Habsburgs in 1619, just before the outbreak of the Thirty Years War.

[28] It is highly unlikely that the rose can have referred to the Tudor-rose which John Dee had tried to serve in the person of Elizabeth I, (as Frances Yates suggested in 1972 in her book *The Rosicrucian Enlightenment*). James I was of course the founder of a new dynasty (as far as England was concerned), that of the troubled Stuarts.

[29] *viz* : the explicitly Hermetic *Rosarium philosophorum; Secunda pars alchimiae de lapide philosophico vero modo praeparando. (*1550).

[30] See page 40 on Sir George Ripley (b. *circa* 1415).

[31] That is the return to spiritual Innocence - Adam's knowledge before the Fall : the aim of Sir Francis Bacon's *The Advancement of Learning. (*1605), as well as the polyvalent circle and centre at the heart of John Dee's *Monas Hieroglyphica* (1564) which symbolised (among other things) the sun at the centre of the cosmos.

[32] Speculative Free Masonry may have been just one of several outflows of this powerful and to a large extent secret movement.

[33] There is no doubt at all that one of the meanings of the word 'Rose' at this point in history was as a suggestive epithet for Elizabeth of Bohemia. This is revealed in a poem by Sir Henry Wotton (1568-1639). The poem is called *Elizabeth of Bohemia*. In the poem Sir Henry compares Nature's many beauties with those gifts indwelling Elizabeth : *You violets that first appear,/ By your pure purple mantles known/ Like the proud virgins of the year,/ As if the spring were all your own;/ What are you when the rose is blown.* This poem is no mere *soubriquet*. Wotton was British Ambassador to the Republic of Venice and an admirer and acquaintance of Trajano Boccalini (as was Andreae) whose work appeared with the first printed *Fama*. The Doge of Venice's attempt at independence from Papal domination and that of the Habsburgs relied on shifting power-patterns in European politics, in particular on whether James I would support his daughter when she and her husband accepted the throne of Bohemia in September 1619 - thereby bringing Protestant political power into southern Europe, something the Habsburg Emperor Ferdinand could

not accept. Wotton used to call in at Heidelburg to see the Elector and his wife on his way back from Venice. See Izaak Walton's *Life* of Sir Henry Wotton (published as a collection of *Lives* in 1670, along with biographies of John Donne, Richard Hooker, George Herbert and Bishop Sanderson and, incidentally, one of Dr. Johnson's favourite books).

[34]   Author : *Impietas Wigeliana*. Tübingen. 1622 - a treatise against Valentin Weigel.

[35]   Author : *Admonitio de Quorundam*. Tübingen. 1620.

[36]   Mögling saying in his *Speculum Sophicum Rhodo Stauroticum* (1618) that those who wished to join should follow the *Imitatio Christi* of Thomas à Kempis.

[37]   Author : *Naturae sanctuarium quod est Physica Hermetica*. Frankfurt. 1619.

[38]   Author : *Epharmosis Mundi.*. Marburg. 1616.

[39]   Homagius was the nephew of Wilhelm Wessel, the Cassel printer, and a student at Marburg when in 1620, he was tried by the university for burning all his books except his Rosicrucian works and the *Arbatel*, (a magical textbook). On the express orders of Landgrave Moritz von Hessen, he was sentenced to "eternal imprisonment" in a frontier fort.

[40] Author : *Fama Syderea Nova*. 1618; *Mysterium Arithmeticum sive Cabalistica et Philosophica Inventio...illuminatissimis laudatissimisque Fratribus R.C...dicta*. Ulm. 1615; and *Himmlische Geheime Magia oder Newe Cabalistische Kunst*. Ulm. 1613. Faulhaber included mechanics, mathematics and perspective in his treatment of Divine Magic and new Cabalist Art. He was one of the first to respond to the *Fama* and interestingly enough, he met and was most impressed by René Descartes in Ulm in June 1620, when the French philosopher, (often regarded as the founder of the mechanistic or materialist philosophy), was looking for the Rosicrucian Brotherhood, while simultaneously journeying with the forces of the Habsburg army of the Duke of Bavaria. This must stand as one of the most ironic encounters in the history of thought.

[41]   Author of *Wohlmeinendes Bedencken der Fama und Confession der Bruderschaft das Rosencreutzes*. Frankfurt, 1616, and a number of other negative responses to the Brotherhood

[42]   Author : *Astronomiae Negeliane*. 1622.

[43]   Author : *Speculum Temporis Zeit Spiegel.*. Freiburg. 1620.

[44]   Author : *Mysterium Iniquitatis Pseudo-Evangelicae*. Goslar 1621.

[45]   Author of *Kurtze Grüdliche Beschreibung...* : on new stars, and *Typus Chemicum*. Strasbourg. 1628.

[46]   *Atalanta Fugiens, hoc est Emblemata Nova de Secretis Naturae Chymica*. Theodore de Bry. Oppenheim. 1618.

[47]   Proclus and Iamblichus both regard the mystical doctrine of the Greeks as deriving from the mystical doctrines of Orpheus. The Orphic mysteries were often linked to the genesis of Gnosis. *Pausanias* IX.XXX.4 describes a statue to Orpheus on Mt. Helicon.

[48]   In particular the Abbot of Sponnheim's book of angel and demon-conjuring, the *Steganographia*.

[49]   Giorgi's (1466-1540) *De Harmonia Mundi* (1525) being a fundamental Renaissance Neoplatonist text.

50 Boccalini's satire was in part aimed at the second Council of Trent, begun in 1562, the history of whose chaotic attempt at Catholic Reform had been written by his friend Paolo Sarpi, a friend both of Boccalini and of Sir Henry Wotton, British Ambassador to Venice (1568-1639), and a portrait of whom hung in John Donne's study. Donne (1573-1631) was chaplain to Elizabeth of Bohemia and Frederick of the Palatinate while they were together at Heidelberg. (Donne's life, like that of Wotton, was written by their friend Izaak Walton (1593-1683).

51 Wense provided Andreae with information and contacts in the Italian liberal scene (especially Venice) through his friend Tobias Adami. Adami brought manuscripts to Andreae and Hess, including the ms. of the *City of the Sun* from the revolutionary friar and magus Tommaso Campanella who was imprisoned in a Naples dungeon at the mercy of the Habsburgs at the time when Haslmayr was arrested at Innsbruck (1612). Andreae was exceptionally well-informed.

52 *Vita ab ipso conscripta*, presented to his friend Duke Augustus of Braunschweig many years later.

53 *Turbo sive moleste et frustra per Cuncta Divagans Ingenium. In Theatrum productum.* (Helicone iuxta parnassum; that is : Zetzner. Strasbourg, 1616).

54 *Civis Christianus sive Peregrini quondam errantis restitutiones.* Zetzner. Strasbourg. 1619.

55 *Reipublicae Christianopolitinae Descriptio.* Zetzner. 1619.

56 *Theca gladii spiritus : Sententias quasdam breves, vereque philosophicas continens* (Zetzner. 1616).

57 Andreae never admitted to anyone in print that he had written any of the Rosicrucian works - but it was widely rumoured in academic circles, and his friends never doubted Andreae's involvement - but when one looks at the consequences, it is not surprising that he refused to attract attention to his part in the play. As stated, his method was to use the interest and energy aroused by the Manifestos for his own purposes.

58 *Invitatio Fraternitatis Christi, Ad Sacri Amoris Candidatos.* Zetzner. 1617.

59 *Menippus sive Dialogorum Satyricorum Centuria inanitatum nostratium speculum. In Gramatticorum gratiam castigatum. Cosmopoli.*

60 *Mythologiae Christianae sive virtutem et vitiorum vitae humanae imaginum Libri tres.* (Zetzner, 1619).

61 This insight could be happily applied to our own situation. How often are we told that we have achieved this, done that, mastered this, that or the other; that we are 'modern', 'advanced', 'up-to-date', technologically superior; that we have the best system, the finest judiciary, civil-service, police-force, public-services, newspapers, television : all the very epitome of Democracy, and so on and on?

62 One thinks of John Lennon & Yoko Ono's declaration of "NUTOPIA" on the *Mind Games* album of 1973 : membership accorded by *awareness* of Nutopia: "no borders, no passports, only people. No laws, other than cosmic."

63 *De Curiositatis Pernicie Syntagma.*

64 *Turris Babel sive Judiciorum de Fraternitate Rosaceae Crucis Chaos* (Zetzner.

1619).

[65] *The Occult Philosophy and the Elizabethan Age.* (Routledge & Kegan Paul. 1979. pp. 169-175)

[66] The fundamental problem is childishly simple and can be solved by a small, but infinitely creative shift in approach. See the world of matter as a manifestation of the spiritual *Nous* and unnecessary dialectical conundra cease to pain us.

[67] This image actually announces itself in the first section of the *Chymical Wedding* where Rosenkreuz dreams that he is in a dungeon full of madmen and only escapes when a rope comes down to him from a light above.

[68] *Jerusalem - the Emanation of the Giant Albion* 11.25. (1804).

[69] Jesus' father Joseph is described as a τεκτων (*tekton* - hence 'architekton' = master mason/builder/architect). Often thought to have been a 'humble carpenter', he could have been a builder in stone involved, as his family was, in the running of the Temple.

[70] The reference here to Christ raising a new Temple "without hands" is directly parallel to the account of the stone in Daniel II.34-35: "Thou sawest till that a stone was cut *without hands*, which smote the image upon his feet that were of iron and clay, and broke them to pieces. ...and the stone that smote the image became a great mountain, and filled the whole earth." The stone can transform itself and anything with which it comes into contact.

[71] Frances Yates discerned unmistakable Rosicrucian references in this work, especially in the allegorical illustrations with their overt use of rose-symbolism.

[72] Comenius was also Hartlib's intermediary in the latter's contact with Jacob Böhme's disciple, Abraham von Frankenburg (the first man in print to identify the Rosicrucian philosophy with that of the Valentinian Gnostics). In a letter from Hartlib to Frankenburg of 1646, Hartlib refers to Frankenburg's pamphlet "with the fourfold and geometrical figures", as well as to Alchemy, Neoplatonism, Qabalistic symbolism, the Jesuit Hermetist Athanasius Kircher, Benedictus Figulus, the *Tabula Smaragdina*, and a request to obtain Gaffarel's *Codicus Caballistarum, Avis sur les Langues* and the *Abdta Divinae Kabala Mysterium.*

[73] Hugh Trevor-Roper in *Three Foreigners & the Philosophy of the English Revolution (Encounter*, Feb. 1960) wrote that Cromwell's supporters were fired by a vision of society "made vivid to them by three philosophers, none of whom was English but who may be called, both in their limited aims and their wild bloodshot (*sic.*) mysticism, the real philosophers and the only philosophers, of the English Revolution."

[74] Descartes had dedicated his philosophical and mathematical *Principia* to Elizabeth of Bohemia in 1644, and went to live in Leiden, Holland, to be near to her - they respected each other - in that same year.

[75] Petty, an academic favourable to Parliamentarian authority in Oxford, had been given rooms in Brasenose College, formerly occupied by a Fellow

of that College who, among a number of other Fellows were forcefully ejected from the College by Cromwellian troops for their Royalist leanings. The significance of this kind of interference in university life will soon become clear. Petty went over to Charles II at the Restoration and was subsequently knighted.

[76]   Dr Everard D.D., a suspected heretic, translated the *Divine Pymander* of Hermes Trismegistus, published by G. Moule in 1650. A year later, Moule published Henry Cornelius Agrippa's *Three Books of Occult Philosophy*.

[77]   This edition contained a peculiar substitution, with which Vaughan or his patron may have played a part. Chapter 34 of the Latin version, dealing with idolatry, refers to the "detestable heresie" of the Templars. In this English version, "The Templars" has been replaced by "old Church-men" (ie : monks or unreformed superstitious Catholics). Someone cared about the reputation of the Knights Templar.

[78]   John Webster, *Academiarum Examen, or the Examination of Academies.* London , 1654.

[79]   *Vindiciae Academiarum*, Oxford, 1654. Ward was later to become bishop of Salisbury and a close friend of Izaak Walton, who was also a friend of Elias Ashmole, and whose *Compleat Angler* (1653) is in many ways a vindication of that spiritual philosophy to which the beliefs of the imaginary Rose-Cross Brotherhood were not inimical. Walton refers with favour to the Rosicrucians and chymists generally. He also acted as a royalist agent (1651) and seems to have been part of a network of pro-Royalist writers and spiritual sympathisers. His *Compleat Angler* reads like a coded message to disaffected and dispersed Royalists and spiritual Anglicans during the Cromwellian Protectorate.

[80]   Margate, 1923. For the Masonic *Societas Rosicruciana in Anglia.*

[81]   Lindsay, a close follower of the Rosicrucian mystery, created a remarkable Garden of the Planets at his home in Edzell. The plaque above the gate to the garden still bears the significant date of 1604, the year of the new stars in *Serpentarius* and *Cygnus* and of the discovery of the Vault of Christian Rosenkreuz.

[82]   Ashmole published his first alchemical book in 1650, *Fasciculus chemicus*, an Introduction to a work by Dee's son, Arthur, then still alive, a physician to the Czar of Russia.

Mercurius Trismegistus

*Quòd Iove sis genitus magno, vis ærthea mentis
Divina, et cœli cognitio alta probat*

Beyond conflict, with the globe at his finger-tips: a popular representation of Thrice Greatest Hermes: a link between earth and the mystery of God.

ALTERIVS NON SIT, QVI SVVS ESSE POTEST.

LAVS DEO, PAX VIVIS, REQVIES ÆTERNA SEPVLTIS.

OMNE DONVM PERFECTVM A DEO, IMPERF. A DIABO.

AVREOLVS PHILIPPVS THEOPHRASTVS

The extraordinary figure of Paracelsus. Note the books scattered on the earth behind him: the universe was the *liber mundi*, (the book of the world), written with the finger of God and open to all those who sought. But Paracelsus had to hide much of his theology for fear of persecution. The 'stone' was everywhere, but remained unseen.

The Portal to the Amphitheatre of Eternal Wisdom: Heinrich Khunrath invites us to penetrate the darkness of Nature to rise to the Light. Nature: a divine revelation to the initiated, hidden in its depth to the profane.

Caspar Schwenckfeld, spiritual hero: "I cannot be one in faith with either the Pope or Luther, because they condemn me and my faith, that is, they hate my Christ in me." Flesh made radically spiritual.

Johann Valentin Andreae, aged 42: intellectual and imaginative genius of the Rosicrucian enterprise at its best.

Two strongholds of faith in the Fraternity of the Rose Cross – one mythical, one real.
(*left*) The Invisible College as 'seen' in Schweighardt's *Speculum Sophicum Rhodo Stauroticum* (1618): signs in the sky (Serpentarius and Cygnus) trumpet the New Age. (*right*) Augustus von Anhalt and his castle at Plötzkau – one of the first men to read the *Fama Fraternitatis*, experience its seductive power, and search for its provenance.

187

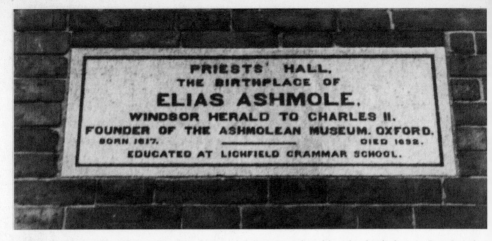

Modest memorial to Elias Ashmole, a 'saint of the gnostic church', at his birthplace in Breadmarket Street, Lichfield, Staffordshire. Three and a half centuries ago, Ashmole was fêted as one of the foremost brains of the world.

(*above*) Carving at St Chad's, Stafford. Could the 'ORM' who established the mason, be Ormus le Guidon, lord of Biddulph, who returned from the crusades with a Saracen mason?

(*left*) Sir William Wilson's carving of Charles II; south door, Lichfield Cathedral. Wilson was made an Accepted Mason in Ashmole's presence on March 11 1682 at Mason's Hall, Basinghall St, City of London.

Two dragons entwine about a ball of fire. Alchemy survives on the wall of a cowshed built from the stones of what was once Dieulacres Abbey, Staffordshire, founded by the earl of Chester in 1214; one of the witnesses to the chartulary was Roger de Meinwarin, ancestor of Ashmole's first wife, Eleanor Mainwaring.

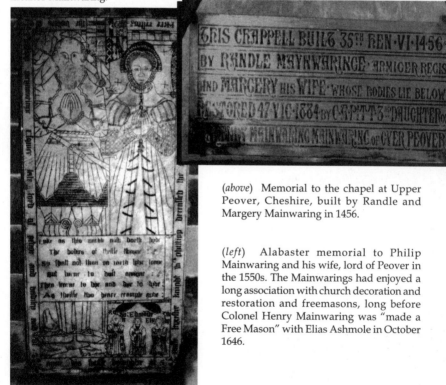

(*above*) Memorial to the chapel at Upper Peover, Cheshire, built by Randle and Margery Mainwaring in 1456.

(*left*)   Alabaster memorial to Philip Mainwaring and his wife, lord of Peover in the 1550s. The Mainwarings had enjoyed a long association with church decoration and restoration and freemasons, long before Colonel Henry Mainwaring was "made a Free Mason" with Elias Ashmole in October 1646.

Part Three

ELIAS ASHMOLE (1617-1692)

ELIAS ASHMOLE.

it is not less absurd, then strange, to see how
some Men... wil not forebeare to ranke True
Magicians with Conjurors Necromancers, and
Witches...who insolently intrude themselves
into Magick, as if Swine should enter into a
faire and delicate Garden, and, (being in
League with the Devill) make use of his
assistance in their workes, to counterfeit and
corrupt the admirall wisdome of the Magi,
betweene whom there is as large a difference
as between Angels and Devils.

(Elias Ashmole :*Theatrum Chemicum
Britannicum.* 1652, p.443.)

Chapter Eleven

A Mighty Good Man

Lichfield is still a beautiful city set in a shallow valley, six miles south of the river Trent in south-east Staffordshire. Surrounded by undulating fields and leafy lanes, the city is laid out on a bed of warm sandstone, the centre of which is dominated by England's only three-spired cathedral, a particularly inviting medieval structure whose heavy (but rarely unhappy) restoration in the seventeenth, eighteenth and nineteenth centuries testifies to the destructive power of the Civil War in England.

A small plaque above an estate-agents in Breadmarket St. commemorates the birthplace of Elias Ashmole and informs us that Ashmole was made Windsor Herald to King Charles II and that he was the founder of the Ashmolean Museum in Oxford. Few would imagine that behind this token record lurks one of the most intriguing and inspiring stories in the whole of English history.

His Life

Elias Ashmole was born on 23 May 1617, the son of Simon Ashmole, saddler and bailiff of the city. At Ashmole's baptism in S.Mary's, the name *Elias* flashed through his godfather's mind and, as a result of this inspiration, he insisted that Elias be the boy's name. Was Ashmole's godfather, Thomas Offey (sacrist of the cathedral church), aware of a prophecy circulating throughout Europe at the time wherein the New Age would be preceded by the return of 'Elias the Artist' : the prophet Elijah? We do not know, but from the day of his baptism to the night of his death, Elias Ashmole's life - for all its exceptional range of interests - would be entwined about the world of prophecy and spiritual magic. He always believed, and was probably encouraged to believe, that there was something special about him.

Elias was an unusually gifted boy, attending and excelling at Lichfield Grammar school and singing in the cathedral choir, thereby imbibing the spiritual flavour of the best of the catholic Church of England. On Elias's maturity, material considerations demanded he make his fortune through practising Law and in 1638, at the age of twenty-one, he began soliciting in Chancery, at which time he also met his first wife Eleanor, daughter of Peter Mainwaring, a Cheshire squire of slender means and, perhaps, a friend of the family. Eleanor Ashmole was to die childless only three years later.

In May 1644 Ashmole was appointed with two others as commissioner for the gathering of excise money in Staffordshire. Later in the same year he was at Oxford, trying to get Parliament to pressure the governor of Lichfield into surrendering excise monies. While at Oxford he became a member of Brasenose College, studying geometry, mathematics, astronomy and judicial astrology. These were all subjects favoured by his hero, the Hermetic magus, John Dee. Dee (1527-1608) had been court astrologer to Queen Elizabeth I and was widely regarded as the most brilliant man of his time, famed in England and on the continent for his knowledge of mathematics and spiritual alchemy. In 1652 Ashmole would write of Dee as a man deserving of "the commendation of all Learned and Ingenious Schollers, and to be remembered for his remarkable abilities" - not the least of which lay in mathematics, of which Dee was "in all parts... an absolute and perfect master." This interest in what he saw as the unjustly neglected Dee inheritance would occupy him on occasion for the rest of his life.

It says something of the character of the English Civil War that while Prince Rupert's Royalists[1] were being routed by a Parliamentary army at Marston Moor (July 2 1644), Ashmole was embroiled in the study of astrology, only to be brought away from his books by his being put in charge of the eastern defences of Oxford in support of the Royalists from May to December 1645. He was then sent to defend Worcester from Parliament, resulting in another failure for Prince Rupert's forces. Worcester fell ten days after Lichfield Close was surrendered to Parliamentary forces (July 14 1646), during which latter siege (and accompanying plague) Ashmole's pious and much-loved mother died. Ashmole returned to Lichfield to bid his mother the saddest farewell. The picture of Lichfield which presented itself to him must have shaken him to the roots. Parliamentarian forces were in the process of completing the demolition of the many ancient art-works both within and without the cathedral, while using the interior as a stable for their horses; that holy place which had once smelt of sweet incense now reeked of horse-manure. There were plans afoot to reduce the cathedral to rubble. The cathedral records - or what survived of them (the Parliamentarians had held the Cathedral Close before) - were being destroyed wholesale, and in the flames Ashmole could see hundreds of years of English history going up in smoke, never to be recovered. Nevertheless, he did succeed in saving some of the cathedral's library-books from the hands of the Parliamentarian vandals. Having saved what he could, there followed a curious interlude in Elias Ashmole's life.

Ashmole retired from the fray to the house of his father-in-law, Peter Mainwaring, at Smallwood, near Congleton in Cheshire, in order to meditate on the shocking events he had witnessed. Less than three months later, on 16 October 1646, at 4.30pm :

> I was made a Free Mason at Warrington in Lancashire with Colonel Henry Mainwaring [a Parliamentarian] of Karincham in Cheshire; the names of those that were then at the Lodge, Mr Richard Penket Worden, Mr James Collier, Mr Richard Sankey [a Catholic], Henry Littler, John Ellam, Richard Ellam and Hugh Brewer.

This is the earliest account of an apparently 'non-operative' or 'speculative' Free Masonic Lodge known to English history, and raises a host of questions pertinent to the history of the Craft. We shall look at these questions in due course.

The year 1646 saw the end of Ashmole as armed opponent of Parliament and the return of the magus-to-be to his books. In 1648 he added the investigation of botany and alchemy to his studies. Alchemy, whose abstruse symbolism permeates the atmosphere of Free Masonry, very soon began to consume his interest.

In the November of the year in which his king was beheaded (1649), Ashmole made a rich marriage to a widow[2] after astrological consultation, a marriage disapproved of by the members of the lady's family who brought a series of lawsuits against him : responsibilities which he later said profoundly restricted his concentration on alchemy. Nevertheless the following year saw the publication of *Fasciculus chemicus*, a translated alchemical text by John Dee's son Arthur (1579-1651) for which Ashmole, as 'James Hasolle' wrote the Introduction. Ashmole had thought that Arthur Dee was dead and was surprised to discover that Dee *junior* had in fact only been away in Russia, as the much-respected physician to the Czar, and had since returned to Norwich. Dee replied to a letter of Ashmole sent on 23 January to the effect that he did not object to Ashmole's use of his work. Friends of Ashmole met Dee in London but Elias missed his own opportunity, for Arthur Dee died the next year (1651). Arthur Dee left a son, Rowland, who was a merchant in London and who gave Ashmole a family pedigree in 1674 during a prolonged period of Dee-interest in Ashmole's life.

Ashmole now began to live up to his self-given title of *Mercuriophilus Anglicus*, the English Mercury-lover. In 1651, Ashmole's diary records his being made 'son', that is to say spiritual heir to William Backhouse[3], an alchemist recluse of Swallowfield, Berkshire, being enjoined thereby to call Backhouse 'father'. The relationship of 'father' to 'son' may well be in imitation of the traditional relationship between the mythic arch-sage of alchemy, Hermes Trismegistus, and his pupils : Asclepius, Tat and Ammon. Ashmole was clearly seeking spiritual initiation[4]. Ashmole wrote a poem[5] which offers ample indication of the depth of spiritual feeling to which his intercourse with Backhouse led him.

> From this blest Minute I'le begin to date
> My Yeares & Happines ...& vow
> I ne're perceiv'd what Being was till now.
>
> See how the power of your Adoption can
> Transmute imperfect Nature to be Man.
> I feele that noble Blood spring in my Heart,
> Which does intytle me to some small parte
> Of...Hermes wealth...

The poem goes on, emphasising that it was alchemy's power to transmute the man rather than the metal which led him to offer his fate over to what he calls the "Hermetick Tribe." Elias clearly followed his own path in his pursuance of alchemical secrets and, considering he had apparently only taken the subject up three years previously, he had made speedy progress. Only five years after meeting Backhouse he was already acknowledged by other independent adepts as the leading British figure in the Art. Ashmole's relationship with Backhouse and indeed Ashmole's career in general was watched with great interest by the Rosicrucian-influenced reformer Samuel Hartlib, who became known to Ashmole personally (some time after Ashmole's initiation). In Hartlib's *Ephemerides* (1650, sect.4. p.6) we also learn that Hartlib enquired of William Petty concerning Backhouse. William Petty frequented John Wilkins' rooms at Wadham College, Oxford between 1648 and 1651, at which meetings the core idea of the Royal Society was established (according to Sprat's official history of the Society). Petty called Backhouse "an Elixir man", and it is difficult to tell whether this designation for an alchemist dedicated to finding the "Elixir of Life" had any pejorative meaning attached to it. One intuits here that Ashmole was not a member of the core group whose associations fostered the Royal Society but was of great interest to at least some of them. Most notably there is the case of Ashmole's desire to join the Rosicrucian Brotherhood.

Ashmole almost certainly believed that the Fraternity of the Rose-Cross actually existed in some form or other. In the Bodleian Library's Ashmole manuscript collection[6] there exists, appended to a hand-written copy of the first 'Rosicrucian Manifesto', the *Fama Fraternitatis* (first published in Cassel, Germany in 1614), a fervent petition to "the most illuminated Brothers of the Rose Cross" that he, Elias Ashmole might be admitted to their fraternity. Professor Frances Yates believed this to have been "an entirely private pious exercise" based on Ashmole's knowledge that the convention for approaching the Fraternity was to understand that the Brothers of the Rose-Cross could detect the true will of the aspirant without themselves seeing any written petition. Unfortunately, we do not know the date of this petition. Ashmole himself, along with the entire British Rosicrucian movement, was entirely ignorant of the true social and political context in which the so-called Rosicrucian manifestos were formed.

In 1652 there appeared Ashmole's *Theatrum Chemicum Britannicum*, the product of a brilliant research enquiry into the English alchemical tradition. In the following year, Ashmole recorded in his diary the astonishing report that his spiritual master William Backhouse (who thought he was dying) had passed on to Ashmole the secret of "the true Matter of the Philosopher's Stone." What this may have been, Ashmole did not say.

Restoration

1660 was the year of the Restoration of Charles II, and one might have thought that the monarch had more pressing business to deal with than to give his assent to the foundation of the Royal Society and to entertain the pleas of Elias Ashmole. But that would be to forget the work of the men who helped ease the way for Charles II : men such as Samuel Hartlib and Sir Robert Moray, liasing with Charles through the court of Elizabeth, ex-Queen of Bohemia in the Hague. The Restoration had meanings other than the return of the Crown. There was the restoration of the dignity of the Church of England, and there was the restoration - one might even say *renaissance* - of the Ancient Wisdom founded upon the Square, that is to say, the Temple : a luminous idea which in its simplicity avoided the more contentious language of magic and the real threat of persecution and social unrest. The puritannical Right was active, but many had been exhausted by it.

Ashmole was in close touch with events in Lichfield. A letter of 19 January 1660 from the churchwardens of S.Michael's Lichfield to Ashmole's chambers in the Middle Temple thanked him for "freely giving £5 towards the building of S.Michael's church in Lichfield" - happily still thriving. Shortly after Charles II's generally welcome return to these islands, Ashmole was granted his first meeting with the new king (16 June 1660). The issue he chose to bring to Charles' attention was the condition of Lichfield Cathedral - that but for the vestry and the chapter-house it was roofless. Nevertheless, the clerks were still keeping the canonical hours amid the ruined interior. Charles II "much lamented" the state of Lichfield Cathedral and made it possible for Ashmole to set about organising its reconstruction. On 18 July, Ashmole wrote of how his friend

> Mr Dugdale moved Dr Sheldon [bishop of London] to become an Instrument for the repaire of Lichfield Cathedral, and proposed that the prebends &c. that were to be admitted should parte with one half of the profits of their living towards the repaire of the Fabricke, which would be no great burden to them, considering their livings are all improved to a treble value at least, and by this example the Gentry might be invited to join with them in some considerable contribution.

Three years later, having urged the appointment of Bishop Hacket[7] to oversee the reconstruction, Ashmole contributed £20 and again £10 towards the restoration of the cathedral. (He was praised for this act in a Latin poem by Thomas Smith, cathedral sacrist). The restoration of the cathedral was understood to be an unmistakable analogy for both the alchemical renewal of the spirit which underpinned Ashmole's life and, possibly, for the practical application of Temple symbolism. In 1662, Ashmole wrote to the cathedral subchanter, outlining a gift of rare sets of church anthems and service-books dedicated *"to the service of your Temple"*. Ashmole was certainly interested in the Temple of Jerusalem. There are among his papers extracts in his own hand taken from John Lightfoot's *The Temple : Especially as it stood in the dayes of our Saviour. With measurements of the second Temple of Jerusalem.* (London. 1650)[8]. It is impossible to say, however, whether this was a personal interest or whether it was connected with his being a Free Mason. A year later Ashmole gave a further £30 to the Cathedral and on 17 March 1666 : "I bestowed on the Bailiffs of Lichfield a large chased silver bowl and cover, cost me £28 8/6d" The letter of thanks from the Bailiffs of Lichfield, John Burnes and Henry Baker, is highly revealing of both the way they saw Ashmole and the way they thought he saw the cathedral. It is very hard to imagine a similar letter being sent today. We have the marvellous picture of Ashmole, a servant and intimate of the King, an astrologer and profound scholar being hailed by a group of bailiffs as nothing less than a magus.

> as if some propitious stars arising in the East had, (at this time) gone before our Magus [Ashmole], steering its course to this our city of Lichfield, and stood over the new-erected **pyramids** of our cathedral, (where as yet a star appears) darting its benign influence on this poor and loyal city, inviting the **Magi** from afar, to offer some tribute to it...like one of those true Magi that offered to Christ in his poorest condition, you have largely offered to the repaire of his Church our ruined Cathedral. But you have likewise Annually and liberally offered, relieved, and refreshed Christ in his members, the poor of our City.

(Ashmole gave at least £5 a year to the poor of Lichfield). The references to Ashmole as a magus and the description of the restored spires as "pyramids" suggest strong Hermetic implications and in-references. His reputation in such matters was now public knowledge - and was approved of. Ashmole may well have thought the New Age of the Brotherhood was well under way - but which Brotherhood?

Charles II bestowed the office of Windsor Herald upon Ashmole in 1660. Significant people were speaking up on Ashmole's behalf. Such men must have included Samuel Hartlib and Sir Robert Moray. As one with the Royal Eye upon him, Ashmole's work began to acquire a new, magisterial and *established* character.

On 2 January 1661, Ashmole was elected to be one of the 114 founders of the Royal Society, to "meete together weekly". Ashmole was judged "willing and fit" to participate in "a designe of Founding a College for the Promoting of Physico-Mathematicall Experimentall Learning." Ashmole probably did not realise that the eventual confining of Royal Society study to purely material phenomena on Baconian experimental lines (Bacon would have been surprised if Magic was to be excluded from Science) would eventually budge Ashmole's beloved Neoplatonic cosmos out of public science and into the private world of the gentleman-scholar or secret Hermetic enquirer. But this long process, thought of in the last century as the 'triumph of science over superstition', was hardly yet underway. Isaac Newton also would have been dismayed at the arrogance of materialism. He was as concerned with the lineaments of the Temple as he was with the gravity which held them in place.

1663 was the date Ashmole had predicted in 1652 by astrological means as the time when the Rosicrucian-style dream of the coming of the "more pregnant and famous philosophers" would be fulfilled. Ashmole may have thought that the Royal Society would be an invaluable aid in realizing this dream. Sir Robert Moray, a man described in his own time as "a great patron of the Rosie-Crucians" would doubtless have shared Ashmole's view. Furthermore, 1663 saw the appearance of a "Fiery Trigon" of Saturn and Jupiter : an unmistakable sign for Ashmole of the 'coming philosophers' who would "Illustrate, Enlarge and Refine the Arts like tryed Gold."

In 1663 Isaac Newton was at Cambridge and after graduating (1664) he spent the two plague years (1665-1666) largely at home in Woolsthorpe in the Fens investigating the properties of light. Why light? Jacob Bronowski wrote in *The Ascent of Man* that it is natural for the physicist to think of the universe in terms of light and matter in energetic inter-action. "We see matter by light; we are aware of the presence of light by the interruption of matter." Suffice to say, Newton became aware of universal gravitation in the period 1665-1666. Newton, alchemist and mathematician, would of course fit the bill as "a more pregnant and famous philosopher".[9]

In the year of Newton's graduation, Ashmole was appointed as a member of the Royal Society's committee charged with "collecting all the phenomena of nature hitherto observed, and all experiments made and recorded."- an activity very much in tune with that of the fictional Fraternity of the Rose-Cross and certainly with the work of Bacon's "Merchants of Light" in the latter's *New Atlantis*. (1627).

On 23 October 1667 Ashmole made a horoscope to determine a propitious time for King Charles to lay the first stone of the Royal Exchange. The masonic researcher E.Conder suggested that Charles II laid this foundation stone "in true masonic form" and that for this reason, Ashmole the Free Mason, was asked to compile the horoscope[10]. In the following year, Ashmole married for the third and last time : Elizabeth, the daughter of his friend William Dugdale. He had no children from any of his three marriages.

In 1672 Elias Ashmole released his *opus magnum* of antiquarian study and research discipline, *The Institution, laws and ceremonies of the most noble Order of the Garter*. This work brought Ashmole even more fame at home and abroad.

Ashmole's magical interests certainly did not come to an end on his becoming friendly with Charles II. On the flyleaf to Ashmole's copy of John Dee's *Liber Mysteriorum 1-V*[11] there is recorded in his own hand the story of how he was brought a valuable cache of John Dee's "spiritual diaries", in particular that magical system called the *Heptarchia Mystica* : a guide to the seven orders of angels and their operations in the governance of the universe :

> Be it remembered, that the 20th August 1672, I received by the hands of my servant Samuell Story, a part of Dr. Dee's manuscripts all written with his own hand; *viz* : his conference with Angello, which first began the 22nd December Ano 1581, and continued to the end of May Ano 1583, where the printed Booke of the remaining conferences (published by Dr Casaubon) begins, and are bound up in this volume.

The story of how Ashmole obtained these manuscripts is itself extraordinary and is told by Ashmole on the fly-leaf. They were brought to him (in exchange for a gilt-copy of the Garter book) by one of the wardens of the Tower, Mr Thomas Wale. Wale's wife had formerly been married to a Mr Jones, a confectioner of Lombard Street, London. Shortly after the latter marriage the couple had gone to look at some stuff put up for sale by a joiner. Among the household items was a chest of fine workmanship, formerly belonging to a Mr John Woodall who had bought the chest "very probably" after Dee's goods were exposed to sale after his death in 1608. About four years before the great Fire of London (1666) the couple had moved the chest, heard rustlings inside and on inspection and with the help of a piece of iron, they discovered a secret drawer full of books together with a rosary. A maid burnt about half of the collection but the then Mrs Jones put the rest safely away. They even survived the Great Fire when the chest itself was destroyed. The manuscripts were taken out with the rest of the saveable goods to Moon Fields and then, after the Fire, finally returned home. On marrying Mr Wale, Mrs Wale informed her husband about the books and he, on hearing that Ashmole had lately passed through London, brought them to him. Ashmole's reputation was pervasive. Whether or not Ashmole ever tried to 're-activate' the angelic calling-system of Edward Kelley and John Dee is unknown, but it is certain that he did take the work very seriously and in no wise found it reprehensible that Dee should have attempted to crown and complete his scientific knowledge by making contact with the spiritual powers believed to be 'behind' those physical manifestations which he had spent his life in observing.

A year later (4 July 1673) Ashmole recorded in his diary that "The learned and ingenious Sir Rob: Murrey died." 'Learned and ingenious' is a phrase reserved by Ashmole for those versed in the Hermetic Art, and that is certainly true of Robert Moray, patron of Thomas Vaughan and friend of Elias Ashmole. Within six months of obtaining the *Heptarchia Mystica*, Ashmole had asked the antiquary John Aubrey (in whose *Lives* Ashmole features) to enquire after contemporary accounts of Dee in Mortlake (Dee's principle place of residence) and received a report from Aubrey on 27 January 1673 with which he was dissatisfied. Aubrey had, however, made contact with an 82 year old widow, Widow Faldo, and Ashmole went to interview her on August 11 1673, a month after hearing of the death of Moray. One wonders what his thoughts were as he approached Mortlake, last home of his Hermetic hero. Widow Faldo told Ashmole that she had known Dee well and had been inside his house, four or five rooms of which had been "filled with bookes." He kept a "plentifull Table and a good Howse" and once permitted Faldo and her mother the vision of "the Ecclips of the Sun in one of his Roomes, which he had made darke."

In 1675 Ashmole executed work on the history of Windsor Castle, notes for a projected biography of John Dee and according to Dr Campbell's biographical article on Ashmole (*Biographia Britannica* 1747), he collected material for a History of Freemasonry, the notes for which existed among Ashmole's papers in 1687. Campbell's account reads as follows :

> As to the ancient history of Freemasons, about whom you are desirous of knowing what may be known with certainty, I shall only tell you, that if our worthy brother E.Ashmole Esq; had executed his intended design, our fraternity had been as much obliged to him as the brethren of the most noble Order of the Garter. I would not have you surprised at this expression, or think it at all too assuming. ...What from Mr E.A's collection I could gather, was, that the report of our Society's taking rise from a Bull granted by the Pope in the reign of Henry III, to some Italian architects, to travel all over Europe to erect chapels was ill-founded. [the 'Comacene theory' of Masonic origins - the architects were supposed to have come from round Lake Como, survivors of the fall into barbarism.] Such a Bull there was, and those architects were Masons; but this Bull, in the opinion of the learned Mr A was confirmative only, and did not by any means create our fraternity, or even establish them in this kingdom.

202

Dr Campbell then went on to suggest that enquirers look into the stories of S.Alban and King Edwin, in whose time masons were supposed to have been active. Campbell asserted that Mr Ashmole was more understanding of, and better acquainted with these stories of masonic origins than those who would ascribe a late date to Free Masonry.

Between 1679 and 1683 Ashmole was busy with another great project. This project was to succeed and bring him the fame on which his name now definitively rests. He was in the process of establishing the first-ever public museum in Britain, a museum of natural science built up from his own purchases and from material inherited through his association with the Tradescant family through his second marriage. The Ashmolean now stands as a great neo-classical structure on Beaumont Street and S.Giles, Oxford. The original building included a unique chemical laboratory in the basement, the first of its kind in a British university. Ashmole was ahead of his time in this work, for after his death the laboratory was reported as being in a disgraceful state of damage and neglect. Ecclesiastical influence prevented the foundation of an Ashmolean Professorship in chemical and natural history but the University did appoint the first Keeper of the Museum, Dr Robert Plot, as Professor of Chemistry. (Plot also wrote the exquisite *Natural History of Staffordshire*, which refers to the very large number of Free Masons in that county[12]). 1,758 of Ashmole's books are today housed at the Ashmolean, and for more than 150 years after its foundation the Museum remained the centre for scientific studies in Oxford - a great tribute to the powerful spiritual impulse which drove Ashmole's great energies into such a life-enhancing and generous direction. If there ever was an invisible spiritual Fraternity, Ashmole certainly paid his membership-dues.

In 1685 Charles II died and his Catholic son James II succeeded him. The bailiffs of Lichfield begged Ashmole to be their MP. Ashmole was delighted to accept. James II opposed Ashmole's candidature, having promised the seat to a favourite and asked Ashmole to stand down, claiming he had known nothing of Ashmole's acceptance. In spite of this, many citizens of Lichfield still voted for Ashmole, deeply regretting that their wishes were so high-handedly overturned. Ashmole wrote the bailiffs a letter, giving money for a coronation party and telling them :

You cannot but imagine I looke upon my selfe as a very unfortunate man, that finde the love of my country men (almost without parallel) so great, and yet cannot accept their votes.

Three years later, in the year that James II fled the country in the bloodless Revolution which ousted him in favour of William and Mary, Dean Addison begged Ashmole to pay for the completion of the Cathedral's ten-bell peal :

Whatever interest this City and Church have in your Birth and Education, hath already redounded, insomuch honour thereby, and in your continual bounty, to both...nor in truth have we any other Argument, but your Charity and our necessity.

Sometime between the 18 and 19 May 1692, Elias Ashmole died. His tombstone in the Howard Chapel of S.Mary's Lambeth reads : *While the Ashmolean endures, he will never die.* John Aubrey, who knew Elias Ashmole, declared, simply, that "he was a mighty good man."

Chapter Twelve

Elias Ashmole and the Origins of Free Masonry

Ashmole's employee, Dr Robert Plot, wrote of 'Free-masons' in Staffordshire in his *Natural History* of that County[13] :

> To these add the Customs relating to the County, whereof they have one of admitting Men into the Society of Free-masons, that in the moorelands of this County seems to be of greater request, than anywhere else, though I find the Custom spread more or less over the Nation;

Why more numerous in the moorlands of Staffordshire than elsewhere? There are a number of significant factors which emerge from close acquaintance and study of the area - factors which were, in the main, well known to Ashmole the antiquarian.

In the Middle Ages the Staffordshire moorlands drew those monks who followed the teachings of the mystic and practical man of genius Bernard of Clairvaux : the Cistercians, the which order began in 1098 when St Robert, the Abbot of Molesmes founded a monastery for the reform of the Cluniacs' Rule of Benedict in the middle of the forest at Cîteaux in the diocese of Langres. In 1112, a young nobleman arrived at Cîteaux with some friends, all of them in search of God. This nobleman was the Bernard who was to become the soul and inspiration of the order of 'white monks', and the unofficial head of Christendom. In 1129 he provided the Knights Templar with their original Rule (based on Cistercian principles) - he was the nephew of one of the founders of the Templars, André de Montbard - and from 1147 organised the Second Crusade, in which the Templars distinguished themselves with legendary valour. By the time Bernard died in 1152, the Cistercian order held 343 monasteries, and before the end of the twelfth century there were 530. One of these monasteries was founded by the crusader-knight, Bertram de Verdon in Staffordshire in 1176, at a place called Croxden near to his castle at Alton, ten miles south-east of Leek.

In about 1214, on returning from the Holy Land, the sixth earl of Chester, Ranulphus de Blondeville, founded the Cistercian Abbey of Dieulacres, just north of Leek with pasturing-rights across Biddulph Moor and elsewhere. In 1223, Henry de Audley founded the Cistercian Abbey of Hulton, five miles south-west of Leek. Adjacent to his lands, a few miles south-west of Hulton, stood (after 1168) a Templar preceptory, at Keele. The relationship between the Cistercians and the Templars was very close-knit. Between them, these three Cistercian monasteries dominated the life of the moorlands of Staffordshire throughout the Middle Ages until the Dissolution of the Monasteries, a century before Ashmole's marriage to Eleanor Mainwaring (1638). Needless to say, they were built and structurally sustained by lodges of masons, stone-cutters and freemasons : sculptors of that chalky stone, so good for fine carving, known as freestone[14].

The rule of the white monks themselves was to keep to the cloister, to be silent, to own no property, to be obedient, to suffer no distraction or murmuring, to confess frequently, to perform the appointed duties and to be bound to one another in mutual love. The appointed duties involved caring for their clothes, their shoes, their kitchen; to rise at midnight and spend the early hours in chant and then to work until sundown when they were to retire to sleep. They did not eat flesh (except when ill), fish, eggs, butter, milk or cheese - except when given in charity. Alongside the monks lived the *conversi* : the masons, smiths, weavers, shoemakers, fullers, tanners and bakers : often the drudges of the establishments. Their domicile was scant (they usually lived at the western end of the building), and their food poor. According to Jean Gimpel[15] the spirit of the Rule of Saint Benedict did not permit the monks to do heavy manual labour such as quarrying, stone-cutting or sculpting.

In 1119 the Cistercians produced a rule of 'usages and customs' with regard to the work of lay brothers, who had to take vows of poverty, chastity and obedience, but who never became priests. While the services of lay-masons were necessary to some of the initial construction and later repair of monasteries, builders, especially specialist sculptors, were often brought in from outside, as the numerous masons marks around many Cistercian monasteries demonstrate. Sculpting was the work of the freemason, a highly skilled man who had graduated from stone-cutting (itself an exact art) and who met his fellows in 'lodges', often constructed in wood on site, where simple economics and pride in their craft dictated that their 'secrets' be transferred only among themselves. It is very important to understand the scope of their craft. To imagine that these freemasons were simply highly skilled workmen (or 'operatives') with little or no intellectual and spiritual grasp of their work would be a great mistake. Among the company of freemasons we do in fact see the origin of the western 'artist' who attempts to emulate the divine Art which his own art has opened his eyes to, and who was naturally disposed to think of the maker of the universe as a 'Great Architect'. As Jean Gimpel expressed the matter :

> By becoming a sculptor, the stonecutter graduated to the intellectual world. He came into contact with theologians and learnt from them; he had the wonderful opportunity of looking through the abbey's precious manuscripts. He learnt to look, to observe and to think. His intellectual horizon broadened, which meant that his carvings benefitted both materially and spiritually. Thanks to the miniatures and manuscripts which he had seen and admired in other abbeys, the sculptor could humbly suggest slight variations to themes put forward by the Fathers. As the sculptor and the theologian were working towards the same end, the former could feel free, for within this association there was no compulsion.[16]

An era (such as the early 17th century), whose intellectuals and others were fascinated by symbols and esoterica, could hardly fail to wonder at what the country's freemasons had been doing for centuries, and who perhaps had begun to miss something of the 'medieval' world, a longing which we, juggled, as it were, differently in time, cannot properly see, or better, *feel*. By Ashmole's time, there was a widespread feeling among the educated that something vital in the ancient world had undoubtedly been lost (and needed to be recovered, *viz* : Francis Bacon's *New Atlantis*, 1627), as the monastic world, with all it involved, and the age of chivalry, had likewise been lost (Ashmole's most famous work in his day was a history of the Order of the Garter - a book which fascinated his contemporaries). The early seventeenth century saw new interest in the mythology of Atlantis, in alchemy, and in the Hermetic 'pristine theology' idea : that kernels of primary wisdom had been handed down from the earliest antiquity in Hermetic, initiated circles. Perhaps to become an 'accepted' mason in Ashmole's day was a way of keeping hold of some sense of rootedness, while the state was busy decapitating itself after a century of religious turmoil.

Freemasons had not vanished from the moorlands of Staffordshire at the time of Elias Ashmole. In spite of the devastating effects of the Dissolution of the Monasteries begun by Henry VIII in 1536, it may be that at the beginning of the following century, some freemason lodges were undergoing a mild revival.[17] Many of the great houses of Staffordshire illustrated in Dr. Plot's *Natural History of Staffordshire* were constructed in that period - and Jacobean architecture delighted in intricate decoration and visual allegory (Inigo Jones is an obvious example of the standard attained and practised in the early seventeenth century). It should not be forgotten that the freemasons were extraordinarily secretive. Had not Ashmole recorded his 1646 initiation in his diary, and had not his employee Plot made reference to Free-masons in the Staffordshire moorlands, this research could never have begun.

The Mainwarings

Ashmole recorded in his diary[18] that on 27 March 1638 :

> I was married to Eleanor Manwaring eldest daughter to Mr Peter Mainwaring (and Jane his wife) of Smalewood in Com'Cest : gent: She proved a virtuous and good wife. The marriage was in St. Benets Church neere Paules wharfe by Mr : Adams Parson there.

While it seems that the couple had met in London (where Ashmole was soliciting in Chancery), Eleanor seems to have spent most of her short married life at her father's house at Smallwood. Ashmole visited regularly and got to know the area and her (extensive) family, in which he took a keen interest.[19] From the point of view of social status, Ashmole's marriage was a 'step-up' in the world. While his grandfather Thomas Ashmole (d.11 Jan. 1620) had been senior bailiff of the City & County of Lichfield, Elias's father had had to make ends meet by working as a saddler. Ashmole's new father-in-law, though relatively poor compared to other gentry families in Cheshire, did struggle to live off his small estate and was part of what had been, since the Norman Conquest, and still was, one of the most significant and wealthy families of Cheshire (with a significant branch at Whitmore, three miles south of Keele in Staffordshire). His wealthiest relatives owned the estate of Peover Superior, amongst other lands in Cheshire, and lived only eight miles to the north of Smallwood.

In 1641 plague broke out in the town of Congleton near Astbury, two miles from Smallwood. From the home of William Laplove, the plague, which had engulfed most of his family, spread about Astbury, the parish records showing that almost 300 people of that village died in this terrible year. Ashmole recorded in his diary that between the fifth and sixth of December 1641[20] :

My deare wife fell sodainely sick about evening and died (to my owne great Griefe and the griefe of all her freinds) the next night about 9 o'clock.

On the 8 December 1641 :

She was buried in Astbury church in Cheshire neere the entrance of the south Isle of that Church. viz. the West end of that isle : Manwarings of Smalewood buried in west end of north isle.[21]

In fact, Ashmole, who was in London while all this was going on, did not hear of his wife's death until he got to Lichfield on 16 December. By the time he reached Smallwood, she had already been interred. On a freezing cold January morning (16 Jan. 1642 - twelve days after Charles I went to the Commons to arrest Pym, Hampden, Hazelrigg, Strode and Holles), Ashmole finally felt able to visit his wife's grave. Although he would marry twice more, Ashmole's memory of Eleanor never dimmed, but was kept alive in his heart through regular visits to his in-laws of whom he was fond[22]. When he made the decision to be initiated a Free Mason in 1646, he travelled to the lodge up the Warrington road (which the Smallwood lane meets at the western end of the hamlet) with Colonel Henry Mainwaring, Eleanor's cousin, who lived four miles away at Karincham[23] where his father had been born, the fifth son of Henry Mainwaring. Not much more than a year after Ashmole stepped out of the porch of S.Mary's Astbury on that cold and bitter morning, Sir William Brereton's Roundheads - who were beseiging Biddulph Hall (which was holding out for the King[24]) - would stable their horses in Astbury church, smash all of the medieval stained-glass, and carry the organ and pre-Reformation furniture to a field and burn the lot. Tumultuous events were on the horizon of Ashmole's life, as they were for the country at large. When things went badly for the Royalist cause (after Naesby in 1645), Ashmole would return again to the Staffordshire-Cheshire border to regain his footing; he had roots there.

As Ashmole stepped down from Astbury cemetery to the village square, he would have passed two unusual medieval tombs - canopied tombs outside a church are not a common sight. There lay the bodies of the knight Richard de Venables de Newbold (*circa* 1342) and of William de Venables, rector of Astbury in the late thirteenth century. An earlier William de Venables, along with Roger de Mein-warin[25] (Mainwaring) witnessed Ranulphus earl of Chester's instruction to his barons regarding the founding of Dieulacres abbey (1214). In fact,

Ashmole was a distant relative of the Venables family, as was his first wife, Eleanor Mainwaring. Eleanor's forebear, Margery Mainwaring, was the daughter of Hugh Venables, baron of Kinderton and, according to Thomas Mainwaring (1656)[26], it was Margery who erected the unusual chapel at the church of S.Lawrence, Upper Peover, over her husband Randle Mainwaring's tomb; Sir Randle (known as Handekyn the Good) died in 1456. Around his helmet is inscribed the motto of the order "Jesu the Nazarene", an order which I have been unable to trace.

The church of Upper Peover is a treasure-house of Mainwaring remains[27], such as the magnificently carved effigies of Randle and Margery's eldest son, Sir John Mainwaring, and his wife Joan. These, like the effigy of Sir William Mainwaring (dated 1399) at Acton church were carved by freemasons out of alabaster. There were alabaster quarries in Derbyshire (Chelleston), in east Staffordshire and near Tutbury, thirteen miles south-east of Ashbourne. Also within S.Lawrence's there are fine alabaster monumental slabs to John Mainwaring, knight (d.1515) and his wife Katherine, who died in 1529. The Mainwarings seem to have enjoyed a longstanding relationship with fine sculptors - freemasons - from the Middle Ages right into the sixteenth and seventeenth centuries. This relationship extended to building.

In 1225, Earl Ranulphus of Chester (founder of Dieulacres), fellow knight of crusading Mainwarings, began building Beeston Castle, possibly designed by Ranulphus himself. The Earl had been in Egypt for two years, hearing at first hand of the crusader castles of Palestine and Syria with their sophisticated defences. Beeston has been compared to Sahyoun in Syria. It was innovative. Unfinished at his death in 1232, the castle was taken over by Henry III whose son Edward I strengthened the castle in major works in 1303/4, known from accounts kept by the king's officials (vol. 59 *Lancs. & Cheshire Records Society*. 1910). The cost of the masons' work, including metalwork, amounted to £38. In charge of the masons working at the castle was Master Warin. The name is suggestive. The Mainwarings were descended from a Norman family who derived their name from the River Guarenne or Varenne and the small town of that name near Arques in Normandy. The name was anglicised to Warenne or Warren and often *Warin*. The name *Mein-warin* appears frequently in the records of medieval Cheshire. *Mein* refers to the *house* of the Warin family, that is to say Upper Peover.

Six miles north of Upper Peover (on land given by the Conqueror to the Venables family) is that church's mother church of Rostherne, some six miles south-east of Warrington (where Ashmole was initiated in October 1646). In 1578 an arbitration award was made to Thomas Legh against Sir Randle Mainwaring who had claimed possession of the Legh chapel in Rostherne church. According to Raymond Richards[28] : "The Legh Chapel at Rostherne stood ruinous in the sixteenth century for want of glass, [and] Sir Randle Mainwaring repaired it at his own expense," assuming possession for himself and his family "only to be turned out by Thomas Legh". The passion for building continued. In 1585 the stately home of Peover was completed and still stands, unspoilt, in the midst of Peover Park, overlooking the church of S. Lawrence.[29]

In 1647, Philip Mainwaring, knight for the Parliamentarian cause, died, and his wife Ellen built the north chapel of Upper Peover to house a magnificently preserved effigy of her husband in armour, and later herself (she died in 1656). Ellen greatly assisted Cromwell with money and influence (local legend has it that Cromwell's troops were frequently billeted in Upper Peover church) but this did not stop the Protestant vandals of the Protectorate period from cutting off her praying hands which, raised upwards on her effigy, were taken as signs of Romish religion by the ignorant. In 1644, while Ashmole was in Oxford trying to get Parliament to pressure the governor of Lichfield into surrendering excise monies, Philip Mainwaring received a letter from Charles I (based that September at Chester), addressed to "Our trusty and well beloved Philip Maynwaringe", expressing concern that Mainwaring was "ill affected to us and our sayd service" and that if he should "answer the contrary", travel across the country would be "at your utmost peril". Philip stayed with Parliament, as did all the fighting-age Mainwarings of whom we have knowledge. There is no record of Ashmole's regarding the Mainwaring's disloyalty to the person of Charles I with censure. Perhaps there was something in him which he felt to be above such partisan concerns. In the lodge to which he would be fraternally bound he encountered a Roman Catholic, an Anglican, a Parliamentarian and himself : a Royalist. A man who could stomach the desecration of a church where his wife lay buried, by associates of his friends was clearly very broad-minded or unusually capable of being in two minds - but then, for Elias (whose motto was *Ex Uno Omnia*) - the Hermetic philosophy united all phenomena, no matter how heart-breaking. Certainly his political position in this instance was enigmatic; Ashmole was an enigma - most of all, probably, to himself.

It is now clear that while freemasons were undoubtedly to be found in the moorlands of Staffordshire, as Dr Plot correctly asserted, and while Ashmole might have been accepted among their number, it was the connection with the mainly Cheshire-based[30] Mainwaring family which provided set and setting for Ashmole's initiation.

On 16 October 1646, Elias Ashmole accompanied his cousin by marriage, Col. Henry Mainwaring on the road north to Warrington, and to Free Masonry.

Warrington - what happened?

The short answer to this question is that we don't know. However, we can partially fill the void thanks to Norman Rogers' investigations, published in 1952 in the *Transactions of Quatuor Coronati Lodge* (vol. 65). Rogers investigated the names of those who appeared in Ashmole's short reference to his initiation in 1646, and it is clear from Rogers' work that the Warrington lodge, whether occasional or not, was largely made up of landed gentlemen from the borders of north Cheshire and south Lancashire : mostly Royalists and a significant number from families with traditions of faithfulness to the 'old religion', ie : Catholicism. It is clear that the contact for Ashmole came through the Mainwaring family and that family's connections with gentry (and probably craftsmen) to the north of the old County Palatine of Chester. Why Warrington?

If, as seems most likely, Ashmole's reference to "Mr. Rich Penket Worden" means that Richard Penket was Warden of the lodge (he is mentioned first), then the Penket family-name may give us a clue. In 1407, a Friar Thomas Penketh (d.1487 : one of the Penkeths who held lands from the lords of Warrington, the Boteler (Butler) family) lived at the Priory of S.Augustine, Warrington (suppressed under Henry VIII). We see here a suggestive connection between gentleman-landowners and the monastic system which we have seen among the Mainwarings and in Staffordshire. (Many relics of the Warrington monastery can be seen in the Warrington Museum). Shakespeare mentions a Friar Penketh, Provincial of his Order, who supported Richard of York against Edward V (*Richard III*, Act III, Sc.5). The Penkeths also patronised the church of Farnworth, to the west of Warrington, and it is now clear that it was the ecclesiastical world which provided the chief medium of contact between gentlemen and operative freemasons. For example, *MS Ashmole*, 1, 125, f.11v-12v contains the copy of an indenture made between the Lord Steward, Lord Chamberlayn, and Sir Thomas Lovell (on behalf of King Charles II) and the Knights of the Garter, and the "fre-masons" John Hylmer and William Vertue, specifying work for the Choir of Windsor Chapel : roof-vaulting and ornamenting with "archebocens, crestys, corses and the Kinges bestes." This kind of work did not come cheaply, and Rogers seems to this author to be quite wrong in thinking that the Richard Ellom of Lymm, co. Chester (close to Warrington, and quite possibly the Richard Ellam present at the Warrington Lodge of 1646) whose will (7 September 1667) describes him plainly as a "freemason", is unlikely to have been an 'operative' due to the fact that his will reveals he had lands to dispose of in a gentlemanly fashion. Rogers seems to be locked into rather Victorian attitudes to 'trade', as well as being surprised that Catholicism played such a part in most of the families mentioned at Ashmole's initiation. Who but the adherents of the old religion would have the greatest concern with old family chapels &c. and their ornamentation? Puritans, and Protestants generally, devalued (at best) the physical representations of God's houses. Rogers makes the point that Ashmole was one exception to the generally Catholic background of the lodge, being "attached" to the Church of England, without realising fully that it was the (for many, welcome) re-catholicisation of the Anglican church ritual under Archbishop Laud which did so much to spark the Civil War in the first place. For men such as Ashmole, the Church of England was not a Protestant Church, but the old (if reformed) church under the King.

Rogers, in a now established tradition of masonic scholarship, confuses the issue by being at pains to demonstrate that the Warrington lodge was "speculative". The use of this word is demonstrably out of context in the seventeenth century. Warrington was a lodge of principally Accepted Free Masons, almost certainly working an operative (ie : traditional) ritual : an old interest of old landed families with private interests in the 'old religion'. It may have been only a part of a larger body, separated for the purpose of initiating gentlemen, or, as stated before, a micro-association formed by accepted Free Masons for their own purposes.

As regards the particular Richard Penket whom Ashmole encountered, Warrington and Farnworth parish records mention a large number of persons of that name for the period, and we cannot be sure which of them was involved in the initiation of Ashmole and Colonel Henry Mainwaring. While Rogers gives copious information about the other brethren present at the 1646 lodge, it is sufficient for our purposes to note that the Littlers were of a gentle Cheshire family, that the Sankeys of Great and Little Sankey held lands - like the Penkeths - from the Boteler (Butler) family, that one of the Ellams, Richard, may have been an operative freemason, that Hugh Brewer may have been the man of Lancashire yeoman stock who distinguished himself as a Sergeant-Major in Lord Derby's Royalist regiment of horse (the burial of a Hugh Brewer is recorded in Warrington parish church records on 29 May 1658) and that Mr. James Collier may have been the James Collier of Newton, gentleman, reported in a certificate taken by Randle Holme (*Deputye to the Office of Armes*) who, on 3 June 1640 - at the age of 32 - married the Elizabeth, daughter of Sir Edward Stanley of Bickerstaffe, Lancashire, whose grandfather was Sir Randle Mainwaring of Peover - a relative of Colonel Henry Mainwaring, and distantly thereby, of Elias Ashmole himself. (*Record Society of Lancs. & Ches.*, Lancashire Funeral Certificates, Vol vi, p.207). Whether or not this was the man, it seems likely that the James Collier of the Warrington Lodge did come from Newton and was a Royalist.

So, having encountered Messrs. Brewer, Littler, Ellam, Collier, Penket and Sankey, what did Ashmole and Mainwaring undergo in pursuit of initiation? The balance of current scholarly opinion is of the view that only two degrees were worked in the seventeenth century : entered apprentice ('interprintice') and 'fellow crafte'. There was, as far as we know, no third degree (nor any reference to the Hiramic legend), and one appears to have been called a 'master' on fulfilling that particular role in the lodge. In short, an accepted fellow craft was effectively a master (there being no further degree). When recording a lodge-summons to Mason's Hall in London, (an operative establishment, note), Ashmole described himself as the 'Senior Fellow' in attendance on Sir William Wilson's (and others') initiation. It may be that 'master mason' was a term more used of a fine sculptor or architect after he had undergone a seven-year apprenticeship and become a fellow craft. In Ashmole's 1682 diary entry, Mr. Thomas Wise is described as *Master of the Masons Company* "this present year", again suggesting that the term 'Master' may generally have been used of those who had undergone operative apprenticeships, and that it was used to describe an office of the operative craft. Gentlemen would naturally wish to attain the lodge's highest position of honour, without the practical apprenticeship - and this honour would be encapsulated in the term 'fellow craft' or, simply, 'Fellow', suitable for a fellowship. Gentlemen would, presumably, already have undergone a

214

gentleman's education - unlikely in the case of practical apprentices. Their education was in the hands of fellow crafts or masters. However, it is still worth considering that Wilson was initiated when already a practising sculptor and architect. Why had he not been initiated before? Had accepted masons created some kind of development of the operative system, or was it that Wilson had been trained as a mason outside of restricted 'freemason' circles with their particular rites of passage? The surprising answer to this question will emerge in the section on the London Masons Company later in this chapter.

Symbolic association with the idea of Free Masonry seems to have been what counted to gentlemen who entered the 'mystery' (skill) of the ancient craft - an association doubtless welcome to practical masons, since these gentlemen were generally in a position to commission work. The monasteries had gone, and most churches and chapels existed under private gentry patronage. House-building and ornamentation constituted another source of freemasons' income. Gentlemen could enjoy the grafting of traditional symbolism and geometrical craft into the very bosom of their habitations : another way, perhaps, of continuing the traditional religious attitudes (which frequently included classical, traditional or 'pagan' themes of one kind or another) of perhaps happier pre-Reformation days. It should be borne in mind that Protestant religious practices and attitudes were imposed on the English people by act of Parliament and the aggression of iconoclasts, where that is, there was no local enthusiasm for Protestantism. (Now that the state no longer enforces religious uniformity, many people in England have returned to ways and thoughts to which the zealous Puritan would have responded with faggots and fire). Gentlemen, then as now, valued privacy and necessary secrecy. The operative freemasons had, unwittingly perhaps, created the ideal gentlemens' club-format : a place (and the 'lodge' was almost an imaginary place) to get away from current religious and political strife and where one could be immersed in more ancient ideals and tried certainties : *on the square.*

Taking all this into account, it is likely that Ashmole and Mainwaring's initiation contained some kind of both entered-apprentice and - swiftly - fellow craft ritual. This is evinced in surviving records of seventeenth century Scottish Acceptations, and it may well have been the case for Ashmole and Mainwaring.

We do not know for certain precisely what words passed by at Warrington in October 1646, but we may get an idea - perhaps an exact idea - from the earliest known English freemasonic catechism :

Sloane Ms. 3329 (British Library), which has been dated to c.1700 or a little earlier, only fifty years or so after Ashmole's initiation. This manuscript (almost certainly referring to operative practices) was bound up by Sir Hans Sloane (1660-1753) in a large volume described as "Loose papers of mine concerning curiosities". Like Ashmole, Sloane was a Fellow of the Royal Society and, being thirty-two when Ashmole died, he had ample opportunity to encounter the grand old man of British antiquarianism.

In his "Narrative of the Freemasons Word and signes" Sloane gives details of various means by which freemasons recognised one another. The grips for fellow crafts and masters are not those employed today (it is significant that the grips for fellows and masters are different). Sloane says that the former grip was made by thrusting the thumb-nail "close upon the third joint of each others' first finger." Could it be that the third degree came about in the early eighteenth century partly because accepted "fellows" required a distinct ritual way of being called a "master mason" - lodges now made solely, even exclusively, of Accepted Free-masons, bent on a wholly symbolic and allegorical interpretation of the craft? Practices seem to have varied; Sloane gives two forms of the master's grip, his information being, apparently, second-hand, so to speak. Sloane does mention the placing of the feet in a manner identical and familiar to Freemasons today. He then gives an example of "their private discourse" which is worth including in full, as it seems not unlikely that something very like it was experienced by Ashmole and Mainwaring on October 16, 1646. (I have put the words in modern spelling and added punctuation - the which is almost entirely absent from the original - not having been designed to be written down, but memorised).

Question : Are you a mason?
Answer   : Yes, I am a freemason.
Q :   How shall I know that?
A :   By perfect signs and tokens, and the first points of my Entrance.
Q :   Which is the first sign or token? Show me the first and I will show you the second.
A :   The first is heal and Conceal or Conceal and keep secret by no less pain than cutting my tongue from my throat.
Q :   Where were you made a Mason?
A :   In a just or perfect or just and Lawful Lodge.
Q :   What is a just and perfect or just and Lawful Lodge?
A :   A just and perfect Lodge is two Interprintices, two fellow crafts and two Masters, more or fewer, the more the merrier, the fewer the Better

Cheer, but if need require, five will serve, that is, two Interprintices, two fellow Crafts and one Master, on the highest hill or Lowest Valley of the world, without the crow of a Cock or the Bark of a Dog.

Q : From whom do you derive your principals?

A : From a greater than you.

Q : Who is that on earth that is greater than a freemason?

A : He it was carried to ye highest pinacle of the Temple of Jerusalem. [note the Christian reference].

Q : Whither is your lodge, shut or open?

A : It is shut.

Q : Where Lies the Keys of the Lodge door?

A : They Ley [sic.] in a bound Case or under a three-cornered pavement, about a foot and a half from the Lodge door.

Q : What is the Keys of your Lodge Door made of?

A : It is not made of Wood, Stone, Iron or steel or any sort of metal, but the tongue of a good report behind a Brother's back, as well as before his face.

Q : How many Jewels belong to your Lodge?

A : There are three. The Square pavement, the blazing Star and the Danty tassley [a corruption of "perpend ashlar" according to Knoop, Jones and Hamer's Early Masonic Catechisms. Manchester University Press 1963].

Q : How long is the Cable rope of your Lodge?

A : As long as from the Lop of the Liver to the root of the tongue.

Q : How many Lights are in your Lodge?

A : Three. The sun, the master and the Square.

Q : How high is your Lodge?

A : Without foots, yards or inches it reaches to heaven.

Q : How Stood your Lodge?

A : East and west, as all holy Temples Stand.

Q : Which is the master's place in the Lodge?

A : The east place is the master's place in the Lodge, and the Jewel resteth on him first, and he setteth men to work. What the masters have in the foornoon [sic], the wardens reap in the Afternoon.

In some places they discourse as followeth (Viz)

Q : Where was the first word given?

A : At the Tower of Babylon.

Q : Where did they first call their Lodge?

A : At the holy Chapel of St. John.

Q : How stood your Lodge?

A : As the said holy Chapel and all other holy Temples stand. (Viz.) east and west.

Q : How many lights are in your Lodge?

A :   Two. One to see to go in, and another to see to work.
Q :   What were you sworn by?
A :   By god and the Square.
Q :   Whither above the Clothes or under the Clothes?
A :   Under the Clothes.
Q :   Under what Arm?
A :   Under the right Arm.

Sloane's notes also include reference to the "master's word", which we may suppose might have been given to fellow crafts such as Ashmole and Mainwaring, since that degree was the highest degree - though it is noteworthy also that the word "degree" does not occur in Ashmole's diary entries, nor in the Sloane Ms.

> Another [salutation] they have called the master's word, and is Mahabyn, which is always divided into two words and Standing close With their breasts to each other, the inside of Each other's right Ankle Joints the master's grip by their right hands and the top of their Left hand fingers thurst [sic] close on ye small of each other's Backbone, and in that posture they Stand till they whisper in each other's ears ye one Maha- the other replies Byn.

THE OATH

> The mason word and every thing therein contained you shall keep secret. You shall never put it in writing directly or Indirectly. You shall keep all that we or your attenders shall bid you keep secret from Man, Woman or Child, Stock or Stone, and never reveal it but to a brother or in a Lodge of Freemasons, and truly observe the Charges in ye Constitution. All this you promise and swear faithfully to keep and observe without any manner of Equivocation or mental Reservation, directly or Indirectly, so help you god and by the Contents of this book. So he kisses the book &c.

The Old Charges

One feature of Ashmole's acception as a 'Free Mason' the which we can be almost certain was experienced by him on 16 October 1646 was the recitation of the 'Old Charges'. This is the name given to the traditional histories of the Craft, of which a number have survived dating from the late 14th century through to the 17th century. They were intended to 'charge' or 'load' the initiate with due gravity, rich colour and acute consciousness of what joining the society of fellow freemasons bound him to. The initiate was to be very much obliged.

Dr Robert Plot, the first curator of Ashmole's epoch-marking Museum in Oxford, had obviously seen a copy of the Charges while producing his *Natural History of Staffordshire* (1686). Judged from the strictly historical point of view, we may not defer from Plot's assessment that the story contained in the Craft history was grossly "false and incoherent".

While it is true that the Old Charges' account of masonry does indeed juxtapose vast tracts of history, rather in the manner of a gay pantomime or quick-fire masque, (a Greek who witnesses the building of Solomon's Temple, for example, proceeds to impart the craft to 'Charles Martill' in France), one nonetheless suspects that Plot may have just missed the point of the plot's original authors, whoever they may have been. It should be noted that the precise wording and content of the Charges varies in different versions, but they are all unmistakable in spirit, emphasis and essential function. They represent a quite peculiar and not a little fascinating form of vernacular literature.

The Old Charges, with great imaginative charm and pleasant innocence delineate the *mythos* of masonry in terms of legend. Legend itself is the precise subject matter of the myth. Masonry is the inscription of history: the emphasis is always on what *survives*. The stones testify, and in doing so transcend the follies of man and the vicissitudes of time. Whoever rules, masonry remains the same dynamic force. Wise counsel dictates friendship with masons. There are those who build and those who destroy; a man is known by his friends.

Legendary achievements of great men past; the initiate was to 'see' in the recitation a kind of *cartoon* of the history of civilisation – even the little scrolls which have come down to us look like reels of film, 'quickies'! The initiate would learn that masonry had first-class, nay unsurpassed *bona fides*. Born in the antediluvian civilisation of the middle east : Egypt, Phoenicia, Babylonia; the knowledge survives the Great Flood, thanks to legendary, larger-than-life guardian figures – and none more potent in mythic and legendary significance than Thrice Greatest Hermes, the 'father of philosophy', 'psychopomp' (Jung) of Alchemy and Patron General of Architecture and natural magic - science surviving to inform the Greeks, the Romans, and even to provide Jewry with her natural and supernatural Temple to crown her seven pillars of Wisdom.

Wheresoever civilisation grew in stone, the golden gift of the masons was present, like a tincture, a catalyst, a magic word and philosopher's stone: an eternal sign in time. It continues through the Dark Ages as the pursuit of wise rulers, giving incomparable form to castle, abbey and palace. Lofty ideals traced out, the Craft had high expectations of the initiate.

Ashmole would have been gratified in his curiosity. As the man who would soon appear to English readers as the *Mercuriophilus Anglicus* – English Mercury Lover - ever attentive lover passionate for the embrace of the Hermetic cosmic vision, suitor to mysteries and the buried yet breathing past, adept of alchemy, astrology and natural magic – Ashmole would have been delighted to hear of the rôle of Hermes as patron-guardian of architecture, with the Almighty himself seen as "heavenly archemaster" of the Craft (as John Dee put it).

And more, we can be fairly sure of the precise wording which met Ashmole's ears on that late autumn afternoon in 1646. For by a curious co-incidence, the manuscript copy of the 'Constitutions of Masonry' formerly in the possession of Sir Hans Sloane (Sloane Ms. 3848, British Library), ends with the following autograph :
"ffinis p.me Eduardu : Sankey decimo sexto die Octobris, Anno domini 1646"
– the very day on which Ashmole and his late wife's cousin Colonel Henry Mainwaring were made Free Masons. Warrington church registers record the baptism of "Edward son to Richard Sankeay [sic], gent., 3 ffebruarie, 1621/2" It seems highly likely that this was the son of the Richard Sankey recorded by Elias Ashmole as having been present at his initiation. We may be permitted to imagine Edward Sankey writing out the Charges – perhaps from memory – as part of his father's preparation for the ceremony. Edward Sankey wrote as follows:

Good brethren & ffellows, our purpose is to tell you, how and in what manner; this Craft of Masonrie was begun; and afterwards founded by worthy Kings and Princes; & many other worshipful men; and also to ym that are heare; wee will declare to ym the Charge yt doth belonge to every true Mason to keep ffor good sooth if you take heede thereunto it is well worthie to bee kept; or a worthie Craft and curious science, ffor there bee seaven liberall sciences;

before Noes flood was a man called Lameth as it is written in ye 4 chapt of Gene, and this Lameth had 2 wives; ye one was called Adar; ye other Sella: and by Adar hee begott 2 sonnes The one was called

Jabell ye other Juball; And by ye other wife hee had a sonne & a Daughter; and these foure children found ye beginninge of all Crafts in ye world; This Jabell was ye elder sonne; and found ye Craft of Geometry;

and these children did knowe that god would take vengeance for sinne eather by fire or water; Wherefore ye writ ye Sciences wch weare found in 2 pillars of stone; yt ye might be found after the flood; The one stone was called Marble that cannot burne wth fire; The other was called Letera that cannot drowne with water; Our intent is to tell you truly how & in what manner these stones weare found; where these Crafts were written in Greek; Hermenes that was sonne to Cus, & Cus was sonne to Shem wch was ye sonne of Noath: The same Hermenes was afterwards Hermes; the ffather of wise men, and hee found out ye 2 pillars of stone where ye Sciences weare written, & taught him forth.

when Abraham and Sara his wife went into Egypt; there weare taught the seaven sciences unto ye Egyptians; And hee had a worthy Schollar called Euchlid and hee Learned right well and was Maister of all ye 7 Sciences;

And there was a King of an other Region yt men called Hyram and hee loved well Kinge Solomon; and gave him timber for his worke; And hee had a sonne that was named Aynon & he was Mr of Geometry; and hee was chiefe Mr of all his Masons; and Mr of all his graved works; and of all other Masons that belonged to ye Temple; & this Witnesseth the Bible in libro 2 Solo capite 5.

And soe it befell that a curious workman; who was named Nimus Graecus & had beene at ye makeinge of Solomons Temple; and came into ffrance; and there taught ye Craft of Masonrie; to ye man of ffrance that was named Charles Martill;

And all this while England was voyde both of any charge or Masonrie; until ye time of St.Albans; And in his time ye King of England that was a Pagan; and hee walled ye Towne wch is now called St. Albans;

until ye time of King Athelstone; yt was a worthy King of England; and hee brought ye Land into rest and peace againe; and hee builded many great workes & Castles & Abbies; and many other Buildings; and hee loved masons well; and hee had a sonne yt was named Hadrian:

And hee held himself assembly at Yorke and there hee made Masons, and gave ym Charges and taught them Mannrs of Masons; and commanded that rule to bee holden ever after: And to them took ye Charter & Commission to keepe;

And from time to time Masonrie until this day hath beene kept in yt forme & order, as well as might gov'ne ye same; And furthermore at dyvrs assemblies hath beene put to and aded certaine Charges; more by ye best advices; of Mastrs and fellowes; Heare followeth the worthie and godly oath of Masons; Every man that is a Masonn take Heede right well; to this charge; if you finde yo'self guilty of any of these; yt you amend you; againe especially you yt are to bee charged take good heed that you may keepe this Charge; for it is a great perill for a man to foresweare himselfe on a book;

And should the reader find this is all terribly old fashioned, consider for a moment the opening to Stanley Kubrick's *2001 A Space Odyssey* (1968). Does the epic not commence with the discovery of a transformative pillar of curious substance – a key to all science awaiting discovery – only this time excavated upon the moon by astronauts, the dark pillar's contents charging these latterday argonauts to mount a quest, a quest that penultimately leads the last survivor "beyond infinity" itself?

The Lodge is in the Head –
The Acception and the London Masons Company

"How high is your lodge?" asks the masonic catechism quoted earlier. "It reaches to heaven" comes the reply. *It reaches to heaven.* Something had happened to the conception of the medieval wooden lean-to, draughty shelter for masons in the shadow of the cathedral-in-the-making. The humble freemason's lodge has acquired some of the universal qualities inherent in the cathedral itself. Even more, the 17th century lodge has in some sense come to represent the dynamic of the infinite cosmos, however simple the locus of the brotherly gathering. The mind of the accepted freemason is to expand with the dimensions of the universe; the sacred book contains the spiritual laws of the universe. He is to dwell in the mind of the Great Architect to learn His Laws and apply them according to His will.

The Edinburgh Register House Ms catechism of 1696 asks of the initiate, "Where is the key?" The answer: "In the bone box", that is to say, inside the skull: the *mind*. It's all in the mind. The cosmic lodge comes alive in the imagination, activated by symbols and signs, as a chessboard may represent all the conflicts of a state, but *this* is the cosmic chessboard interiorised, then projected.

The freemason is drawn into a basic mnemonic system in which his mind partakes mysteriously of the 'lost word' that is, the *logos*. The familiar English translation of the Greek as 'word' is misleading. The dynamic logos (very close in conception to the alchemical *mercurius*) is the "second God" or "son of God" of the pagan and Christian Hermetists, the active, intelligent mind who is both responsible for and implicit in creation: the source of intelligence and creative power. This logos, or stone, comes from heaven and is to be found throughout the world, though invisible to the fool who 'trips' on it. (See Luke XX, 17-18) In the beginning was the *logos*, and He is incarnate in chapter one of John's Gospel and typified in Christian and masonic tradition as "the stone the builders rejected". The logos is the "precious cornerstone" of the prophetic tradition, rejected due to human spiritual blindness. The logos is that stone which has now and will become "the head of the corner" of the new Temple, built when the 'lost children of Israel' return to Zion, that is, God's House: in the bone box and beyond it. "The higher you fly, the deeper you go" (John Lennon). I did not 'read all this in'; freemasons did. Take, for example, a mason's grave in the west of England, dated 4 May 1639, inscribed as follows:

> Christ was thy Corner-stone, Christians the rest,
> Hammer the word, Good life thy line all blest,
> And yet art gone, t'was honour not thy crime,
> With stone hearts to worke much in little time,
> Thy Master saws't and tooke thee off from them,
> To the bright stone of New Jerusalem,
> Thy worke and labour men may esteem a base one,
> Heaven counts it blest, here lies a blest free-Mason.

> (*Devon & Exeter Gazeteer*, 8 Oct. 1909, p.7, brought
> to my attention, as with that following, by Matthew Scanlan)

Again, we have the plaque raised to the memory of John Stone, now at S.Giles, Sidbury:

> An epitaph upon ye Life and Death of JOHN STONE, FREEMASON, who, Departed Ys Life ye first of January, 1617, & Lyeth heer under buried.

On our great Corner Stone this Stone relied,
For blessing to his building loving most,
To build God's Temples, in which workes he dyed,
And lived the Temple, of the Holy Ghost,
In whose lov'd life is proved and Honest Fame,
God can of Stones raise seede to Abraham.

To call the Almighty Himself a 'Freemason' was neither an unknown nor empty epithet. Witness Cawdrey's *Treasure of Similes* (London, 1609, p.342): "As the Freemason heweth the hard stones... even so God, the Heavenly Free-Mason, buildeth a Christian Church."

Few have fully grasped the gnostic import and transformative power of these symbolic ideas and ideal symbols. The accepted freemason is to be a microcosm wherein the mystery of cosmic redemption is to be enacted and realised. "Who is that on earth that is greater than a freemason?" asks the Sloane Ms. catechism, sternly. "He it was carried to ye highest pinnacle of the Temple of Jerusalem", that is, Jesus, the slain Master, tempted of Satan but raised and triumphant.

These and related ideas permeate what has become known as 'speculative' freemasonry, generally regarded as something independent of the so-called 'operative' craft – as if the tool could be meaningfully detached from the mind that made it. Christianity was born of free theology forged in the spirit. An analagous case may be made for freemasonry.

Professor David Stevenson's *The Origins of freemasonry: Scotland's century* makes a good case for the Hermetic inspiration behind some of William Schaw's reforms of Scottish masonry in the 1590s (Schaw's Statutes). He also highlights the probable hoped-for inclusion of some aspect of the Art of Memory in a Scots mason's utility kit. Frances Yates has shown how this Art was related to neo-Neoplatonic symbology by Hermetists such as Giordano Bruno (1548-1600). Bruno spread the mnemonic magic about Europe during the 1580s, believing it to be linked to a liberating gnosis of Egyptian provenance.

It is now clear that the love of Renaissance men of learning for polyvalent symbolism, riddles, metaphors, paradoxes and hidden keys was not alien to the life of the architect and sculptor – the apostle of the substantial Renaissance.

Masons, associated with so many medieval lay confraternities across Europe had been 'speculating' (geometry, mathematics, plus symbolic theology) for centuries. Indeed, the term could simply mean mathematics, *viz*: *The City and Country Purchaser and Builder's*

Dictionary: or the Compleat Builder's Guide (TN Philomath, London 1703) in which the author, Richard Neve, writes in his fifth section on the 'Freemason's Work': "Some ingenious Workmen understand the Speculative Part of Architecture or Building: but of these knowing sort of Artificers there are few because few workmen look any further than the Mechanical, Practick or Working part of Architecture; not regarding the Mathematical or Speculative part of Building,..."

In fact, the earliest known use of the appellate 'speculative' to distinguish Grand Lodge from the world of practical architecture, occurs as late as 12 July 1757. It appears in a letter from Dr Manningham, Deputy Grand Master of the Premier Grand Lodge in London, writing to a Brother Sauer at the Hague.

For the man who most inspired Elias Ashmole, namely John Dee, as well as for many other men of learning in the 16th and 17th centuries, mathematics was simply a branch of what was called 'natural [or non-demonic] magic'. This conception derived from the Sabians of Harran and Baghdad, as described in the first part of this book, and was restated by Renaissance *genii* of the calibre of Pico della Mirandola.

Serious knowledge, then as now, simply holds the ignorant spell-bound, that is, bound by a spell. ('Spelling' means getting the words *right*.) Such ignorance persists to this day. In some parts of India, masonic lodges are called by locals, 'magic houses' (Jadu Ghar), while in Britain anti-masonic propaganda still asserts some mysterious relationship between the Craft and witchcraft, in spite of every contrary assertion. Sound education, for masons and non-masons alike, is of course the cure for such fears. Electricity holds little mystery to the man who has made his own wireless.

Elias Ashmole was not the first 'speculative mason', nor was the Warrington microcosm the first speculative lodge. Ashmole's record concerning 1646 has come to represent the first known record of a lodge of Free Masons apparently unrelated to the 'operative' craft. But was it really unrelated to the sculptors and architects?

As we have seen, it is highly likely that the Richard Ellam mentioned in Ashmole's record was a freemason as full-time occupation. (The will of Richard Ellom of Lymm, Cheshire, 7 September 1667, describes him as a 'freemason', which can only mean the Art and Craft. The will mentions brothers John and Peter, to whom Richard left his messuage and tenement in Lymm. Ashmole refers to Richard Ellam's brother, John.) A copy of the Old Charges from the 1660s among the Harleian Mss. (Ms. 1942, British Library) requires a lodge to consist of one warden, five brothers and a minimum of one other "of the

Trade of ffreemasonry". Warrington would have had the blessing of all freemasons, whether 'accepted' or not – and we must get used to thinking of accepted masons rather than 'speculatives'. Being 'speculative' as opposed to 'operative' constitutes the basis for the claims of the United Grand Lodge of England to govern Free and Accepted Masonry in England and Wales, ie: that it is the first wholly speculative masonic institution.

Architecture, since the heyday of the Renaissance, was not only a freemason's business; it was a gentleman's accomplishment. Furthermore, the Craft needed patrons: informed patrons who appreciated the true value of the freemason – people, one suspects, who looked with horror at the Tudors' pillage of the ancient religious houses of England and Wales. People, perhaps, like Penketh, Ashmole and Mainwaring. Or – before we get too romantic – people who had done well out of the Dissolution of the monasteries and had new houses to renovate and construct, from the stones of the old.

This line of enquiry would probably remain purely conjectural were it not for Elias Ashmole's second surviving record of masonic involvement, dated 10 March 1682. This record makes all the difference to the way in which we must see the first record of masonic activity in Ashmole's life. It also helps us to understand exactly what is meant by the term 'accepted' Free Mason, an epithet unique to English freemasonry in the period. It is noticably lacking in 17th century Scottish practice, even though the quantity of 17th century Scottish evidence greatly exceeds English masonic evidence for the same period, as David Stevenson is at pains to emphasise in his study.

Ashmole gives us a living snapshot of an afternoon in the heart of the busy City of London in the 1680s, a place pullulating with well-paid masons, eighteen years after the Great Fire created an architectural vacuum.

March 10. 1682 : About 5pm I received a summons, to appear at a Lodge to be held the next day at Mason's Hall London. Accordingly I went, and About Noone were admitted into the Fellowship of Free Masons, Sir William Wilson Knight, Capt. Rich: Borthwick, Mr Will: Woodman, Mr Wm Grey, Mr Samuell Taylour & Mr William Wise. I was the Senior Fellow among them (it being 35 years since I was admitted). There were present beside my selfe the Fellowes after named. Mr Thos. Wise Mr. [Master] of the Masons Company this present year. Mr Thomas Shorthose, Mr Thomas Shadbolt, Waindsford Esq. Mr Nich: Young. Mr: John Shorthose, Mr William Hamon, Mr John Thompson, & Mr. Will: Stanton.

We all dyned at the Halfe Moone Taverne in Cheapside, at a Noble
Dinner prepared at the charge of the New-accepted Masons.

The Masons Hall referred to stood in Mason's Avenue, Basinghall
Street, the headquarters of the London Company of Masons (formerly
the Company of Freemasons) since 1463. The Company was awarded
its arms in 1472, its main feature being the outstretched compasses
and three castles so familiar to students of the Craft. By the time of
the Stuarts, the London Company of "ffreemasons" consisted of a
master, two wardens, a court of assistants (the ruling body), a livery,
and a body of freemen or yeomen. Before we look more closely at this
hoary Company, the name Sir William Wilson, mentioned by
Ashmole, should be noted.

Wilson (1641-1710), architect and stone-mason, had been knighted
a few days before. A native of Sutton Coldfield, eight miles from
Lichfield, he had carved a still-extant statue of Charles II. It used to
stand at the very top of the western façade of Lichfield cathedral,
looking over all who entered therein and clearly linking the
reconstruction of the cathedral to the patronage and care of the
restored monarch, guardian of the privileges and tradition of the
Church of England. (Charles is boldly described as *Restaurator* at the
foot of the statue). The statue may still be seen by the south door of
the cathedral, its provenance a mystery to visitors and locals alike.
Who would have thought that this eroded larger-than-life-size
monument, sculpted by an architect of Nottingham Castle, might yet
represent Ashmole's union of Monarchy, Church and Free Masonry
in a single lump of durable sandstone?

Some years ago, when I first came to consider the case of Sir William
Wilson's becoming an accepted mason, I could not see how a
practising stonemason-architect could have been initiated into a
freemasonic fellowship, long after becoming a fully functioning,
professional master freemason. More research was required.
Fortunately, the requisite clues have been uncovered.

In his article *Nicholas Stone and the Mystery of the Acception*,
(Freemasonry Today, Spring 2000), masonic historian Matthew Scanlan
has written of how another and even more illustrious professional
freemason-architect apparently became an Accepted Fellow in 1638,
while at the time holding the position of King Charles I's master
mason. This was Nicholas Stone the elder (1586-1647), whose father's
memorial plaque we had cause to quote from earlier.

Given the paucity of evidence, Scanlan is to be congratulated for penetrating the mystery and recognising its historical significance. When one grasps this significance, it renders one incredulous as to how it could have taken so long to put 'two and two together'. Then again, the path had been obscured by masonic historians (who have enjoyed a virtual monopoly of the subject) with peculiar vested interests in separating as far as possible the lineage of 'speculative' (Grand Lodge) from 'operative' (respectable working-class) masons. The reasons for this can only have been academic, social and political, deriving perhaps from the extraordinary period of confusion and obfuscation following the establishment of Grand Lodge in 1717 during the long sunset of the Jacobite challenge to the House of Hanover. Furthermore, there was an attested desire among Grand Lodge apologists to transform their masonic inheritance into a proto-enlightenment moral club system, while squeezing its mystical theological basis into what Blake and Coleridge – to name but two – considered the dull, reasonable tick-tock philosophy of 'natural religion'.

William Blake parodies the god of the oh-so-rational natural religionist in his famous watercolour, *The Ancient of Days* (1793), even giving "Old Nobodaddy" some rather pointed compasses with which to bind and limit his universe. If this quasi-deity had been asked 'how high is your lodge?', he might have replied, "Oh, about 100 million miles, give or take a few feet." The Lodge in the Head is, of course, like the imagination, infinite.

Contemporary English freemasonry, not surprisingly, does not appear comfortable with the muddying of its version of the historical water which a reconsideration of the word 'speculative' involves. Masonic historian John Hamill's standard account, *The Craft* (Crucible 1982), for example, regards the locus of Ashmole's second masonic diary reference as little more than incidental. According to Hamill, the lodge which accepted Wilson in the presence of "senior Fellow" Elias Ashmole was most likely "an occasional lodge", his summons to that place doubtless due to the Masons Company connections of some of those present. It is as if a group of dairy farmers had dinner at the offices of the National Farmers Union, of which they were nearly all members, and then it was denied that there was any serious link between the NFU and dairy farming! In retrospect, the lack of interest displayed in such connections is to say the least, surprising.

Thankfully, Scanlan finds the connections worthy of scholarly attention, keenly aware how much contemporary masonic history of pre-1717 conditions has been composed with the latterday phenomenon of Grand Lodge in mind.

Scanlan examined the Renter Warden accounts for the London Company of *ffreemasons*, now held in the Guildhall Library, London. Records for 1638 describe a meeting that took place some time between March and midsummer 1638, the year, incidentally, in which Elias Ashmole married Eleanor Mainwaring.

> *Pd wch the accompt [accountant] layd out*
> *Wch was more than he received of them*
> *Wch were taken into the Accepcon*
> *Whereof xs [ten shillings] is to be paid by*
> *Mr. Nicholas Stone, Mr Edmund Kinsman*
> *Mr John Smith, Mr William Millis, Mr John Coles.*

Nicholas Stone was no footnote to history. King's master mason, close working colleague of Inigo Jones, architect of the magnificent Banqueting House, Whitehall, "ffreemason and citizen of of the City of London", sometime Master of the London Company of Freemasons, sculptor of one of the finest sepulchral monuments known to 17th century history, (the effigy of John Donne, S.Paul's), Stone was learned in classical mythology and theological symbolism, and encouraged his son to travel to Italy to further such and related practical studies. Nicholas Stone the younger (a Royalist) was the author of the *Enchiridion of Fortification* (1645) – a most suggestive title when one realises that in the year prior to publication, Elias Ashmole was put in charge of the City of Oxford's eastern defences and a year later, made a Free Mason .

And yet, for all this, Stone, along with the four other men referred to in the Renter Warden's accounts, while still a member of the London Company of Freemasons, had yet remained a stranger to the "Accepcon" until 1638, when he, along with his colleagues, were prepared to pay the large sum of 10 shillings for the privilege. At that price, it was unlikely to have been a long-service award ceremony!

Ashmole, in 1682, is specific about the events that took place on March 11th – the "new *accepted*" masons paid for the noble dinner at the Half-Moon Tavern. What was this Acception, which had apparently grown up within the London Company? Scanlan writes: "From the scant records, it appears to have involved some kind of a meeting, followed by a dinner paid for by those who had been 'accepted'. Was it that the acception dealt with the symbolic and so-called 'speculative' side of architecture?" Scanlan saved his definitive 'sting in the tail' for the last paragraph of his article:

"It is perhaps curious to note that in 1718, when the Grand Master [of the Grand Lodge] George Payne requested brethren to bring to Grand Lodge "any old writings and Records concerning Masons, ...to shew the usages of Antient Time", that it was also recorded that "several very valuable manuscripts" were tragically lost. Interestingly, the Rev. James Anderson specifically records that one particular manuscript, "writ by Mr. Nicholas Stone the Warden of Inigo Jones, were too hastily burnt by some scrupulous Brothers, that those Papers might not fall into strange hands" (Anderson's *Constitutions*, 1738, p.111).

"Could it be that there was a ritualistic form of Accepted Free Masonry prior to 1717 that was unpalatable to those who wished to 'revive' the movement in the 1720s?"

Obviously, Scanlan thinks so. The implication, surely, is that an earlier movement was in some way 'hi-jacked', rather than having simply, or even complicatedly, evolved from antecedent conditions. However, thanks to the "scrupulous Brothers", we may never know for sure. How convenient, a cynic might think, for a new kind of Freemasonry, severed from its paternity, to so inherit – or acquire – the title deeds.

————————

Ashmole's references to his fellowship with the Free Masons are few indeed, and this has led some commentators rashly to imagine Ashmole's commitment to the craft was slight. They would do well to remember not only the prohibition on committing to writing masonic rituals, but also that Ashmole's diary - vitally interesting as it is - is a highly selective work, accomplished for personal reasons of which we are ignorant. We do know that he wished to write a history of the craft, and made notes for the same, the which have disappeared.

Free Masonry bound him in fellowship to men great and small in his time. A man of Ashmole's attested sociable and good character would be unlikely to disregard his obligations - and those obligations demanded secrecy. It is highly possible that the circles in which Ashmole moved included more than a few accepted masons (the example of Sir Robert Moray - another Hermetic enthusiast and accepted mason stands out), of whose fellowship we are ignorant simply because they kept their obligations in the matter. We must be grateful indeed for the few clues Ashmole did choose to leave to posterity.

Furthermore, Ashmole never stopped contributing to church restoration - especially in Lichfield - and were we to have the records of construction-work, our knowledge of seventeenth century freemasonry, in its united operative and accepted aspects would be that much the richer. (Acceptation directly suggests an invitation to the operative world. Symbol and allegory permeate the operative catechism given above - and it is operative; Sloane mentions the placing of tools in special ways on site to indicate a summons for help from other freemasons). There was no such thing as 'speculative Freemasonry' at the time Ashmole was initiated, though it seems reasonable to suppose that having been initiated, accepted (and educated) masons did 'speculate'. However, the term 'speculative Freemasonry' has been used to make a spurious distinction between post-1717 'symbolic' masonry and the old trade which 'preceded' it, in effect drawing a cautious (and unnecessary) veil over the movement's genuine past. Speculation on secret allegorical and symbolic riddles was a general characteristic of the Renaissance in both its continental and English phases. Classicism, the Greek Mysteries, old English and Scottish pagan (country) traditions and Hermetic philosophy all played a part in this. For in that melancholy twilight later seen as the dawn of rationalism, these traditions could all be viewed as interweaving parts of the 'old religion' : hearty, gargantuan, fair. It would be surprising if, after the removal of the Puritan-dominated Protectorate of Cromwell, Renaissance modes of thought did not attempt a re-emergence, but how far such a movement may have influenced Free Masonry - or to what degree Free Masonry was indeed a part of that movement - is unclear, especially as one must consider that the operative freemason was himself the very practical instrument of the Renaissance. While philosophers dreamed, freemasons cut. For all the benefits of modern research, there is still a mystery in the matter.

One thing is clear : Ashmole stayed with Free Masonry for the rest of his long life; it was bound up with his deepest roots and his essential - and mercurial - conception of himself and his life's great work. Three and a half centuries after initiation, that life stands today as an inspiring example to all those persons of good-will who would make a lasting temple out of the base elements of their earthly lives.

Notes to Part Three

[1] This Rupert was the son of Elizabeth of Bohemia, whose court in the Hague drew learned men from all over Europe who wished to see a spiritual and scientific reformation.

[2] Mary, sole daughter of Sir William Forster bt. of Aldermaston in Berkshire, widow of Thomas Mainwaring knt, one of the masters in Chancery - and a relative of Ashmole's in-laws. Mary died on April 1st. 1668. There were no children.

[3] William Backhouse (1593-1662), Rosicrucian philosopher; educated at Christ Church, Oxford; adopted Ashmole as his son; left in manuscript (*Ashmole MSS.*) translations in verse and prose of French works on occult philosophy. (*Concise Dictionary of National Biography*. O.U.P. 1992).

[4] See *Freemasonry, Hermetic Thought & the the Royal Society in London*, by Michael Baigent, delivered to Quatuor Coronati Lodge of Research on 27 June 1996. Baigent suggests that Ashmole's relations with Backhouse mark the inception of Hermetic interests into his Free Masonry - and Free Masonry in general. This is a slender twig on which to hold such a large bird. Ashmole had been interested in Hermetic subjects since he was a youth. There is a distinction between *conversion*, and *regeneration*. His initiation at Warrington could have 'put him on the road' (conversion) while Backhouse seems to have actualised spiritual regeneration : the life of God in the soul - but this process would surely have begun in Ashmole's childhood; its Hermetic definition may in part have been the work of the mysterious Backhouse.

[5] Ms. dedicated to "my worthily honour'd William Backhouse Esquire Upon his adopting of me to be his Son." Bodleian Library *MS Ashmole*, 36-37ff. 241v-242.

[6] Ashmole Mss, 1459; ff 280-2; ff 284-31.

[7] It is interesting to see the rewards of service offered after the Restoration. When Dr. John Hacket had been rector of S.Andrews Holborn, London under the Protectorate, he had been ordered to refrain from the traditional Anglican liturgy by Puritans. At one point, a soldier entered the church and put a pistol to Hacket's head, ordering him to cease. Hacket continued, indifferent to the threat of death, saying, in a calm and grave voice : "Soldier, I am doing my duty; do you do yours". The soldier, abashed, fled the field. (Reported in Harwood's Introduction to Sampson Erdeswick's *Survey of Staffordshire* (1598) (London. 1844).

[8] Dr. John Lightfoot, learned divine and one of the editors of the *Polyglot Bible*, was born in Stoke, Staffordshire in 1602. Since he and Ashmole were contemporaries, it is not unlikely that they not only knew of one another but possibly were acquainted : both being Staffordshire men of great attainments.

[9] Note that Newton's alchemical writings far outweigh his purely physical investigations, and that his most prominent alchemical source was Ashmole's 1652 publication : *Theatrum Chemicum Britannicum*.

[10] *King Charles II at the Royal Exchange. London. 1667. Quatuor Coronatorum.*

London. 1898. vol. XI.pp.138ff.

[11] Sloane MS 3188, British Museum.

[12] "To these add the Customs relating to the County, whereof they have one, of admitting Men into the Society of Free-masons, that in the moorelands of this County seems to be of greater request, than anywhere else, though I find the Custom spread more or less all over the Nation; for here I find persons of the most eminent quality, that did not disdain to be of this Fellowship. Nor indeed need they, were it of that Antiquity and honor, that is pretended in a large parchment volume they have amongst them, containing the History and Rules of the craft of masonry. Which is there deduced not only from sacred Writ, but profane story, particularly that it was brought into England by Saint Amphibal, and first communicated to S.Alban, who set down the Charges of masonry, and was made paymaster and governor of the Kings works, and gave them charges and manners as St. Amphibal had taught him. Which were after confirmed by King Athelstan, whose youngest son Edwyn loved well masonry, took upon him the charges and learned the manners, and obtained for them of his father a free-charter. Whereupon he caused them to assemble at York, and to bring all the old books of their craft, and out of them ordained such charges and manners, as they then thought fit : which charges in the said Schrole or parchment volume, are in part declared : and thus was the craft of masonry grounded and confirmed in England. It is also there declared that these charges and manners were after perused and approved by King Hen.6. and his council, both as to Masters and Fellows of this right Worshipfull craft.

Into which Society when they are admitted, they call a meeting (or Lodg as they term it in some places) which must consist at least of 5 or 6 of the ancients of the Order, whom the candidates present with gloves, and so likewise to their wives, and entertain with a Collation according to the custom of the place : This ended, they proceed to the admission of them, which chiefly consists in the communication of certain secret signes, whereby they are known to one another all over the Nation, by which means they have maintenance whither ever they travel : for if any man appear though altogether unknown that can shewe any of these signes to a Fellow of that Society, whom they otherwise call an accepted mason, he is obliged presently to come to him, from what company or place soever he be in, nay tho' from the top of a steeple, (what hazard or inconvenience soever he run) to know his pleasure, and assist him; viz. if he want work he is bound to find him some; or if he cannot do that, to give him money, or otherwise support him till work can be had; which is one of their articles; and it is another, that they advise the Masters they work for, according to the best of their skill, acquainting them with the goodness or badness of their materials; and if they be in any way out in the contrivance of their buildings modestly to rectify them in it; that masonry be not dishonoured : and many such like that are commonly known : but some others they have (to which they are sworn after their fashion) that none know but themselves, which I have reason to suspect are much worse than these, perhaps as bad as the History of the craft it self; than which there is nothing

I ever met with, more false or incoherent." (*The Natural History of Staffordshire by Robert Plot.LLD. Keeper of the ASHMOLEAN MUSAEUM And PROFESSOR of CHYMISTRY in the UNIVERSITY of OXFORD. 1686. Chapter Eight*).

[13] *The Natural History of Staffordshire by Dr Robert Plot LLD. Keeper of the Ashmolean Musaeum And Professor of CHYMISTRY in the UNIVERSITY of OXFORD. 1686. Ch. 8.*

[14] Jean Gimpel (*The Cathedral Builders*. Michael Russell. 1983.p.68ff.) : "The expression 'freestone mason' was gradually replaced by the simpler term 'freemason'. The word 'freemason' then clearly refers to the quality of the stone and not some franchise granted to the cathedral builders. ...there was in London, in 1351, a *maître maçon de franche peer* [stone] which is roughly the Anglo-French equivalent of two Latin expressions : *sculptores lapidum liberorum* (London, 1212) and *magister lathomus liberarum petrarum* (Oxford, 1391). The modern English...translation of this expression would be : 'a master mason of freestone'".

[15] *The Cathedral Builders* (Michael Russell. 1983). p.102.

[16] Ibid. pp.71-72.

[17] Biddulph Parish Registers are full of names of people connected with quarrying and masonry. For one unique year, Biddulph's Rector gives us the occupations of those named. Thus we learn that in "1600. Baptismata. Mar. 6 Joanna, fa. Rumbaldi DURBAR, **freemason**." Rumbald Durbar was interred in Biddulph Church on April 23 1610. It is to be presumed that Rumbald was not alone in his trade.

[18] MS. Ashm. 1136, f.7.

[19] Ashmole recorded the Mainwaring pedigree in MS. Ashm. 846, f.43. & MS. Ashm.1763, f.32v.

[20] MS. Ashm. 1136, f.10.

[21] Where once Eleanor's stone lay, now there is a set of box-pews. Likewise, the Mainwaring memorial stones have also disappeared, and while there is at Astbury an exceptionally large number of 17th century graves, there is no longer to be found any mention of the Mainwarings of Smallwood in their church at Astbury. 19th century restoration-work has spoiled this along with so many ancient English churches.

[22] Ashmole found his second wife from the Mainwaring family also. This wife was Mary, widow of Thomas Mainwaring, knt., one of the masters in Chancery where Ashmole began his professional life. Mary was the sole daughter of Sir William Forster bt., of Aldermaston in Berkshire, through which connection with Berkshire it is possible that Ashmole met his 'spiritual father', William Backhouse of Swallowfield.

[23] Karincham today (now called Kermincham and pronounced by locals as 'Kermidgum') is not even a place as such, just a few farm-houses and converted cottages on the road from Swettenham, at which church people from Kermincham have been buried since at least the 17th. century. Records from the Consistory Court in Chester reveal that Henry Mainwaring of Karincham (Ashmole's father-in-law's father) was involved in a dispute over burial places and seats at the church of S.Luke, Goostrey, two miles away.

Henry Mainwaring was permitted to build an out aisle or aisles on the north side of the chancel. One wonders who undertook the building-work. Incidentally, the Advowson of Goostrey had been held by Dieulacres Abbey. (The church was rebuilt 1792-6). Mss. held in the Stafford Record Office prove the longstanding pre-Reformation commitment among the Mainwarings to joining confraternities. Guilds of masons enjoyed confraternal identification with religious sites.

24   The lord of Biddulph, Sir Francis Biddulph, was a direct descendent of Ormus le Guidon. Ormus or one of his children reputedly returned from the crusades with a Saracen stonemason (John Sleigh, *A History of the Ancient Parish of Leek*, J.R. Smith, 1862). In Stafford's 12th cent. St Chad's Church is an inscription, ORM VOCATUR QUI ME CONDIDIT ("He who established me is called Orm"), close to an oriental style carving of Ishtar and Tammuz. Ormus was married to the daughter of the Norman sheriff of Stafford, Nicholas de Beauchamp. Sir Francis's hall stood by the church where five unique Templar gravestones have been found. (Land was given to the Templars at Keele in 1168 or 1169, see *Testa de Nevill*).

25   In Ashmole's friend William Dugdale's collection, *Chartularium Mainwaringianum* (1668), it is asserted that there are no less than 133 variant spellings of the family name - surely an exaggeration.

26   Reported in the account of S.Lawrence church, Upper Peover in Raymond Richards' classic *Old Cheshire Churches* (Batsford. 1947).

27   It may also interest readers that Upper Peover was also a command-camp of the US Third Army during World War II, and that General George Patton and his staff worshipped in the little church for many months; Patton presented a US flag to the church in gratitude.

28   Following Randle Holmes. Holmes' knowledge of this matter is particularly interesting and possibly suggestive since he was himself an accepted gentleman member of a lodge of freemasons based in Chester in the mid-seventeenth century. (See Q.C. Transactions on Randle Holmes, and *Old Cheshire Churches*. Batsford. 1947. p.874).

29   On the tomb of Philip is a coat-of-arms consisting of an eight-pointed star above a crescent, suggestive of some oriental involvement in the family.

30   See *Transactions of the Quatuor Coronati Lodge : The Lodge of Randle Holme at Chester* by Coulthurst & Lawson. *Harleian MS*. No. 2054 at the British Museum contains a collection of papers in the handwriting of the Royalist Randle Holmes which reveals the existence in *circa* 1655 of a lodge of freemasons in Chester. The members include both operative masons and other tradespeople, as well as the gentleman Randle Holmes. There is however no way of knowing if this lodge had any connection with the possibly 'occasional' lodge held at nearby Warrington in 1646. Interestingly, Randle Holmes was elected to the dignity of 'sewer' (similar to the ancient role of dapifer or steward) in the household of Charles II at the Restoration. Holmes had been mayor of Chester and had grieved at having been able to do so little to ameliorate the sufferings of the inhabitants after Sir William Brereton's destruction of so much of the city in 1645.

Bibliography

AGRIPPA. Heinrich Cornelius. *De Occulta Philosophia*. (Eng. trans. London. 1651).

ANDREAE Johann Valentin. *Peregrini in Patria errores. Utopiae*. (Strasbourg. Lazarus Zetzner.) 1618.

Civis Christianus sive Peregrini quondam errantis restitutiones. Strasbourg. Zetzner. 1619.

Reipublicae Christianopolitanae Descriptio. Strasbourg. Zetzner. 1619.

Turris Babel sive Judicorum de Fraternitate Rosaceae Crucis Chaos. Strasbourg. Zetzner. 1619.

Invitatio Fraternitatis Christi Ad Sacri Amoris Candidatos. Impensis Heredum. Strasbourg. Zetzner. 1617.

Christianae Societatis imago. Tübingen. Eberhard Wild. 1620.

Christiani amoris dextera porrecta. Wild. 1620.

Mythologiae Christianae sive virtutem et vitiorum vitae humanae imaginum Libri tres. Strasbourg. Zetzner. 1619.

Menippus sive Dialogorum Satyricorum Centuria inanitatum nostratium speculum. In Grammatoricum gratiam castigatum. Cosmopoli (Zetzner). 1618.

Turbo sive moleste et frustra per Cuncta Divagans Ingenium. In Theatrum productum. Helicone iuxta parnassum. (Zetzner). 1616.

Theca gladii spiritus, Sententias quasdam breves, vereque philosophicas continens. Zetzner. Strasbourg. 1616.

De christiani cosmoxeni genitura ludicium. Zetzner. 1619.

Tobias Hessi, viri incomparabilis, Immortalitas. Strasbourg. Zetzner. 1619.

Chymische Hochzeit : Christiani Rosencreütz. Anno 1459. Arcana publicata vilescunt : et gratiam prophanata amiltunt. Ergo : ne Margaritas obijce porcis, seu Asino substerne rosas. Strasbourg. Lazarus Zetzner. 1616.

Allgemeine und General Reformation der gantzen weiten Welt. [extract from Trajano Boccalini's *News from Parnassus*. Venice. 1614.] *Beneben der Fama Fraternitatis, Dess Löblichen Ordens des Rosenkreutzes, an alle Gelehrte und Haüpter Europae geschrieben. Auch einer Kurtzen Responsion* [not by Andreae] *von dem Herr Haselmeyer gestellet, welcher desswegen von den Jesuittern ist gefänglich eingezogen, und auff eine Galleren geschmiedet : Jtzo öffentlich in Druck verfertiget, und allen trewen Hertzen communiciret worden*. Kassel. Willhelm Wessel. 1614.

The Asclepius. Translated & edited by Nock & Festugière.

ARNOLD. Sir Thomas. Ed. : *The Legacy of Islam*. Oxford. 1931.

ASHMOLE. Elias. *Theatrum Chemicum Britannicum*. 1652.

Fasciculus Chemicus (Arthur Dee). Ed : Ashmole ('James Hasolle') 1650.

The Way to Bliss (Anon.) 1658.

The Institution, laws and ceremonies of the most noble Order of the Garter. 1672.

BENY. Roloff. *Iran. Elements of Destiny*. Collins. 1977.

BESOLD. Christoph. *Collegii Politici (Passim Juridicis et Philosophicis digressionibus illustrati) Classis prima, Reipublicae Naturam et Constitutionem XII. Disputationibus absolvens. [Classis Posterior, De Republica in omnibus partibus*

gubernanda, IX. Disputationibus] ...Accessit nunc primum Frid. Rich. Mockelii Doctrinae Politicae synopsis. Tübingen, I.A. Cellius, 1616.
De verae Philosophiae fundamento Discursus. Tübingen, I.A. Cellius, 1618.
Dissertatio Juridico-Politica, De augenda curandaque Republica ...Ingenii exercendi causa discutiendam exhibet. M.Ioan. Martin Rauscher. Tübingen, I.A. Cellius, 1613.
Axiomatum Philosophiae Christianae, vitam vere philosophicam utcumque adumbrantium. Strasbourg. Zetzner. 1627.
Motive seiner Rückehr zur römisch-katholischen Kirche. Bearbitet, übersetzt und herausgegeben von P.W.K., Augsburg . Ch. Kranzfelder. 1828.
BIBLIOTHECA PHILOSOPHICA HERMETICA. (Ed : Joost Ritman; Frans Janssen; Frank van Lamoen) *Hermes Trismegistus. Pater Philosophorum.* Amsterdam 1991.
Les symboles spirituels de l'alchimie. (M de Jong). Amsterdam. 1988.
The Hermetic Gnosis. (van Lamoen) Amsterdam. 1988.
Kabbale et philosophie hermétique. (François Secret) Amsterdam. 1989.
Johann Valentin Andreae 1586-1986. Die Manifeste der Rosenkreuzer-bruderschaft. (Carlos Gilly) Amsterdam. 1986.
BLAIR. H.A. *The Kaleidoscope of Truth. Types and Archetypes in Clement of Alexandria.* Churchman Publishing. 1986.
BOHM. David. *Wholeness and the Implicate Order.* Routledge & Kegan Paul. 1981.
BURCKHARDT. Titus. *An Introduction to Sufism.* 1976.
BURKITT. F.C. *Church and Gnosis.* University of Cambridge Press. 1931.
BROCARDUS. Jacobus. *Mystica et prophetica libri Geneseos interpretatio. Bremen.* Th. Gluichstein. 1585.
CAMPANELLA. Tommaso. *Città dell'O sole, cioé Dialogo di Republica, nel quale si dissegna l'Idea della Riforma della Republica Christiana conforme alla promessa da Dio fatta alle sante Catarina e Brigida* (ff. Iro-45vo); DERSELBE, *Cento cinquanta Concetti metodici dell'Universa scienza Politica di Fra Tomaso Campanella P[iae] m[emoriae]* ff. 47ro-91vo. Mss. at *Bibliotheca Philosophica Hermetica.* Amsterdam.
CASAUBON. Meric. (Ed.) *A strange relation of what passed between Dr John Dee and some spirits.* 1659. (Reprint. Daniel & Co. 1977).
CHADWICK. Henry. *The Early Church.* Pelican 1978.
COPLESTON F.C. *A History of Medieval Philosophy.* Methuen & Co. Ltd. 1972.
CLULEE. Nicholas. *John Dee's Natural Philosophy.* Routledge & Kegan Paul. 1988.
DEE. John. *Monas Hieroglyphica.* Antwerp. 1564.
Documents of the Christian Church. Edited by Henry Bettenson. Oxford. 1977.
DOMINI. Donatino. *Chymica Vannus.* Longo Editore. Ravenna. 1986.
EDIGHOFFER. Roland. *Rose-Croix et Société Idéale.*
The Book of Enoch. Translated by R.H. Charles. SPCK. 1984.
EUSEBIUS. *Ecclesiastical History.* Translated by Kirsopp Lake. Loeb Classical Library. 1975.

237

FLUDD. Robert. (as Rudolfus Otreb). *Tractatus Theologo-Philosophicus, In Libros tres distributus, Quoram I. de Vita, II. de Morte, III. de Resurrectione. Cui inseruntur nonnulla Sapientiae veteris, Adami infortunio superstitis, fragmenta ... Fratribus a Cruce Rosea dictis, dedicata. Oppenheim. H.Gallerus impensis J.Th. de Bry.* 1617. (as Joachim Frizius) *Summum Bonum, Quod est Verum Magiae, Cabalae [et] Alchymiae Verae, Fratrum Roseae Crucis verorum, Subjectum. In dictarum Scientiarum laudem, et insignis calumniatoris Fratris Marini Mersenni dedecus publicatum.* Frankfurt. 1629.

FOWDEN. Garth. *The Egyptian Hermes.* Cambridge University Press. 1986.

FRENCH. Peter. *John Dee.* Routledge & Kegan Paul. 1972.

GABELLA. Philippus A. *Secretioris Philosophiae Consideratio brevis et nunc primum, una cum Confessione Fraternitatis R.C. in lucem edita.* Kassel. W.Wessel. 1615.

GILLY. Carlos. *Cimelia Rhodostaurotica.* Bibliotheca Philosophica Hermetica. 1995. 2nd Edition: 1998.
Theophrastia Sancta - Paracelsianism as a religion, in conflict with the established churches (BPH, Amsterdam, 1995).

GIMPEL. Jean *The Cathedral Builders.* Michael Russell. 1983. *The Medieval Machine.* Victor Gollancz. 1976.

GODWIN. Joscelyn. *Athanasius Kircher.* Thames & Hudson. 1979.
Robert Fludd. Thames & Hudson. 1979.

GUTMAN. Aegidius. *Offenbarung Göttlicher Mayestat, Darinnen angezeygt wird, Wie Gott der Herr Anfänglich sich allen seinen Geschöpffen mit Worten und Wercken geoffenbaret, und wie Er alle seine Werck, derselben Art, Eygenschafft, Krafft und Wirckung, in kürtze Schrifft artlich verfasst, und solches alles dem Ersten Menschen, den Er selbst nach seiner Bildnus geschaffen, uberreycht, welchen dan biss daher gelangt ist.* Frankfurt. J. Wolff Däschen im Hanawischen Buchladen. 1619.
Hermetica. Translated by Walter Scott. Reprint : Shambhala Press. 1986.
The Hermetick Art. by a lover of Philalethes. London. 1714.

HAERI. Shaykh Fadhlalla. *The Sufi way to self-unfoldment.* Element. 1987.

HIRST. Désirée. *Hidden Riches.* Eyre & Spottiswoode. 1964.

HOLROYD. Stuart. *Magic, Words and Numbers.* Aldus. 1976.

HUGHES. David. *The Star of Bethlehem Mystery.* Dent. 1978.

INGE. William Ralph. *Personal Idealism and Mysticism.* Longmans. 1907. *Truth and Falsehood in Religion.* John Murray. 1907. *Mysticism in Religion.* Hutchinson University Library (undated) *The Philosophy of Plotinus.* (2 vols.) Longmans.

IQBAL. Sir Muhammad. (Ed.) *The Mathnawi.* Maulana Jalal-ud-din Rumi. 1983.

JOHNSTON. Arthur. *Francis Bacon.* Batsford. 1965.

JONAS. Hans. *The Gnostic Religion.* Beacon Press (1958). *The Imperative of Responsibility.* University of Chicago. 1986. *Philosophical Essays.* University of Chicago. 1974.

JOSEPHUS. *The Works of Flavius Josephus.* Trans. Will. Whiston. Nimmo. 1865.

JOSTEN. C.H. (Ed.) *Elias Ashmole (1617-1692)* (5 vols. Oxford, 1966).

KEE. Howard Clark. *Medicine, Miracle and Magic in New Testament Times.* Cambridge University Press. 1988.

JUNG. C.G. *Psychology & Alchemy*. Routledge & Kegan Paul. 1981.

KHUNRATH. Heinrich. *Amphitheatrum Sapientiae Aeternae, solius verae, o.O.* [Hamburg?] 1595.

De igne magorum philosophorum [herausgegeben von Benedictus Figulus], Strasbourg. Zetzner. 1608, pp. 107-123. Also contains : JOHANNES ARNDT : *Iudicium und Bericht eines Erfahnen Cabalisten und Philosophen über die 4 Figuren dess grossen Amphitheatri D. Heinrici Khunradi.*

MAHÉ. Jean Pierre. *Hérmes en Haute Egypte.* 2 vols. University of Quebec Press. 1978.1982.

MINO. Gabriele. *Alchimia. La Tradizione in Occidente Secundo le Fonti Manoscritte e a stampa.* Edizione La Biennale. Electa Editrici. 1986.

KELLY. JND. *Early Christian Doctrines.* A&C Black. 1977.

MAIER. Michael. *Silentium post Clamores, Das ist, Apologi und Verantwortung wieder etlicher ungestümmer Clamanten (so sich in die Fraternität R.C. auffzunehmen begehret, aber ihres Gefallens keine Antwort erlangt) Verl ästerungen und Schmachreden, welcher sie wider dieselbige aussgegossen : Beneben Gründlicher Anzeige, warum gedachte Fraternität bissanhero auff solcher Clemanten unzeitiges Anhalten zu antworten, und nach ihren jedem Begehren sich zuoffenbaren, wenigers dieselbe zu ihrer Gesellschafft auffzunehmen. Bedenckens getragen. Erstlich in Lateinischer Spraach beschrieben, und nachmals ins Teutsche übersetzt, Durch R.F.M.* Frankfurt. Luca Jennis. 1617.

Themis Aurea, Das ist, Von den Gesetzen und Ordnungen der löblichen Fraternitet R.C. Ein aussführlicher Tractat und Bericht, Darinenn gründlichen erweisen wird, dass dieselbige Gesetz, nicht allein in Warheit beständigt, sondern auch an sich selbst, dem Gemeinen und Privat Ntzen nohtwendig, nützlich und erpriesslich seynd ... Jetzt und ins Teutsche übersetzt, durch R.M.F. Frankfurt. N.Hoffmann, in Verlegung Lucas Jennis. 1618. *Sophicum Rhodo-Stauroticum, Das ist : Weitläuffige Entdeckung dess Collegii unnd Axiomatum von der sondern erleuchten Fraternitet Christ. Rosen Creutz : Allen der wahrn Weissheit Begrigen Expectanten zu fernerer Nachrichtung, den unverständigen Zoilis aber zur unauslöslicher Schandt und Spott.,* o.O., 1618.

McINTOSH. Christopher. *The Rosicrucians* (Weiser, 1997)

The Rose Cross and the Age of Reason - 18th Century Rosicrucianism in Central Europe and its Relationship to the Enlightenment (E.J. Brill, Leiden, 1992).

MOORE. R.I. *The Origins of European Dissent.* Basil Blackwell. 1985.

MORSIUS. Joachim. *Nuncius Olympicus Von etzlichen geheimen Bücheren und Schrifften, so ein fürnehmer Gottesgelerter und hocherleuchter berümbter Theosophus und Medicus, in Theosophia, Cabala, Magia, Chemia, Medicina und Philologia, durch viel beschwerliche Reisen ennd grosse Unkostung, Ecclesiae und Reip(ublicae) litterariae commodo, zusammen gebracht, darin die gröste Himmilische unnd Jrrddische Weissheit begriffen ist.* Gedruckt Philadelphiae [Amsterdam] Anno CIVXMIILLVCCIILI [1626].

Occult and Scientific mentalities in the Renaissance. Edited by Brian Vickers. University of Cambridge Press. 1984.

PARACELSUS. Theophrastus. *Erster [-Zehender] Theil Der Bücher und Schrifften*

239

des Edlen, Hochgelehrten und Bewehrten Philosophi und Medici, Philippi Theophrasti Bombast von Hohenheim, Paracelsi genannt. Jetzt auffs new auss den Originalien, und Theophrasti eigner Handschrifft, soviel derselben zu bekommen gewesen, auffs trewlichst und fleissigst an tag geben : Durch Iohannem Huserum Brisgoium, Churfürstlichen Cölnischen Rhat und Medicus. Basel. K.Waldkirch. 1589-90.

PHILALETHES. Eugenius. Trans. by Thomas Vaughan. *The Fame and Confession of the Fraternity of R:C: Commonly, of the Rosie Cross. With a Praeface annexed thereto, and a short Declaration of their Physicall Worck.* London. Printed by J.M. for Giles Calvert, at the black spread Eagle at the West end of Pauls. 1652.

PICKFORD. D. *Staffordshire: Its Magic and Mystery.* Sigma Books. 1994.

QUISPEL. Gilles. Review of *Neues Testament und Gnosis* (Schmithals, Walter. 1984) in *Vigiliae Christianae* 39 (1985) E.J. Brill. Leiden.

RABELAIS. François. *The Heroic Deeds of Gargantua and Pantagruel.* Trans. Sir Thomas Urquhart. J.M. Dent. 1929.

The Renaissance Philosophy of Man. Edited by Kristeller and E.Cassirer. University of Chicago. 1948.

RUDOLPH. Kurt. *Gnosis.* (Trans. R.Mc L.Wilson). Harper & Rowe. 1985.

SCHOLEM. Gershom. *Major Trends in Jewish Mysticism.* Schocken Books. 1961.

SCHWENCKFELD. Caspar. *Catalogus oder Register der Bücher Herren Caspar Schwenckfelds, die er mehr dann von XXX jaren her geschriben, und was durch ihn selbst, und hernach aus seinem befeel durch seine mitbekenner und liebhaber der Glorien und warheit Jesu Christi inn truck ist khommen* [herausgegeben von Johann Heid von Daun] *Von newen getruckt* [wohl auf Kosten des Daniel Sudermann], o.O. 1595.

Select works of Plotinus. Translated by Thomas Taylor. Edited by G.R.S. Mead. Bohm's Popular Library. 1914.

SHAH. Idries. *The Secret Lore of Magic.* Abacus. 1972.

SINGER. Dorothea. *Giordano Bruno - His Life and Thought with annotated translations of his work On the Infinite Universe and worlds.* Schuman. 1950.

SPENCE. Lewis. *The Encyclopaedia of Occultism* (US, 1920).

SPERBER. Julius. (Attrib.) *Echo Der von Gott hocherleuchten Fraternitet dess löblichen Ordens R.C. Das ist : Exemplarische Beweis, Das nicht allein das jenige, was jetzt in der Fama und Confession der Fraternitet R.C. ausgebotten, möglich und war sey, Sondern schon für neunzehn und mehr Jahren solche Magnalia Dei, etzlichen Gottesfürchtigen Leuten mitgetheilet gewesen, und von ihren privatschrifften depraediciret worden. Wie dessen ein fürtrefflich Magisch Scriptum und Tractätlein, der Hochlöblichen Fraternitet R.C. dediciret und offentlich durch den Druck evulgiret wird. Durch dess Deutschen Abecess Laut ...* Danzig. A. Hünefeld. 1615.

TURNER. Robert. (Ed.) *The Heptarchia Mystica of John Dee.* Aquarian Press. 1983.

VAN DEN BROEK, Roelof, and Cis van Heertum (Ed.) *From Poimandres to Jacob Böhme: Gnosis, Hermetism and the Christian Tradition* (BPH, Amsterdam, 2000).

VON ESCHENBACH. Wolfram. *Parzifal.* (Ed. A.T. Hatto) Penguin Classics. 1980.

WEIGEL. Valentin. [Benedikt Biedermann] *Studium Universale, Das ist, Alles dasjenige, so von Anfang der Welt biss an das Ende je gelebet, geschrieben, gelesen, oder gelernet und noch geschrieben oder gestudieret werden möchte; Was das rechte Studieren und Lernen sey; was alle Menschen in dieser Zeit studieren sollen; Wie gantz leicht, wie gantz schwer die Theologia und alles zu lernen sey, dass wir einig und allein durch Gebeth all Dinge ohne Verdruss und Arbeit erlangen und lernen; Dessgleichen vom Schulgange oder Studieren aller Menschen.* Frankfurt. S. Müller. 1695.

WHITE. Ralph. (Ed.) *The Rosicrucian Enlightenment Revisited.* Essays by John Matthews, Christopher Bamford, Joscelyn Godwin, Nicholas Goodrick-Clarke, Clare Goodrick-Clarke, Robert Powell, Paul Bembridge, Rafal Prinke, Christopher McIntosh (Lindisfarne Books, 1999).

WIDEMANN. Karl. *Sylva Scientiarum et artium laudabilium. Thesaurus inaestimabilis.* (Ms. IV 341 from the Niedersächsischen Landesbibliothek, Hannover).

WILLIAMS. George. *The Radical Reformation* (Westminster, US, 1962).

WIND. Edgar. *Pagan Mysteries in the Renaissance.* Oxford. 1980.

YATES. Frances. *Giordano Bruno and the Hermetic Tradition.* Routledge & Kegan Paul. 1964.

The Occult Philosophy of the Elizabethan Age. Routledge & Kegan Paul. 1979.

The Rosicrucian Enlightenment. Routledge & Kegan Paul. 1972.

"If you look very carefully, you may find Damcar ..."

INDEX

243

Lethe, 52
Lexicon alchemiae, 63
Libavius, Andreas, 131
Liber de causis (Plotinus), 36
Liber de confirmatione religionis ethnicorum, 28
Liber perfecti magisterii (Geber), 39
Libri de vita (Ficino), 78
Lichfield, 77, 193ff.
Lightfoot, John, 232
Littler, Henry, 195, 214
Lindsay, Sir David, Earl of Balcarres, 173
Lorenzo the Magnificent, 49
Lovell, Sir Thomas, 213
Louis VII, 73
Lull, Ramon, 123
Luther, Martin, 104
Lux in Tenebris, (Comenius), 164, 177

Madimi, 97
Magdeburg, 90
Mahabyn, 30
Mahé, Jean Pierre, 6, 70
Maier, Count Michael, 128, 135, 140, 173
Mainwaring, (née) Eleanor, 208, 209
Mainwaring, Col. Henry, 209, 212
Mainwaring, Peter, 194, 195 208
Mainwaring, Philip, 211
Mainwaring, Randle, 210
Mainwaring, Thomas, 210, 234
Mainwaring, Sir William, 210
Mandaeans, 72, 73
Mani, 73
Marie de Champagne, 73
Martill (sic), Charles, 221
Masons Hall (Basinghall St), 226ff.

Mathematical Preface, (1570), 172
Maurice, F.D., 153
Maximilian, Archduke, 81, 89
McIntosh, Dr Christopher, 104, 158
Medulla Alchimiae, 40
Menippus, 62, 111, 114, 120, 147
The Merchant of Venice, 83
Mercurio da Correggio, Giovanni, 45ff.
Merian, Matthieu, 136
Mersenne, Marin, 154
Merula, 49
Methuselah, 50
Meyerhof, Max, 29, 38
Milton, John, 166
Mithra, 158
Monas Hieroglyphica, 29
Moray, Sir Robert, 168ff., 197, 199, 200, 202
Morsius, Joachim, 133, 135, 158
Münster, 121
Mutawakkil, 27
Muthadid, 28
Mysticism in Religion (Inge), 72

Nag Hammadi, 55, 124
Nagel, Paul, 132
Naometria, 101, 107
Nasoreans, 72
Naudé, Gabriel, 139
Nazirite, 158
Nebuchadrezzar, 159
Neoplatonism, 14-16, 136, 155
New Atlantis, 35, 192
News from Parnassus, 91, 123, 125
Newton, Isaac, 62, 114, 154, 200
Noah, 50
Nollius, Heinrich, 131
Norton, Thomas, 75